READING THE NEW TESTAMENT

Reading the New Testament

An Introduction

by

PHEME PERKINS

PAULIST PRESS
New York, N.Y./Ramsey, N.J.

NIHIL OBSTAT
Rev. Msgr. Matthew P. Stapleton
Censor Librorum

IMPRIMATUR
✝ Humberto Cardinal Medeiros
Archdiocese of Boston

November 28, 1977

Library of Congress
Catalog Card Number: 78-51892

ISBN: 0-8091-9535-6

Published by Paulist Press
Editorial Office: 1865 Broadway, New York, N.Y. 10023
Business Office: 545 Island Road, Ramsey, N.J. 07446

Printed and bound in the
United States of America

CONTENTS

v

Part I

INTRODUCTION

Chapter One

___

WHY STUDY THE BIBLE?

What Is the New Testament?

Very often when I ask a beginning class what the New Testament is, no one has a clear idea. Some say, "the stuff they read in church"; others, "the gospel," or "the last part of the Bible." If you open a copy of the New Testament and look at the table of contents, you will see a list of 27 different titles. Here is that list with a brief indication of when each is usually thought to have been written and to whom. You will notice that we often do not know anything about who wrote particular books. The traditional practice of early Christians was to assign writings to famous apostles. At the time of Jesus, people often wrote "in the name of" some famous person. Disciples would often continue the work of their teacher by writing in his name. That is what some of the disciples of the apostles have done.

I. Gospels and Acts

(1) *Matthew:* (ca. A.D. 90) This gospel was written by a Jewish convert to Christianity. He used Mark and other traditions about Jesus to picture him as the Messiah and true teacher of the Law.

(2) *Mark:* (ca. A.D. 70) This is the earliest gospel. Because of its many references to suffering, people used to think that Mark was written for Christians during Nero's persecu-

3

tion in Rome. Now that further study and archaeology reveal the extent of suffering in Palestine during the Jewish war against Rome (A.D. 66-70), many scholars suggest that Mark may have been written for Christians in that situation. Jesus is portrayed as the suffering Messiah.

(3) *Luke:* (*ca.* A.D. 90) This gospel was written by a well-educated, Gentile convert to Christianity. Luke used Mark and other material about Jesus, some of it similar to Matthew's additional material. He stresses the general, ethical side of Jesus' teaching to show that he had a message for everyone, rich and poor, Jew and Gentile.

(4) *John:* (*ca.* A.D. 90) This gospel is quite different from the other three. The fourth evangelist stresses the divinity of Jesus as the Word of God.

(5) *Acts:* The author of Luke followed his gospel with the story of the founding of the Church. He wants to show how the Holy Spirit led the apostles—especially the great heroes Peter and Paul—to spread the message from Jerusalem all the way to Rome.

II. Pauline Letters

(6) *Romans:* (*ca.* A.D. 55-57) Paul wrote this letter to the Church at Rome. He was hoping to visit them after a trip to Jerusalem and, since he had never been there before, he wanted to introduce himself and his message. He was hoping that the Roman Christians might support him in missionary work further to the West in Spain. Because of its general character, Romans has been the most important of Paul's letters.

(7) *I Corinthians:* (*ca.* A.D. 52) Paul wrote this letter to a Church he had founded in Corinth. Many practical problems about Christian life and worship had arisen there that Paul wanted to settle until he could go and visit that Church.

(8) *II Corinthians:* (*ca.* A.D. 54) After I Corinthians and before this letter, Paul had visited Corinth and had had a very difficult time there. In addition, other Christian missionaries had come into that Church and challenged Paul's authority. One of his assistants, Titus, had been able to win the Corin-

thians back to Paul, so Paul writes to express his gratitude and to defend his apostleship against those who attack him.

(9) *Galatians:* (*ca.* A.D. 55) Sometime after Paul had left the Church he founded in Galatia, other preachers had come and told these Gentile converts that they would have to be circumcised and follow Jewish customs in order to be Christians. This letter is an angry reply to their view.

(10) *Ephesians:* (Date uncertain.) This letter seems to be an exposition of the cosmic unity of the Church as body of Christ written by one of Paul's students. Many expressions used in this letter are copied from another letter to the Colossians.

(11) *Philippians:* (*ca.* 52-54) Paul wrote this letter to the Church at Philippi from prison (in Ephesus?). He wishes to thank them for aid they sent him and to remind them of his teaching.

(12) *Colossians:* (Date uncertain.) The language and style of this letter are so unlike Paul's other letters that many feel that Paul had a disciple write it. The Colossian Church was troubled by false teachers who apparently wanted to turn Christianity into a form of Jewish mysticism.

(13) *I Thessalonians:* (*ca.* A.D. 51) Christians in Paul's Church at Thessalonica wondered why members of their Church had died. Paul wants to reassure them that departed Christians will share in the second coming and to congratulate them on the good report that Timothy had made about them.

(14) *II Thessalonians:* (Sometime after I Thessalonians.) Christians in the Church began to think that the end of the world was so near that they should give up work—just like the people today who give up everything to wait for people on flying saucers. Either Paul or a student of his wrote to tell them to go about their occupations. He tells them that many mysterious signs would have to be fulfilled before the end of the world.

(15-17) *I, II Timothy, Titus (the Pastoral Epistles):* (*ca.* A.D. 110) These letters were written in the name of the apostle by a second-generation follower of his. They use the language that had developed in that generation to codify rules and regulations for the various offices in the Church. They show us how the Pauline Churches were becoming institutionalized.

(18) *Philemon:* (ca. A.D. 52-54) A short private note that Paul sent the master of a runaway slave when he returned the slave. Although Paul did not demand that Christians abolish slavery, this note shows that he did understand slaves and their masters to be equals in their Christian faith.

III. Other "Apostolic" Letters

(19) *Hebrews:* (ca. A.D. 90) Even in ancient times people realized that this letter did not come from the Pauline school. One of the most elegant writings in the New Testament, Hebrews is not really a letter at all but a sermon or theological treatise. It portrays Christ as the eternal, heavenly high priest, and was written to Christians who were becoming "lukewarm" in their faith—perhaps even going back to Judaism.

(20) *James:* (ca. A.D. 60) Again, more a homily than a letter, James represents the ethical teaching of early Christianity that has largely been taken over from Judaism. It also shows that the early Christians practiced confession of sins and anointing of the sick.

(21) *I Peter:* (ca. A.D. 100) A brief statement of Christian faith and practice at the turn of the century. This writing may contain parts of an early baptismal homily.

(22) *II Peter:* (ca. A.D. 110) Sometime after I Peter, this letter was written to reiterate Christian belief in the end of the world against false teachers who claimed that Christ's failure to return soon had proven that teaching wrong.

(23-25) *I, II, III John:* (ca. A.D. 110) Written by the disciples of the fourth evangelist, I John is sometimes called the first commentary on the gospel of John because it shows what practical conclusions Christians drew from the teaching of the evangelist.

(26) *Jude:* Written sometime before II Peter, it uses passages from this brief warning against false teachers.

(27) *Revelation:* (ca. A.D. 90) This account of a revelation to a Christian prophet named John opens with seven general letters to different Churches warning Christians against false

teachers and lukewarmness. That shows how important the use of letters was in early Christianity. The visions that follow the letters encourage Christians who were having to undergo martyrdom for their faith.

A brief inspection of this list points out several important things about the New Testament. First, its writings are of several different types. Second, they were written over a span of 50-75 years. Third, the earliest, the letters of Paul, are already over 20 years later than the death of Jesus. The first account of the life of Jesus is some 40 years later. Finally, all the New Testament writings—however strange some of them may seem to us—were addressed to specific communities and dealt with specific problems that people faced. The New Testament authors were not writing just for the sake of writing, nor even to leave a literary monument to posterity—indeed, many of them thought that the world would end within a short time. They were writing to nourish, safeguard and develop the faith of fellow Christians. This observation means that we should always try to understand a New Testament book in terms of the specific situation that the author is addressing. How is he meeting the problems and challenges of Christian faith in his day? Once we have done that, we can then ask how he might address himself to the problems and concerns that we have. Studying the Bible in its own, historical context does not destroy its relevance for Christians today. Rather, it helps us to really hear what the author is saying without covering his message with our own concerns, pieties and perhaps even misapprehensions of the Christian faith. People are usually amazed at how much they discover when they read the Bible carefully in this way. They find a richness and variety in the New Testament that had been covered over by years of sermons that treat only a few of the many themes found there.

Language, Text and Translation

In the past decade or so, both Catholics and Protestants have been subjected to a dizzying variety of new translations of the Bible. People constantly ask, "Why all the new translations?" Often they object to the popular tone and the colloquial language of the translations because they feel that a sacred book should use a more elevated, solemn or poetic style than that of everyday speech. First, we should realize that much of the New Testament was not written in "good Greek." For the most part its authors used the common language and expressions of their day. An educated person in antiquity would have been just as offended by some of its language as we are by some of the new translations. Perhaps we should remember that the saving power of the gospel message does not depend upon eloquence—as Paul was already having to remind the Corinthians (I Cor. 1:17-25; 2:1).

Many new translations try to use language that will roughly correspond to the original in emotional impact. We should remember that every translation is also an interpretation. There are no perfect one-on-one matches between the words of one language and those of another. Even the Greek word *euangelion* and its English translation "gospel" have a different set of meanings. The translator chooses words on the basis of what he or she thinks the author is trying to convey in a passage. Here is an example: In II Corinthians 10:10 Paul reports an accusation that some are making against him. A fairly literal translation would be:

> They say, "On the one hand, his letters are weighty and strong; but his bodily presence is weak and his speech contemptuous."

The New American Bible (NAB) has:

> "His letters," they say, "are severe and forceful, but when he is here in person he is unimpressive and his word makes no great impact."

And the Jerusalem Bible (JB):

> Someone said, "He writes powerful and strongly worded letters, but when he is with you, you see only half a man and no preacher at all."

Both modern translations are trying to make Paul's point in such a way that a person listening will understand the point of the argument immediately and not have to stop and think about what Paul is referring to. In this example, the NAB has the edge in being closer to the original, but some might argue that the JB has captured the angry ironic tone of these chapters better; that if Paul had written in American English, that is the way he would have spoken. These examples show you how much interpretation is involved in translating a text from one language to another.

Most of our quotations will be from the NAB with modifications where it does not accurately reflect the Greek text. However, the analysis has been done on the basis of the Greek so the reader may consult any translation that he or she wishes.

Modern Historico-Critical Study of the New Testament

Our previous sections have indicated the importance of historical research in understanding the Bible. Study of non-literary Greek papyri helps us understand the language in which the New Testament is written. We also look at popular writings of the time to discover how biblical writings compare with their contemporaries. We shall see that Paul's letters represent a unique departure from the way in which private letters were written.

We also look to historical study for information about the content of the New Testament. Information about people, places, events and customs shows us the context within which Christianity was born and developed. But there is even more. We want to understand how people in New Testament times thought about their world. What explanations did people give for the meaning of existence; for the possibilities of divine, human and even demonic action; for the final goal and destiny of human life? What did they experience as the frustrations and limitations of existence in this world? What did they hope for? How was their experience and hope shaped and answered by the various philosophies and religions competing with one another throughout the Mediterranean world? With the

plethora of philosophies, of new and old but westernized eastern cults, of astrologers and magicians that flood our culture,
we are in a good position to empathize with the religious
pluralism of the 1st century. Some theologians have suggested
that Christianity will lose its privileged place and have to
compete on equal footing with all these other modes of "salvation." Christians should not be uneasy at such a prospect. That
was the situation when Christianity was born, and it did very
well. The religious pluralism of the time also left its mark in
the New Testament. Many different symbols were taken over
from the philosophical and religious language of the time and
used to express the reality of salvation found in Jesus. There
was no "official" theological language. Instead, the various
New Testament authors worked out their own ways of proclaiming the gospel. These different visions cannot and need
not be made into one amorphous lump. Doing so would be like
mixing together all the paints on your palette to get some
muddy color rather than enjoying the wide spectrum of colors.
In order to understand the concepts and symbols used in the
New Testament, we must find out everything we can about its
world.

The collection of canonical Christian writings is called
"new testament" to distinguish it from those canonical writings inherited from Judaism that Christians call "Old Testament." (Since "Old Testament" has negative overtones that are
unfair to Judaism, Christians are beginning to use the more
ecumenical expression "Hebrew Bible.") The parallel expressions imply, of course, that the most important source of New
Testament religious thought and language was the Jewish
tradition from which Jesus and his followers came. For the
New Testament authors there was no other "Word of God," no
other "Sacred Scripture" than the Old Testament. They quote
and allude to it constantly as evidence for what God requires of
humanity. But when we speak about the relationship between
Christianity and Judaism, we must remember several things.
First, just as you cannot find out about 1st-century Christianity by going to a 20th-century church, so you cannot find out

about 1st-century Judaism by going to a 20th-century synagogue or Seder service. You might find out more about both by going to an out-of-the-way Arab village in the Middle East where life goes on much as it did centuries ago. Both religions have had a long—and in many respects diverging—history. Each is now a distinct religious option with its own unique vision. Further, present-day Judaism and Christianity are the descendents of two among several religious options that existed within 1st-century Judaism.

One of the major efforts of present-day scholarship has been to recover the religious diversity of 1st-century Judaism. The discovery of the library of a sectarian Jewish group, the Essenes, near the Dead Sea in 1945, drew worldwide attention to the diversity of 1st-century Judaism. In the early enthusiasm for the new finds, people speculated that John the Baptist and Jesus had been Essenes, or even that Jesus and the mysterious "teacher of righteousness," who founded the sect, were identical. Subsequent study of the documents has shown these hypotheses to be incorrect. But we have found important parallels to the language and customs in the New Testament suggesting that both groups drew on religious expressions that later passed out of use in Judaism, just as the language of the Church Fathers was quite different from much of the New Testament. This same Qumran library has also provided our oldest copies of the Hebrew Bible and thus aided scholars in understanding the Hebrew text. Currently, excavations around Jerusalem, in Caesarea, in the old synagogues of Galilee and in the major Mediterranean cities associated with the rise of Christianity may all yield further insights into the world of the New Testament. Of course, archaeological discoveries are not our only source of information about the times. The literary output of the Hellenistic and Graeco-Roman period, while not as well-known as that of classical Greece and Rome, was vast. Both Jewish and pagan authors continue to provide new insights into the world in which Christianity came into existence.

Literary Analysis of the New Testament

Obviously, historico-critical study of the New Testament demands that a person master several languages and a wealth of detailed information. General readers must look to commentaries, dictionaries and encyclopediae to summarize the results of such research. At the same time, we cannot do without such research if we are to hear the Bible speak in its own language and time. But there is another side to New Testament study which is more readily accessible to the general student without a strong background in ancient history: internal literary analysis.

Historico-literary analysis compares biblical works with other literature being written at the same time. It provides us with clues as to how contemporary readers might have understood the New Testament books. Internal literary analysis, on the other hand, seeks to analyze the individual works themselves. What are the author's main themes? How has he structured his work? What patterns of composition can be discovered there? Sometimes, as in the case of structuralist analysis, a rather arcane vocabulary and unfamiliar technique is employed. In other cases, more conventional modes of literary analysis are used on the biblical text. The potential advantage of the kind of work being done by the structuralists is that much of the material on which they work is folklore and myth, that is, material derived from oral and popular story-telling. Such material is closer to the milieu of New Testament narrative than more recent literature. But the simpler types of literary analysis have the advantage of producing results that can be easily "checked" by the general reader. He or she is asked to attend carefully to the main patterns and techniques that structure biblical narrative. Anyone can become a more discerning bible reader by learning the themes, patterns and techniques used in the various books. Throughout this book we will be asking you to look at specific passages. If you analyze them as we suggest, you should then be able to apply the same methods to other passages.

Existential and Theological Analysis

The New Testament is not, of course, simply or even primarily a work of ancient history or literature. Its authors want to persuade us to see Jesus Christ as the final revelation of God and to adopt a style of life in accord with that revelation. The vast differences between their culture and ours and the long centuries of Christian tradition have led people to seek further methods of bringing out the meaning of the Bible for today. Existential or phenomenological analyses seek to describe the human experience of being-in-the-world that is reflected in the pages of the Bible. What does the text show us about the hazards and possibilities of human existence? Using philosophical language to describe the message of the Bible on these points, such interpretations seek to show the relevance of the biblical witness for our common human experience. Although the language of the Bible belongs to earlier cultures, it may—indeed, must, if it is to retain its role as revelation— address fundamental human concerns and experiences. The interpreter, then, must locate the same experiences and concerns in his or her own experience. They, too, must be described in existential or phenomenological language. Then both contemporary and biblical evaluations of the human situation may be compared. While this method may seem unnecessarily complex, it makes an important point. The Bible must be interpreted in order to be understood. Indeed, all human communication involves the hearer or reader in interpreting the message received. We make our interpretations on the basis of a shared language and cultural assumptions about the world, society, humanity, etc. First-century authors and readers shared a different set of assumptions. Unless we look for a common meeting ground between their experience of being human and our own, their witness cannot really challenge us. These observations have a further corollary: Interpreting the Bible *does not* mean repeating 1st-century phrases and metaphors whose import is quite different in our own culture. In other words, it is not necessarily truer to the gospel message

to use only words and phrases derived from the New Testament. We may need to use quite different words and expressions to make the same point today that the New Testament
made in the 1st century. All such interpretations depend upon
the careful historical exegesis described above to ensure that
they are not merely the fanciful applications of an individual
interpreter or preacher.

Just as existential or phenomenological interpretation
seeks to bridge the gap between New Testament times and our
own by describing the human situation in which we are all
involved, so theological interpretations seek to bridge the gap
between the religious and theological insights of the Bible and
our own religious and theological questions. Because the New
Testament is a religious text, historico-critical interpretation
will already have given a descriptive analysis of the religious
and theological positions of the various authors. But our religious and theological problems are often not the same as
theirs. The theologian must look for analogies between New
Testament situations and problems and our own. He or she
may then claim scriptural warrant for a contemporary solution
on the basis of that analogy. The status of the Bible as canonical Scripture necessitates such appeals whether in theological
books or in the preaching and teaching of the Church. All the
other methods described could be—and often are—practiced
by scholars interested in antiquity but without any commitment to the Christian tradition. But theological interpretation
can only properly take place within the context of the Christian community.

New Testament as Scripture:
The Problem of the Canon

We have already pointed out the diversity among the New
Testament writings. They all presuppose the Old Testament as
God's revelation, but only the revelation of John claims to have
been revealed. Actually, whenever we speak of the "New Testament" we are referring to the process by which the Church
selected these writings from its earliest period to be a norma-

tive standard for Christian belief and praxis. In A.D. 367, the festal letter of Athanasius fixed the boundaries of the Christian canon for both the Old Testament and the New Testament. We cannot trace all of the fascinating history behind that final selection but must be content with reviewing the main lines of development.

Like many religions, Christianity did not begin with a new Sacred Scripture. It began with the person and preaching of Jesus, who presupposed the Scripture of his people. For a few decades after his death, that teaching was handed down from person to person either orally or in small collections of sayings or miracles. The move to write accounts of the life of Jesus did not arise until the last quarter of the 1st century, perhaps motivated by the growing number of converts and the deaths of many of the first generation. The developments that will lead to the formation of a specifically Christian Scripture of Old and New Testaments only occur about a century later. Before that, the gospels, letters of Paul and other writings from the early period were circulated among the various Churches but were not defined as revelation in the same sense as the Old Testament.

Christians were forced to clarify their stance on these writings by developments—all felt to be heretical—that occurred in the second half of the 2nd century. The Jewish roots of Christianity were attacked by the heretic Marcion. He used those passages where Paul speaks of Christ as ending the Law to argue that the loving Father of Jesus was not the God of the Old Testament. Consequently, the Old Testament and any Christian writings inspired by it could not serve as Sacred Scripture. Instead Marcion proposed a "canon" comprising expurgated versions of Luke and ten Pauline epistles. This heresy led Christians to reaffirm the Old Testament as the true revelation of God.

During the same period, Christian Gnostic groups arose who claimed that Jesus had secretly taught the disciples Gnostic doctrines about humanity's true destiny in a light world beyond this evil one and beyond the reach of its evil god. Like

Marcion, they rejected the Old Testament and its God. They used elaborate allegorical interpretations of the Bible to prove that it taught the truth about a higher God. The problem that the Gnostics posed for the development of the Christian claim followed from their claim to possess secret teaching that the risen Jesus had given to the disciples. The most famous Gnostic work is the *Gospel of Thomas*. It is a collection of sayings attributed to the risen Jesus and begins thus:

> These are the secret words which the living Jesus spoke, and which Didymus Thomas wrote down. And he said: "The one who finds the interpretation of these words will not taste death."

To provide some basis for their arguments against such heretical views and secret gospels, the orthodox Christians settled on our four gospels as the only ones in which authentic teaching could be found. They realized that there are many differences between the four gospels but accepted all four as genuine apostolic witness rather than adopt just one. By A.D. 180, Bishop Ireneus of Lyons defended the existence of a four-gospel canon by claiming that it corresponded to the order of the world. In his great work *Against Heresies*, he wrote:

> It is not possible for there to be more or fewer gospels than there are. For, since there are four zones of the world in which we live and four principle winds, while the Church is scattered throughout the world, and the pillar and ground of the Church is the gospel and the spirit of life; it is fitting that she should have four pillars, breathing out immortality on every side. . . . He who was manifested to men has given us the gospel under four aspects, but bound together by one Spirit (III.xi.8).

Ireneus goes on to describe the "aspects of each gospel" and to condemn both Marcion and the Gnostics.

He also rejects a third group, the Montanists, whose doctrines also influenced the development of a Christian canon. A prophet called Montanus had started the sect that claimed inspiration of the Holy Spirit and the imminent coming of the end of the world. Even if he, himself, did not make such a claim, Montanus' followers soon argued that he was the Spirit-Paraclete promised in the gospel of John. Their claims led Christians to realize that the presence of the Spirit in the Church could not imply new revelations. Revelation was said to have been completed with the apostolic age. Therefore, all writings revered as Christian Scripture had to have an apostolic origin. Many Church Fathers knew that Paul did not write Hebrews, for example, but they included it in the canon under his name to guarantee its apostolicity.

The two other major criteria in arguments about the canon were that a writing had to be widely used in the Church and that its teaching had to be in line with the rule of faith. Some very popular early Christian writings like the *Shepherd of Hermas* — which is quite old and was frequently copied into New Testament manuscripts even into the Middle Ages — could not meet these criteria. The earlier Church Fathers like Ireneus do not use inspiration as a criterion for including or rejecting a work. They assume that any work accepted into the canon is inspired by the Spirit. Ireneus used the Spirit in the passage above to explain the unity of the four gospels. These observations make it clear that the reason we have a New Testament is because the Church felt the need to single out certain writings from the earliest period as authentic and reliable guides to her faith in Jesus Christ. They did not all have to be apostolic in the same sense; nor did they all have to present exactly the same picture of Jesus. But they did all have to reflect the Spirit and present a true picture of the faith.

The Church and the Study of the Bible

The Vatican II constitution, *On Revelation* (1965), began to bring the Bible back to the attention of Catholics. Translation into modern languages is encouraged; the Old Testament is accorded its rightful place as Scripture; bishops and clergy are exhorted to preach on Scripture and to see to it that opportunities for study of the Bible are made available to the faithful. Catholic biblical scholars are encouraged to pursue their studies using the best methods of research available. That document gave Scripture a place of honor parallel to the sacraments: "The Church has always venerated the divine Scriptures just as she venerates the body of the Lord" (vi: 21). In the past decade, Catholic biblical scholars have produced a wealth of scholarly and popular studies of the Bible. They serve equally with Protestant colleagues in national and international societies for the study of the Bible and on the editorial boards of scholarly journals. A Catholic no longer has to defend his or her scholarly integrity against the suspicion that dogmatics or an uninformed magisterium is controlling the results. Undergraduates elect courses on the Bible, and the Bible is one of the most frequently requested topics in adult education. When I recently asked my High School CCD class what changes they would like to see in the liturgy, they replied that they would like sermons that really explained the biblical readings. Music came second. Clearly the Council's decree hit on a need in the Church.

But the Council was only summing up two earlier decrees on bible study. In 1943, Pius XII issued an important encyclical, *Divino Afflante Spiritu*. There, he encouraged biblical scholars to use all the methods of language study, historical research and archaeology. They are to study ancient forms of writing when seeking the literal meaning of the biblical text. He urged them to set out carefully the theological doctrine on faith and morals contained in the individual writings. The Pope said that interpretations should be sought that are both in accord with church teaching and that also fit the requirements of historical research. He pointed out that there are very few biblical texts whose meaning has been definitely established by the magisterium. Pius XII realized that if Scripture is truly the Word of God, honest inquiry into its meaning cannot undermine its divine teaching, and his confidence has meant a great deal to biblical scholars.

In 1964, the Pontifical Biblical Commission issued an instruction "On the Historical Truth of the Gospels." This in-

struction was occasioned by the growing realization that the
gospels were not intended to be historical or biographical reports. It points out that the teaching of Jesus passed through
three stages:

(1) Jesus used the language and concepts of his day to
explain his teaching to his audience and to his disciples.

(2) After the resurrection, the apostles clearly recognized
the divinity of Jesus. They, too, used the language of their time
to proclaim his saving death and resurrection. When they
looked back on his life from the post-resurrection perspective,
they were able to relate what he had done to his divine status
as it had become clear to them after the resurrection. Further,
we must study the various forms in which they cast their
preaching.

(3) The *gospel-writers* (note that they came after the apostles) put this instruction in writing. It had been passed on
orally and in pre-gospel written collections. The evangelists
selected things from this oral tradition. Sometimes they interpreted it to fit the situation in the Church at their time. This
adaptation and reinterpretation did not destroy the truth of the
life and teaching of Jesus. That teaching was never intended to
be "remembered" by rote repetition but was intended to serve
the Church as a basis for her faith and action.

In sum, then, the Church is concerned to have Scripture
play a vital role in the life of all people. Biblical scholarship
has played an important role in that revitalization. But the
second Vatican Council was not concerned with scholars. It
was addressing all Catholics. The Church does not venerate
the Bible because of its antiquity. Rather, as the living Word of
God, it continues to guide Christians to an understanding of
God and salvation; to inspire them to live in obedience to the
Word of God. Or, as Ireneus said of the gospels, Scripture goes
on "breathing out immortality on every side."

Using this Book

Since the reason for studying the Bible is to help you read
the New Testament, this book is not to be read through like a
novel. Instead, you should read it along with your New Testa-

ment. Most chapters are about a particular book in the New Testament. Read that book through quickly before beginning the pertinent chapter. Within each chapter we have picked out certain passages for analysis. These analyses are designed to help you learn what to look for in reading biblical material. They should also help you understand and evaluate some of the claims made about the Bible by popular speakers and in the media. Many false claims can be easily dismissed by anyone who has a clear understanding of the New Testament. We have included a great deal of historical material in our analyses because that material is the most difficult for the non-specialist to find. But we have also given examples of literary and theological interpretation. The study questions at the end of each chapter will help you check your understanding of the material presented. Try to answer each question in your own words just as you might explain it to someone else. If you have to keep looking up the words of the chapter, then you have not yet really made the ideas your own so that you can use them.

STUDY QUESTIONS

1. What is the New Testament? When was it written?
2. Why are there so many new translations of the Bible?
3. Why do Christians consider the "Hebrew Bible" Sacred Scripture?
4. List four different ways of analyzing a biblical text. Give a brief description of each one.
5. What led the early Christians to make a collection of Christian writings that would be considered Sacred Scripture?
6. What criteria did a writing have to meet in order to be included in the New Testament?

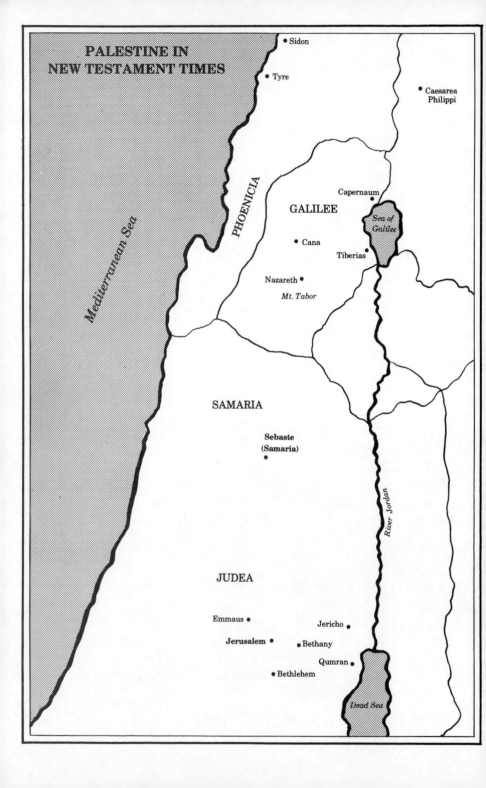

Chapter Two

THE WORLD OF JESUS

In order to understand Jesus and the first disciples, we must learn something about the world in which they lived. We need to understand the political situation that controlled their lives as well as the various religious groups that were also seeking to teach people about God and salvation.

Political History

Although Judea was just a small country, it lay on major trade routes. Throughout its history, major empires, Syria to the North, Egypt to the South and Persia to the East have fought to control its territory. Alexander the Great's conquest of the East (333 B.C.) brought Western empires into the power struggle. His successors dominated the scene until Pompey conquered Palestine for the Romans in 63 B.C. As the Jews looked back to the great empires of David and Solomon, they continued to hope for independence; for a state dedicated to God that would take its place among the nations of the world. For about a hundred years before Pompey, they had seemed close to that ideal. When the revolt against Rome was crushed in 70 A.D., such dreams became more remote. The Romans destroyed the splendid temple at Jerusalem, which figures in so many New Testament stories. The religious parties mentioned in the New Testament as well as many popular beliefs developed during the struggles of the previous two centuries.

Two problems confronted Jewish people. One was political; the other, cultural. The Greek conquerors had brought their culture with them. Other peoples in the East assimilated it. They organized their cities along Greek lines. The wealthy adopted Greek names and clothes. The gymnasium, the race track and the theater as well as temples and statues to the gods and goddesses, who patronized those activities, were all signs of that assimilation. Men from the East began to appear in Athens as founders and members of philosophical schools. Some of the wealthy Jewish aristocrats wanted to take the same route. Judaism, too, was to become Hellenized, and, to varying degrees, it did assimilate Greek culture even in Palestine itself. (*See* I Macc 1:13-15; II Macc 4:10-15.) Other Jews saw Hellenization as the abandonment of everything Judaism stood for. They called for devoted observance of the Law (cf. I Macc 2:42). Ben Sirach argued that human wisdom could not replace divine revelation. He admonished Jews not to be ashamed of or transgress their Law (Sir 10:19; 42:20).

Social distinctions drawn in this period continue into New Testament times. The wealthy aristocracy was the source of the move to turn Jerusalem into a Greek city. It was divided into two groups. At the top, the priestly families headed by the High Priest controlled the temple, which not only gave them religious importance but secular as well. The temple treasury, for example, served as a deposit bank for wealthy individuals. The secular aristocracy—probably the older of the two groups—lived off agricultural holdings and high administrative posts. New Testament readers will recognize the "masters" and absentee landlords in this category.

The scribes develop as the priests become an aristocratic caste that is no longer concerned with interpreting the Law. The scribes took over that important role. One became a scribe by learning and not by birth. They tried to interpret the Law so that it could apply to every detail of life. A group called "the Pious" and later the Pharisees were offshoots of that movement.

Most people in Judea were small peasants, the farmers,

fishermen and housewives of many of Jesus' parables. The urban population of Jerusalem included craftsmen, some merchants and those involved in the various forms of taxcollecting. Anyone who reads the New Testament can see that its traditions stem from this peasant majority. The wealthy landlords, the priests, and even the scribes and Pharisees were looked upon as "others," outsiders. They rarely do anything praiseworthy. Some 200 years earlier, Ben Sirach wrote of the unrest and conspiracy in the cities that was being caused by the sharp division between rich and poor (26:5). He does grant, however, that a rich person who does not exploit the poor might be considered good. However, the antagonisms mentioned in his work had solidified by New Testament times. Economically, rich oppose poor; morally, the sinners oppose the righteous, and religiously the unbelievers oppose the pious.

The Maccabean Revolt (175–135 B.C.)

Around 175 B.C., Antiochus IV became the ruler of the Syrian part of Alexander's legacy. Judea had been under Syrian control since 200 B.C. Antiochus pursued policies of Hellenization and expansion throughout his empire. He appropriated the large sums of money needed to support the military forces necessary to subdue the state of unrest throughout his empire. Certain families of High Priests supported Antiochus and would pay him large sums to hold the office. The once hereditary position was now a political "pay-off," given to the highest bidder or current royal favorite. (Such an arrangement may have existed between Caiaphas and Pilate since Caiaphas lost his office soon after Pilate was removed.)

The political intrigues and Hellenizing policies of these aristocratic High Priests lost them popular support. Revolts occurred during Antiochus' campaigns against Egypt (169/68 B.C.). These uprisings may have been led by "the Pious," whose rallying cry was "the Law of Moses." Antiochus retaliated by confiscating property, introducing pagan settlers and establishing a garrison of Syrians in the fort, the Acra, on the temple mount in Jerusalem. Naturally the settlers also brought their Syrian gods with them. But Antiochus' retaliation did not stop there. On his return from the second Egyptian campaign (168 B.C.), Antiochus launched a full scale effort to wipe out the Jewish religion, that barbarian superstition.

(1) The temple was renamed for Zeus Olympius.

(2) An altar to Zeus, "the abomination" (Dn 9:27; 11:31; 12:11), was set up there.

(3) Circumcision and keeping the Sabbath were prohibited.

(4) Copies of the Torah were burned.

(5) High places and altars were built on which swine were sacrificed.

(6) Jews were forced to celebrate the king's birthday once a month.

(7) They were also forced to take part in festal processions in honor of Dionysius.

Those items of Jewish belief and practice that Antiochus singled out took on immense symbolic significance for the pious Jew: the temple, the Torah scrolls, the Sabbath, circumcision, the dietary ban against eating pork. It is often very difficult for Christian students to understand why the abandonment of such requirements occasioned such terrific debate within the 1st-century Church. But heroic Jews had died rather than give them up during Antiochus' attempt to supress their religion. People knew stories about these heroic martyrs, that they treasured. Read the story of the martyrs in II Maccabees 6-14.

The resistance might have remained sporadic and fruitless if the Maccabee family had not emerged as leaders. (Read 1 Maccabees 1-7.) From 167-160 B.C., Judas Maccabee led the Jewish resistance in a series of guerilla actions against the Syrians. They also had to help fellow Jews who lived in or near pagan cities in Palestine and were persecuted by the inhabitants. In 164 B.C., Judas had gained control of the temple but not of the Syrian garrison. He was able to rededicate the temple to Yahweh. The Jewish feast of Hannukah commemorates that rededication. He also reestablished the Torah as the law of the land. A treaty signed in 162 B.C. recognized the freedom of the Jews to follow their own laws but not their independence from the Syrian garrison.

War continued for most of this period. Judas was succeeded by his brother Jonathan. In this early period, Jewish rulers were still confirmed in office by the Syrian king. (Read 1 Maccabees 10:65, Jonathan is made general and governor of Judea.) They were deeply involved in the power struggles for the Seleucid throne. In 152 B.C., the Syrians made Jonathan High Priest even though he had no legitimate claim to that office, since he was not descended from a high priestly family. The previous legitimate High Priest had been a rampant Hellenizer, Alcimius. There is a gap in our historical records between the end of his priesthood and that of Jonathan. Some scholars think that the High Priest, then, was a man whose name is lost to history and who survives only as the mysterious "Teacher of Righteousness," the founder of the Jewish sect at Qumran. If so, he must have come from among the ranks of "the Pious," who supported the Maccabees in their revolt but who became suspicious of their later policies and their political ties with the Syrians. Jonathan carried his search for political allies to the point of negotiating with Sparta and Rome (1 Macc 12:1-23).

Jonathan was murdered in 143 B.C. and succeeded by his brother Simon. Simon (143-134 B.C.) was able to abolish the Syrian garrison in Jerusalem, but he was still plagued with the problem that he did not come from a legitimate kingly or high priestly family. In 140 B.C., a great assembly of Jews was called to establish Simon and his sons as High Priest, governor and commander of Israel (1 Macc 14:41-47). Even though 1 Maccabees is pro-Maccabeean, its author hints that there was resistance to that policy. We learn that a decree was issued forbidding opposition to Simon whether by priest or layman. Private assemblies were forbidden. Further, Simon and his descendants were granted the high priesthood only "until a faithful prophet shall arise"—a tacit recognition that the legitimate priesthood was being set aside. 1 Maccabees 15:21 tells us that Simon also had trouble with certain "political criminals or dissidents" who fled to Egypt.

Simon was murdered by his son-in-law, Ptolemy, in 134 B.C. and succeeded by his son, John Hyrcanus I (134-104 B.C.). John Hyrcanus undertook a systematic conquest of the country beginning in Samaria. He captured Greek coastal cities to open the trade routes and imposed severe penalties on those who would not convert to Judaism. But his policy seems to have been motivated by economic and nationalistic concerns, not religious ones. His ideal was to have all Palestine united and Jewish as it had been under King David. His son, Alexander Janneus (103-76 B.C.) continued this warlike policy and brought all Palestine under his control. He came close to restoring the old boundaries of David. However, he did not have popular support. When Jerusalem revolted against him, he was only able to retain power because he maintained mercenary troops. The rift between the Jewish kings and the people was intensified as the kings took on Greek names and the other trappings of Hellenistic monarchs.

Political Parties and Sects

During these years the major sectarian divisions that we find in New Testament times came into existence. Although they had begun as populist leaders, the Hasmonean monarchs became a new, wealthy aristocracy. The Sadducees were an aristocratic party who supported Hasmonean policies. Although the first historical reference to this group does not occur until the time of John Hyrcanus, they probably included survivors of older aristocratic families. A conservative party, they guarded their priestly prerogatives jealously. As the reader of the New Testament can observe, they did not enjoy popular support.

Possibly as early as Simon's reign, the party of "the Pious" (Hasidim) split. The Teacher of Righteousness led his followers out to the wilderness near the Dead Sea, Qumran, where they established a sectarian community. They claimed that the Jerusalem temple and cult had been corrupted by a false priesthood. They sought to observe the Law in strict purity according to the teachings of their founder, and expected a true prophet as well as a priestly and royal Messiah to usher in the messianic age. At that time, the truly righteous—members of the sect, not all of whom lived in the desert community— would be vindicated, while evil and those who had given into it would be destroyed. Although no Essenes are mentioned in the New Testament, their writings, the Dead Sea Scrolls, have provided important parallels to some of the language and customs we find in the New Testament.

Another group of "the Pious," the Pharisees, were a populist movement whose origins probably lay close to that of the scribes with whom they are associated in the New Testament. Their opponents called them the "separated ones" because they avoided Gentiles and sinners. They come in for bad press in the New Testament where they are portrayed as hypocrites who did not care about the people. However, that image is the result of bitter controversy between Christians and Pharisees. Historically, the Pharisees would be considered the religious liberals. Unlike the Essenes, they did not think that withdrawal was the only way a person could be faithful to the Law. They claimed that along with the written Law, God had also established the oral Law, which allowed one to interpret the written law in such a way that it could be followed in changed circumstances. The Pharisees had a vision of all Israel following the Law faithfully. The Essenes considered their way of interpreting the Law too liberal. They referred to the Pharisees as "interpreters of smooth things." Jesus, on the other hand, does not reject the idea of interpreting the Law but the way in which they went about it in specific instances.

Christians often think of Sadducees and Pharisees as though they belonged to a single party. In fact, they were often bitter opponents. The religiously conservative Sadducees rejected such Pharisaic views as the existence of the oral Law and belief in the resurrection of the dead (cf. Mt 22:23). The rivalry between the two groups had its social and religious aspects. Socially, the Pharisees represented the interests of the populace against the wealthy aristocracy. But the rivalry also represented conflict between two religious institutions within Judaism: the temple, controlled by the Sadducees, and the synagogues, where reading and studying the Law was the focus of worship. Archaeological investigation of Galilean synagogues may eventually provide more information about the development of that institution. At present, our earliest example of a synagogue is the one in Herod's fortress at Masada. After the devastation of the war with Rome in A.D. 66-70 when the Jerusalem temple was destroyed, the Pharisees would be the ones to direct the future history of Judaism. But for most of this earlier period it is the aristocratic Sadducees who have the upper hand.

Roman Conquest

The Roman conquest of Palestine in 63 B.C. forced the separation of religious and political authority. Judea was annexed to the Roman province of Syria. Herod the Great was the most interesting and influential political figure in this period. He survived several changes of allegiance during the power struggles between Pompey, Julius Caesar, Mark Antony and Octavius. In 40 B.C., he was declared King of Judea by the Roman senate, but he still had to use Roman troops to conquer his province so that his reign did not begin until 37 B.C. As a vassal of Rome, a *rex socius*, an allied king, Herod was independent of the Roman legate in Syria. He had full domestic autonomy and did not have to pay tribute. However, he was subject to the emperor in matters of tribute and foreign policy. Herod spent the first years of his reign (37-25 B.C.) ruthlessly consolidating his power. The middle years (25-13 B.C.), he devoted to a variety of cultural improvements financed, of course, by taxes.

Herod was a Hellenist at heart. Many of his cultural endowments served to spread Greek culture. He built temples, theaters and race tracks in established cities and even whole cities. He endowed the Olympic games. Jerusalem received gardens, parks, fountains, a theater, an amphitheater, a royal palace and a fortress (Antonia) at one corner of the temple. He also built a chain of fortresses throughout the country. Masada, the last stronghold of Jewish resistance to Rome (it did not fall until A.D. 73) is the most spectacular. Today, Israeli soldiers take their oath atop the ancient fortress whose defenders all committed suicide rather than be taken alive by the Romans. Today's soldiers promise never to let Masada fall again. Around 20 B.C., Herod began a massive project to restore the temple in Jerusalem. This project was not completed until A.D. 63. But that project could not buy Herod popularity. His court was completely Hellenized, and people remembered that he was only half Jewish. The Pharisees twice refused to pledge allegiance to Herod and to the emperor. Herod was only able to hold his people in check by force.

The last years of Herod's reign were marred by fear and paranoia and violence over succession within his own family. Before he was finished, Herod had had three of his own sons executed. Since there is no independent record of the story about the slaughter of the innocents (Mt 2), some scholars believe that that story comes from a legend about Herod that had grown up after he had murdered his own sons for allegedly plotting to seize his throne. Certainly the reaction to a threat against his kingship (Jesus) reported in Matthew's story is typical of Herod's behavior in his later years.

Herod died in 4 B.C. A codicil to his will asked the Roman senate to divide his territory between three surviving sons. Augustus honored the will but refused to give any of the sons the title of king. Philip (4 B.C.–34 A.D.) became tetrarch of the regions North and East of the lake of Galilee. His kingdom was the buffer between the Nabateans and the Parthians, Rome's long-time enemies. He was a good ruler, praised for his benevolence and justice. Herod Antipas (4 B.C.–A.D. 39) was Tetrarch of Galilee and Perea. He built the city of Tiberias on the western shore of the lake of Galilee as his capital. He was known for his indolence and vanity. His repudiation of a wife, who was the daughter of the Nabatean king, in order to marry his brother's wife, Herodias, drew the condemnation of John the Baptist. Although an angry Herod could have the Baptist beheaded, he could not dispose of the angry Nabateans so easily. They defeated him in A.D. 37. In A.D. 39, Caligula, the emperor, exiled him to Lyons. Most of the references to Herod in the New Testament are to this Herod, not to his father Herod the Great. Archeleus (4 B.C.–A.D. 6), the oldest, was the least successful. As ethnarch, he had inherited half of his father's kingdom, Judea, Samaria and Idumea. His high-handed aristocratic ways made him extremely unpopular despite his attempts to curry favor with extensive building projects. The Jews finally sent a delegation to Rome asking for his removal. In A.D. 6, he was exiled to Vienna in Southern Gaul and his territory turned into a province governed by a Roman official.

The Province of Judea

When Judea was made a province, the Syrian legate, P. Sulpicius Quirinus ordered a census. Resistance to the census was lead by someone known as Judas, the Galilean. Perhaps he and his followers looked back to the ideals that had inspired the Maccabees. In older books and in some popular works, one sometimes reads that Galilee was the home of an organized resistance movement, the zealots. Some have tried to justify Christian involvement in political revolutions by claiming that Jesus, himself, was a zealot. Recent historical studies have pointed out the following facts:

(1) Although Judas is called "the Galilean," his resistance activity was in Judea. Perhaps "the Galilean" was a negative epithet of his opponents, since Judeans considered Galilee "back woods"; their religious devotion might even be suspect. There were so many Gentile cities in Galilee that it was called "Galilee of the Gentiles."

(2) Our first real evidence for an organized zealot movement comes from Judea in the A.D. 60's just before the outbreak of the Jewish war against Rome. In that war, the resistance in Galilee collapsed easily. Therefore, it is more likely that Judas, the Galilean, was operating the kind of sporadic

resistance that we find off and on in the area throughout the
Hasmonean period. People never forgot the ideals of the Maccabees. They never lost their desire to be free from foreign
domination. Since the zealots did not come into being as an
organized party until the 60's and then did so in Judea, Jesus
cannot have been a zealot. Judeans would have looked down on
someone of Galilean origin as ill-educated and possibly religiously suspect. The New Testament gives us plenty of examples of that sort of prejudice. Galileans could be recognized by
their accent.

Census and the Birth of Jesus

The attentive reader will notice that there is a chronological problem associated with the two stories of Jesus' birth.
Matthew associates it with events in Herod's last years. Herod
murdered his sons in 7 B.C. and died in 4 B.C. Luke, on the
other hand, associates it with the census under Quirinus in
A.D. 6. The two cannot be reconciled. The historian may decide
that one or the other is the right date, or that both are using
different traditions about Jesus' birth. In our age of birth cer-
tificates that bear not only the day but the time of birth, we
forget that in cultures without such record keeping, people do
not know exactly how old they are. Instead, the birth of a child
may be associated with some major event that occurred around
that time. There probably was some simpler story about the
time of Jesus' birth being one of political unrest in Judea. Later
stories record this in two separate events: Herod's slaughter of
"the innocents" and the political unrest that followed his death
(7-4 B.C.) and the unrest associated with the census under
Quirinus (A.D. 6). Without accurate records, people would not
be certain about the exact chronological relationship between
those events. If the tradition that Jesus was in his 30's when he
died is correct, then both dates are slightly off. But people in
antiquity would hardly have shared our concern over matters
of precise dating. It was sufficient to know the "great events"
associated with the time of Jesus' birth.

Prefect and Procurator

As a Roman province, Judea was ruled by an official appointed by the emperor. There was no stipulated term of office for such officials. Although Pilate is sometimes referred to as "procurator" of Judea, that title was not used until the time of the emperor Claudius. Thus the gospels are using the later terminology. Archaeologists have found an inscription on a building in Caesarea Maritima which tells us that Pilate was *prefect* of Judea. The prefect had full authority over his province. He could even order capital punishment. He was expected to collect the tribute owed to Rome and to maintain order. If he needed military help, he could call on the legate of Syria. The prefect usually lived in Herod's palace in Caesarea. When he came to Jerusalem, he either lived in the palace Herod had built in the western part of the city or in the fortress Antonia overlooking the temple. Thus, historians are not quite sure of the location of Jesus' trial. Perhaps future archaeological investigations will bring new evidence to light.

Pilate

We have enough information about Pilate in Christian, Jewish and Roman sources to draw a fairly accurate picture of the man who sentenced Jesus to death. The fact that he was appointed by Sejunus, the anti-Jewish advisor to the emperor Tiberius, should already warn us that Pilate will not be sympathetic to the sensibilities of his subjects. Indeed, his administration shows a consistent pattern of brutal acts against the Jews. Herod Agrippa complained to the emperor Caligula that Pilate was wanton, cruel, took bribes and executed people without trial (Philo, *Gaius* 38:301-302). Specific examples of Pilate's brutality include:

(1) Smuggling Roman standards into Jerusalem at night when he knew that it would offend the Jewish prohibition against images. The Jews protested for five days and were even willing to die to get them removed (Josephus, *Wat* 2.9,2-3: 169-74; *Antiquities* 18.3,1: 53-59; Philo, *Gaius* 38: 299ff.).

(2) Taking money from the temple treasury to pay for a

new aqueduct for Jerusalem. Private individuals were expected to pay for such projects, and the temple was used as a
"bank" by the wealthy aristocracy. Pilate probably saw that
move as a logical way to obtain the money from them. But the
people perceived his action as an attack against the public
treasury used to maintain the temple. They demonstrated outside Pilate's palace. He retaliated by sending soldiers disguised
as demonstrators out into the crowd to beat them (War 2.9,4:
175-177).

(3) Mingling the blood of some Galileans with their sacrifices. We have no further information about this incident
referred to in Luke 13:1.

(4) Slaughtering a group of Samaritans who had gathered
on Mt. Gerezim in expectation of seeing lost temple treasures
discovered. This act of hostility (A.D. 35) led the Jews to com-
plain to the Syrian legate. Pilate was sent to Rome to account for
his actions and was exiled (Antiquities 18.4,1-2: 85-89). No
more is known about him. Possibly the anti-Christian persecution that led to the death of Stephen occurred in A.D. 36 while
Pilate was in Rome and before the new procurator had arrived.
A similar gap between the procurators Felix and Festus (ca.
A.D. 60) allowed the martyrdom of James and kept Paul in
prison.

We do not need to go into the details of the rest of the
history of the province. Unrest and hostility against Rome fes-
tered throughout the period. In the late 50's or early 60's the
zealots emerge as an organized insurrectionist group. A particularly ruthless segment of the party, the sicarii, murdered
prominent people who were thought to be collaborating with
Rome. Their first victim was the High Priest, Jonathan. Naturally the procurators retaliated in kind. They tried to extermi-
nate the zealots and plundered the province. Finally under
Eleazer and his aide Menahem, the Jews organized for war. An
initial victory over the procurator and the Syrian legate in
A.D. 66 raised hope that the Maccabean success could be repeated. But the Roman empire did not have the internal
weaknesses and civil wars that had plagued the Syrians 200

years earlier. Nero sent Vespasian, an experienced field commander, to quell the disturbance. Galilee fell easily. When spring came in A.D. 68, Vespasian was ready to move on Judea. The death of Nero in June, A.D. 68, led him to delay while waiting for developments in Rome. There the succession was chaotic. 68-69 A.D. is known as the year of the four emperors. But the Jewish resistance was also in chaos. Its leaders were fighting among themselves. In June, A.D. 69, Vespasian moved against Jerusalem with four legions. He had to return to Rome when he was acclaimed emperor and he left his son Titus in charge of the war. The Jewish historian Josephus tells gruesome stories of life inside the besieged city. Titus had erected a wall around it and he crucified anyone who tried to escape in sight of the defenders. Between August 8-10 his soldiers burned the temple and slaughtered its inhabitants. To many Jews the destruction of the temple was a great shock. Why had God not stepped in to save his temple as Jewish legend said he had done under the Maccabees? The walls of the city were levelled and most of it razed. Titus took captured Jewish leaders and the seven-branched candlestick from the temple sanctuary that had been lit to celebrate the liberation of the temple by the Maccabees every year for 200 years back to Rome where he marched them in his triumphal procession. You can still see this procession carved on the arch of Titus in Rome.

We do not know much about what happened to Christians during the war. A relatively late legend holds that they fled to Pella before the siege. Nothing either in the accounts of Jewish historians or in the gospel descriptions of the fall, suggests that they participated. If the war was interpreted ideologically as the messianic war before the end of the world, Christians would not participate because they knew that the Messiah had come. Later Christian writers tend to view the destruction of Jerusalem as punishment for Jewish rejection of Jesus (e.g. Lk 19:41-44). The Jewish historian, Josephus, on the other hand, claims that God had caused the Jews to lose the war because the nation as a whole had sinned and been led astray by the fanatical zealots. The fact that the fall of Jerusalem did not leave much of an impact on the New Testament is not—contrary to an argument recently advanced by J. A. T. Robinson—evidence that most of the New Testament was written before the war but shows that most of its writings stem from the Hellenistic Church, not from Judea. Even James, whose work is sometimes taken as a Jewish homily, shows by his style and exposition that he had received a Greek education. For all we know, the fall of Jerusalem may not have been any more traumatic for Jews living in the diaspora than it was for Christians. What Christianity did lose as a result of the war was the strong presence of Jewish Christians and the visible link with her past symbolized earlier by the Church in Jerusalem. Twenty years earlier Paul had labored to keep his Gentile converts mindful of that link by having them contribute to a collection for the poor in Jerusalem—just as a pious Jew was obliged to send offerings to the temple (cf. 2 Cor 8-9; Rm 15:25-29). In later centuries, when Jerusalem again becomes a holy city, it is not because of its associations with Judaism but because of Jesus' passion and death there.

Religious Parties and Sects

Our historical survey has introduced the major religious divisions within Judaism. The history of these various groups is deeply entwined with Judaism's response to the cultural and political forces that shaped her destiny in the Graeco-Roman period. They show us that Judaism was not homogenous but diversified. Our historical sources suggest that that diversification went even further than the main parties and sects. There seem to have been smaller sects as well. For Christians, the most obvious example is John the Baptist. We tend to think of him as a long-haired loner preaching repentance to crowds. However, the New Testament mentions that he had disciples who carried on after his death and may have been in conflict with early Christian missionaries. They seem to have asserted that John was superior to Jesus, the latter merely being a somewhat aberrant disciple of the Baptist (cf. Mt 11:11a; Lk

7:28a). In later times we hear of Jewish baptismal sects in Palestine. John the Baptist may have founded such a group.

J. Neusner subtitled a book on the Pharisees "from politics to piety." That subtitle reflects the tension in which many of these groups found themselves. Because Jews sought to create a nation ruled by the Law God had revealed in the Old Testament, religious and political issues were entwined. The Old Testament prophets had often announced political disasters as the result of national disobedience to the Torah. The increasing powerlessness of Jews to determine their own fate elicited a variety of responses. The Sadducees who still had access to some power and had control of the cult, rejected innovations in the religious sphere. The most common response seems to have been embodied in the rise of what we call "Apocalyptic," new revelations about the continuing course of history and the end of the world. Such writings held that evil is so radically embedded in the present age—indeed it is on the increase—that it cannot be eradicated by human effort. The pious must hang onto their holiness against terrific odds and wait for the day when God himself will intervene, the "day of the Lord (Yahweh)," when evil will be defeated and all people judged. The later prophets in the Old Testament give several examples of such apocalyptic speculation. Read Isaiah 60-62. There you will find a description of the ideal Israel that God will establish in the future. Pay particular attention to Isaiah 61:1-11. This passage occurs frequently in New Testament descriptions of the ministry of Jesus. Now turn to Isaiah 63:7–64:11. Here the prophet describes the oppression under which the Jews are living. He first recalls the covenant God had made with his people (v. 7) and then prays that God will again save them as he had done under Moses. Isaiah 58:1-12 and 59:1-20 show that the prophet sees the present suffering of Israel as due to the people's disregard for God's Law. But these early passages still hold that the vindication by God will occur within the realm of socio-political history. The new Israel will be a political entity among or superior to the other nations of the world. Now turn to Zechariah 9-14. Here we find the day of Yahweh described as a fearsome war. Not only will the political enemies of Israel be destroyed, but God will also turn and judge the people themselves (12:1–13:6). The image of God as a warrior received even more elaborate treatment in later texts. Read Daniel 7 and 8. Here the foreign nations have become terrible beasts as they will be described in later apocalyptic writings including the book of Revelation in the New Testament. Such powerful, poetic imagery was shared by many of the groups we have described. But they often drew different conclusions as to how a person was to live in the present time of evil. The more terrible and mythological the description of present reality became, the more difficult it is to tie the description to actual historical events.

For some people the descriptions were ways of saying that God would surely vindicate his people and reverse their status. But they still expected that action to come about through human agents who would be active in the socio-political realm. The following pharisaic psalm written slightly before the time of Jesus describes how an ideal ruler will come and purify Israel:

> . . . we hope in God our deliverer.
> For the might of our God is forever with mercy.
> And the kingdom of our God is over the nations in judgment forever.
>
> You, O Lord chose David as king over Israel, and swore that his kingdom would never fail before you.
> But, because of our sins, sinners rose up against us . . .
> They did not glorify your name . . .
> They destroyed the throne of David in tumultuous arrogance . . .
>
> Look on their plight and raise up for them their king, the son of David . . .
> And gird him with strength so that he can destroy the unrighteous rulers,
> And throw out of Jerusalem the nations that trample her to destruction . . .
>
> And he shall gather together a holy people and lead them in righteousness . . .

And he shall force the pagan nations to serve under his
yoke;
And he shall purify Jerusalem, making it holy as of old:
So that nations will come from the ends of the earth to see
his glory.

(Psalms of Solomon 17, selections)

While they are waiting for the salvation to be brought by the
new king, the people should strive to be righteous and keep the
Law of God (= being a "son of God" in these texts) so that they
will not be judged and cast out of the holy people as sinners.

Other people thought that God would have to take more
radical action. They thought that this whole creation would be
destroyed at the judgment. Here is a passage from a work
called *The Assumption of Moses*. (Notice that most of these
Jewish writings from New Testament times claim to be revelations of past heros.) It uses the expression "kingdom of God,"
which was a favorite one in the preaching of Jesus:

And His (= God's) kingdom will appear throughout creation,
And then Satan will no longer exist,
and sorrow will depart with him.
And the hands of the angel appointed chief
will be filled,
and he will avenge them against their enemies.
For the Heavenly One (= God) will arise from His royal
throne
and He will go forth from his holy dwelling,
with indignation and wrath on account of his sons.
The earth will tremble and be shaken to its depths.
The high mountains will be leveled
and the hills be shaken and fall.
And the horns of the sun be broken and it will turn dark;
The moon will not give her light and be turned to blood . . .

For the Most High, the only Eternal God, will arise,
and He will appear to punish the Gentiles,
and He will destroy all their idols.
Then you, O Israel, will be happy . . .
And God will exalt you,
and bring you near to the stars,

And you will look down from above and see your enemies
    in hell
And you will recognize them and rejoice,
And you will give thanks and praise to your creator.

(The Assumption of Moses 10)

This passage draws the division between the good (saved) and
evil as a division between Israel and the Gentiles. The Gentiles
who worship idols and are without the revelation of the Law,
cannot be anything but sinners. It is important to remember
this perspective in order to understand the controversy in the
early Church over the admission of Gentiles to the community.

Finally, the Essenes, like the Pharisees, thought that Israel herself would be purged. We have seen that historically
both groups sprang from circles of the pious in Maccabean
times. Those who withdrew to the desert no longer were a
political force but only a religious sect. They saw themselves as
the true and only heirs of the covenant with God. The following
selections come from their community rule:

Everyone who joins the community must enter into a
covenant before God to do everything He has commanded and not to turn away from Him through fear
or through any trial to which he may be subjected by
Belial (= Satan) . . .
Then the priests are to recount the bounteous acts of
God and to recite His tender mercies toward Israel.
The levites are to recite all the sins and transgressions
that the children of Israel have committed as a result
of the dominion of Satan. Everyone who enters should
make a confession, saying: "We have acted wickedly;
we have transgressed; we have sinned and done wickedly, we and our fathers before us by going against the
truth. God has been right to bring His judgment on us
and on our fathers before us. But from ancient times,
He has been merciful to us and always will be." Then
the priests are to bless all those who have cast their lot
with God . . . and the levites to curse all who have cast
their lot with Belial.

Notice that humanity is now divided into two categories, mem-

bers of the sect ("cast their lot with God," elsewhere called
"sons of light") and all others who are under the dominion of
Satan ("sons of darkness"). Later in the Rule this dualism is
attributed to two spirits God has established in the world:

> Now God created man to rule the world and appointed
> two spirits whose direction he would follow until the
> final Judgment: the spirits of truth and perversity. All
> who practice righteousness are under the domination
> of the Prince of Lights and walk in light; whereas all
> who practice evil are under the Angel of Darkness and
> walk in darkness. Through the Angel of Darkness,
> however, even those who practice righteousness are
> made prone to error. All their sins and deeds of trans-
> gression are the result of his domination, which is
> permitted by God's inscrutable design until the time
> He has appointed. But the God of Israel and His angel
> of Truth are always there to help the sons of light. God
> created these spirits of light and darkness and made
> them the instigators of every action and thought.

Here the two spirits are spoken of as angels. In other passages,
they are interpreted in terms of the inner conflict each believer
suffers.

Notice that repentance and purification from sin are required of new members. They are to keep the Law as they look
toward the final judgment which will separate good and evil,
light and darkness. The combination of repentance; a type of
baptism for sin, and the announcement of judgment led early
investigators to think that John the Baptist might have been
an Essene. However, although he had a circle of disciples and
lived in the wilderness, John baptized people at large. They
came; heard his preaching; repented and were baptized and
then returned home. They were not called to enter a new religious community. Therefore, it seems more likely that the sect
of John the Baptist represents an independent expression of
the piety that inspired many Jews in this period. We will now
turn to some of the basic beliefs and practices shared by Jews.

Religious Customs and Feasts

Most people are aware that Jews kept the Sabbath, that no work was allowed from sundown Friday to sundown Saturday.

Some Jews took that obligation so seriously that during wartime they would not fight on the Sabbath even if they were attacked. Although the Old Testament contains many dietary laws, the Syrian attempts to force Jews to eat pork quickly elevated that rule to a symbolic level. It came to be said that a Jew who was a swineherd—which would mean working for a Gentile or for a person of little Jewish religious conviction—lost all status as a member of the chosen people.

Synagogues are also familiar to most people. The origins of synagogue worship are not clear. It was a post-exilic development. We know of a synagogue in Egypt in the 3rd century B.C. and one in Antioch in the 2nd. Archaeologists uncovered a 1st-century A.D. synagogue at Masada. But most other synagogues come from the late Roman and Byzantine periods. The synagogue was a place for worship, study of the Torah and the education of children. The "president" of the synagogue and a "servant" were the only officials. Any adult male could be called upon to read the Scripture and perhaps to comment as well. The details of synagogue services at this time are not known. The real liturgical focus of religious life in Jesus' time was the temple in Jerusalem. Christians are sometimes confused by the present-day practice of calling the synagogue "temple" and think that the synagogue was the successor to, and modeled on, the temple in Jerusalem. The liturgy of the temple was, in fact, quite different. Priests are required only for the sacrificial rituals that were confined to the temple in Jerusalem. No sacrifices could be offered anywhere else. Once the temple was destroyed by the Romans, sacrifices were no longer offered. The Rabbi today is not the descendant of the Old Testament priests but of the teachers, the scribes and Pharisees. The High Priest and the chief priests under him presided over the temple cult. Other priests rotated duty in the temple and returned home after their term was up. In addition there were temple musicians and other lesser functionaries. People to sell animals for the offerings and to change currency could be found in the huge outer court. During Jesus' lifetime, the temple was still under renovation so there were many workmen employed there as well. The temple had its own police to keep order in the crowds.

The crowds of pilgrims made their own personal offerings. In addition to these, certain daily offerings were mandated in the Law: a daily offering of incense and an unblemished lamb. These offerings were maintained even during the Roman siege. Sometimes we find it difficult to imagine offering animals as sacrifices to God. Most of the religions of that time had a place for such offerings. So much of the meat sold in the market in Corinth came from sacrifices to the pagan gods and goddesses, that it caused a problem for early Christians: could they buy such meat? (1 Cor 8 and 10) We often forget that the ancient economy was not built on money. Many wealthy people would have little money. Their wealth was measured in land and livestock. A person might well go through a whole year without needing to use money at all. Thus, people are being asked to offer what really counts—livestock.

Every adult, male Jew contributed to the temple. (This is the "temple tax" referred to in Matthew 17:24.) Ideally, he was expected to go up to Jerusalem for the three pilgrimage feasts, Pentecost, Passover and Tabernacles. Many Jews did make the journey. Attempts to calculate the number of people in Jerusalem at Passover from the area of the temple court and the number of lambs sacrificed suggest that the population at least quadrupled during the feast. It is no wonder that the Passover was a time of tension when officials were concerned about avoiding any disturbances.

PASSOVER was a spring festival commemorating the exodus of the chosen people from Egypt. The feast begins at sundown. The ritual meal was celebrated in groups large enough to eat a whole lamb. We do not have evidence of how the passover meal was celebrated in Jesus' day. The ritual was later standardized so that two cups of wine open the meal; the

story of the Exodus is recited followed by the Hallel psalm;
then the meal; the third cup of wine; Hallel psalm completed
and a final cup of wine. The mishnah tractate dealing with
Passover gives an example of how the feast was understood in
the 2nd century:

> R. Gamaliel used to say: "Whoever has not said the
> verses concerning these three things at Passover has
> not fulfilled his obligation. They are: Passover, un-
> leavened bread and bitter herbs. 'Passover' because
> God passed over the houses of our fathers in Egypt;
> 'unleavened bread' because our fathers were redeemed
> from Egypt; 'bitter herbs' because the Egyptians em-
> bittered the lives of our fathers in Egypt. In every
> generation a man must so regard himself as if he him-
> self came forth out of Egypt, for it is written, 'And you
> shall tell your son on that day, It is because of what
> the Lord did for me when I came out of Egypt.' " (m.
> Pesahim 10.5)

You can see from this passage that the commemoration of
Passover asked the individual to put himself back into the time
of the Exodus.

PENTECOST occurred fifty days after Passover. The
firstfruits were brought to the temple. That feast was also tied
to the Exodus motif by being made the commemoration of the
giving of the Law on Sinai.

TABERNACLES, the third pilgrimage feast occurred in
the fall. Like Pentecost, it had an agricultural origin. It was a
thanksgiving for the harvest. Part of the ritual required that
water be brought up to the temple from the pool of Siloam and
poured out on the altar. On the first day of the feast a large
candlestick was lit in the women's court. (In John 7, Jesus
gives a discourse on the Feast of Tabernacles which employs
the light and water symbolism.) During the eight days of the
feast the Jews were to dwell in tents. That custom may go back
to the agricultural origins of the feast, but it was interpreted as
a commemoration of the years the Israelites spent wandering
in the wilderness.

Thus the three great pilgrimage feasts reminded the Jews of the deliverance from Egypt, the giving of the Law and the wandering in the desert prior to their entering the promised land. New Testament authors frequently pick up these themes of salvation history as analogies for Christianity. 1 Corinthians, John and Hebrews all have similar treatments of the wandering motif so it may even have been a set theme in early Christian preaching.

Once a year on the Day of Atonement (Yom Kippur), Jews fast and pray for God's mercy. As long as the temple was standing, the atonement ritual included two sacrifices. The High Priest first sacrificed a goat for his own sins and then another goat was driven out into the desert bearing the sins of the people. Yom Kippur was the one day of the year when the High Priest entered the innermost sanctuary of the temple, the holy of holies. Hebrews 7:1–10:8 uses that imagery to describe the ministry of Christ.

The reader should remember that much of the activity in the Jerusalem temple—or any other temple where sacrifices were carried out—took place outside in the large courtyards. The building itself was the center of several concentric courts. Gentiles were only allowed in the outermost court. Signs warned that those who ventured further would be put to death. Women were also confined to an outer court. The building itself stood in an inner court. In front of it stood the altar of sacrifice with a ramp leading up to it and a large laver for the priests. Israelite males were allowed into the court in front of the temple. Excavations in the temple area since 1968 have shown that the paved platform on which it stood comprised some 35 acres. A paved street ran along the west wall, which was 32 feet wide and was lined with small structures on both sides. Archaeologists think that it may have been the central market. An inscription found in the southwest corner tells us that a tower stood there from which a priest would blow a trumpet every Friday evening to announce the beginning of the Sabbath. The famous royal portico ran along the south wall. There money-changing and other such activity was carried on. It may also have served as the location for the court. In the large cities of antiquity, people lived outdoors in such porticos and market places. Someone like Jesus might well gather a crowd in some corner of the temple court. The apostles later gathered crowds in the market places of the cities they visited.

Whatever their particular beliefs may have been Jews were united in their devotion to Jerusalem; its temple and its great feasts. The Essenes were an exception. That sect had broken away from worship in Jerusalem, claiming that the true priestly line had been lost and that the cult celebrated there was corrupt. They used their own calendar to determine feasts and expected a priestly messiah who would restore true worship. But Jerusalem is still the holy city. They did not try to set up a rival temple.

God and the Chosen People

Most people know that the Jews believe they have been especially chosen by God. Not only did he promise Abraham a great nation of descendants; he delivered them from Egypt and gave them the promised land. Since Christians have come to consider themselves heirs to those promises, it is sometimes hard for them to remember that in Jesus' day a person had to be Jewish or a convert to Judaism to belong to the chosen people. All others are Gentiles.

Holiness and the Law

The condition of that special election was that the chosen people be set apart, different from the other nations. The Law was seen as part of a covenant (treaty) between God and his people. It established the conditions for holiness. Many people today think of the Jewish religious Law as a bunch of picky details that no one in his or her right mind would want to follow. They suppose that all Jews were hypocritical legalists. Nothing could be further from the truth. They see the Law as God's gift—a gift that set them apart from others because it taught them about the true way to worship God and saved them from the sinfulness and idolatry of pagan society. Read

Psalm 119 and you will see how devoted to the Law the pious Jew was. God's commandments show his mercy to a sinful people (vv 129-136).

By the time of Jesus, some of the precepts of the Law were difficult to follow because they had been formulated in a much earlier time. The Pharisees were concerned with interpreting the Law in such a way as to apply it to contemporary problems. They held that God had given Moses two laws, a written one and an oral one. The oral one enabled people to interpret what had been written:

> The torah was given to Moses chiefly in writing, a small portion in oral form (TB Grittin 60B).
> As the sea has little waves between the large ones, so the Torah has many details of oral law affecting commandments of the written law (Shekalim 6.1).

The Sadduccees rejected the concept of oral law. The Essenes, on the other hand, believed that the Law could be interpreted, but that God had made its true interpretation known to their teacher: he is referred to as "him who taught the Law aright" or "the true interpreter of the Law" (1 QpHab ii.8,14; viii, 4f). They described the attempt to fulfill the Law perfectly as preparing the way of the Lord in the wilderness (1 QS viii, 14-16).

Many of Jesus' controversies with his opponents concerned the interpretation of the Law. An example of how the various groups approached a problem may be found in the following discussions of Sabbath law. Jesus justified his Sabbath healings by saying to the Pharisees: "What person among you if he has one sheep and it fall into a pit on the Sabbath will not lay hold of it and lift it out?" (Mt 12:11; Lk 14:5). The Pharisees obviously interpreted the Law prohibiting work on the Sabbath to permit recovering an animal that had fallen into a pit. One of the Essene rule books takes the following position on this issue:

> No one is to foal a beast on the Sabbath day. Even if it drop its young into a cistern or a pit, he is not to lift it out on the Sabbath (CD xi.13-14).

Their position is even more stringent than the rule to which the Pharisees were granting an exception. Not only could one not rescue an adult animal, but a newborn must be left in a pit on the Sabbath. That could, of course, lead to the death of the animal and hence loss of property for the owner. If you react negatively to the Essene view, you should remember that they felt that they could not keep the Law in all its purity without assistance from God. They viewed the Law as part of God's covenant with his people, as one of his saving gifts to humanity and felt that people should be thankful to God for it. They should not try to interpret it as the Pharisees did.

History and the End of the World

The importance of the history of Israel—especially the events of the Exodus—lay in its evidence for the character of God. God is defined by what he does for his people. The Jew could learn from the past that those who failed to keep the Law would be punished. At the same time, many Jews believed that God's covenant with his people was an eternal one. No matter how unfaithful they might be, God's mercy and loving-kindness would sustain some; there would always be a faithful remnant who would be saved. While this picture of God as one who is active in the history of particular people has continued to force both the Jewish and Christian traditions to grapple with historical and social issues in a way that other religious traditions do not have to, it also leads to severe religious problems. If God has declared himself the deliverer of the people when they are oppressed, why are they continually subject to foreign powers? If God demands justice for the poor, the oppressed, the widow, why do the evil and the rich who neglect his Law prosper? Those who expected a judgment at the end of the world, were not trying to threaten people with damnation. The Gentiles, the rich and the sinners who are the damned in their apocalypses never heard that preaching. Rather, those who felt themselves among the righteous oppressed like the Essenes preached a universal judgment as their own vindication. Although their righteousness and fidelity to the Law did not seem

to "pay off," the judgment at the end of the world would prove
that God did in fact demand obedience to his revelation. Thus,
the descriptions of judgment are a way of professing faith in
the righteousness and justice of God, the creator.

Messianic Figures

Because Christians believe that Jesus is Messiah, they
look for *the Messiah* in Jewish writings. They often suppose
that the primary form of Jewish hope for the future was centered on the coming of the Messiah. In fact, Jews were much
more interested in the coming age of salvation. God, himself,
might be pictured as inaugurating the new age, or he might be
said to employ a variety of human and/or angelic figures to
bring salvation. The word "Messiah" simply means "anointed";
it could be used of king or priest. We have already mentioned
that the Essenes expected both an anointed king and an
anointed priest in the new age. Therefore, we should not look
for "the Messiah" in Jewish writings but for the various functions that had to be fulfilled in that age. Many of these functions could be fulfilled by human or angelic agents. The imagery varies widely from one writing to another.

(1) *Davidic king*, political ruler. We have already read
some descriptions of this new king who was to arise over Israel.
The following passage is an Essene description of the messianic
king: It takes the form of a commentary on the Old Testament
text in Genesis 49:10:

> This (= the Old Testament passage) means that
> sovereignty will never depart from the tribe of Judah
> ... the throne will never be taken from the line of
> David. Until the coming of the legitimately anointed
> king, the offspring of David. For the eternal kingship
> over his people, the covenant was given to David and
> his seed—the covenant which the Lord has kept ...
> with the members of this community.

You can see from this passage that the interpretation of the
Old Testament played an important role in formulating mes-

sianic expectations. Most of the promises of salvation in the Old Testament referred to the present. But when people began to expect that God would inaugurate a new age of salvation, they began to reinterpret those promises and prophecies. Another scroll from Qumran simply lists Old Testament prophecies that were thought to refer to the new age. Still another gives a messianic interpretation of 2 Samuel 7:10-14 using other texts from the Old Testament. The New Testament shows that Christians made their own collections of Old Testament texts. They used them to interpret each other and to interpret the life of Jesus. You can also see from this passage that the Essenes felt that their community was the heir to the covenant and to all the promises God had made to Israel. The New Testament shows us that the Christians made the same claim for themselves. Sometimes people are embarrassed by those claims because they think of Christianity as the non-Jewish community it soon became and they feel that Christians had no right to make such a claim. The Essene case shows us that at least one Jewish sect before the Christians made the same claim—one which they based on their claim to be the only faithful interpreters of the Law. Since Christianity originated as a Jewish sect, it is not surprising that they, who knew the Messiah, might insist that they were the heirs to those promises of salvation.

(2) *Prophet like Moses.* We have already seen that disputes over the true interpretation of the Mosaic Law were an important element of Jewish religious life in this period. Such problems would not exist in the messianic age when everyone would follow the Law. Deuteronomy 18:18f. has Moses predict that God would give his people a prophet like himself. The Essenes expected such a prophet in the new age. The prophet was the key messianic figure in the Samaritan sect and it occurs as a designation of Jesus in the Fourth Gospel.

(3) *Priest.* We have seen that the Essenes considered the contemporary priestly line hopelessly corrupt. They expected an anointed priest in the new age. The messianic priest ranked above the messianic king. The following description of this

ideal priest is taken from a Jewish work known as the *Testament of Levi*:

> Then the Lord will raise up a new priest.
> All the words of the Lord will be revealed to him,
> and he will judge the earth righteously for many days.
> His star will arise in heaven like that of a king,
> and light the light of knowledge as the sun does the day.
> He will be magnified in the world,
> and shine forth on the earth like the sun,
> and remove all darkness from under heaven.
> There will be peace in all the earth,
> and the heavens will exult in his day,
> and the earth will be glad.
> And the glorious angels of the Lord's presence will be glad
>   in him.
> The heavens will be opened,
> and sanctification will come upon him from the temple of
>   glory,
> with the Father's voice as from Abraham to Isaac.
> The glory of the Most High will be uttered over him,
> and the spirit of understanding and holiness will rest upon
>   him.
> And no one shall ever succeed him.
> In his priesthood the Gentiles will increase in knowledge
>   (NB knowledge = religious devotion to God)
> and be enlightened through the graciousness of the Lord.
> In his priesthood sin will come to an end,
> and the lawless will stop doing evil.
> He will open the gates of paradise;
> remove the threatening sword against Adam,
> and give the holy ones the tree of life to eat,
> and the spirit of holiness will be upon them.
> He will bind Beliar,
> and give his children power to tred on evil spirits.
> And the Lord will rejoice in his children,
> and be pleased with his beloved ones forever.
> Then Abraham and Isaac and Jacob will exult,
> and I (= Levi, to whom the revelation is attributed) will be
>   glad,
> and all the holy ones will clothe themselves with joy.

We have quoted this long passage because so many of the images used in it are found again in Christian stories about Jesus. You can find some of them easily in the Christmas and Baptism stories.

(4) *Leader of the eschatological war* against Satan and evil people. Many Jewish texts expect a great cosmic war between the forces of good and evil to come before the new age. The Essenes had a writing (the War Scroll) that stipulated the arrangements for the battle. Although one might expect the Davidic Messiah to be cast as the leader of the righteous—as he is in other texts—there the messianic priest seems to be in charge. Usually the war against evil, the Gentile oppressors and the Jews who sided with them, was only part of a cosmic conflict between the angelic army and Satan's army. Thus we find angelic figures in charge of the heavenly armies. An angel of light or Michael leads them in the War Scroll. Another Qumran text has the heavenly figure Melchizedek in charge.

(5) *Judge.* Most pictures of the end of the world assume that a great judgment will condemn the wicked. Sometimes God himself is the judge. In other cases, like the *T Levi* passage we just read, the anointed priest or the anointed king performs that function. The Melchizedek text from Qumran has him perform that function. Still others introduce another figure the Son of Man as judge. Daniel 7:13f. pictures "one like a son of man" (i.e. a human figure) ascending to the throne of God where he receives an eternal kingdom. Daniel 7:18 interprets the vision to mean that the righteous Jews, who will eventually be liberated from their oppressors and have an eternal kingdom, are represented by the "son of man" symbol. Although son of man is interpreted in Daniel as a collective symbol, later Jewish writings seem to interpret the Daniel passage as referring to an individual heavenly figure. IV Ezra 13, a work written toward the end of the 1st century, describes the messianic redeemer as arising from the sea and flying with the clouds. Fire from his mouth destroys evil. A somewhat earlier use of the Daniel passage occurs in 1 Enoch 62:2-15 where the son of man is enthroned as judge:

And the lord of spirits seated him on his glorious throne
and the spirit of righteousness was poured out upon him
and the word of his mouth slays all the sinners . . .
and they shall be downcast.
Panic will seize them when they see the son of man
    sitting on his glorious throne
The kings, the mighty and all who possess the earth
    will glorify and praise him who rules over all
    and who was hidden,
for the son of man was hidden from the beginning;
the Most High preserved him in his mighty presence,
and revealed him to the elect . . .
And the righteous and the elect will be saved on that day,
and they shall never again look upon the sinners and un-
    righteous.
The Lord of Spirits will abide over them;
and they will eat with the son of man . . .
And the righteous and the elect will have risen from the
    earth,
and cease to be downcast.
And they will be clothed with glorious garments.

Again you can see that the primary focus of this image is the vindication of the righteous who will be saved and exalted into the presence of the Son of Man. The same imagery from Daniel is often used in the New Testament to describe Jesus' exaltation into heaven and his future role as judge. It is important to realize that when the New Testament author uses the expression son of man to describe Jesus in this way the expression does not contrast his humanity with his divinity (= Son of God) as later patristic exegetes who did not have access to Jewish religious language of the time mistakenly thought. When Son of Man comes from the metaphor in Daniel 7:13f., it is referring to a heavenly figure, not to an earthly one at all. This heavenly figure sits on the divine throne, executes God's judgment against sinners and establishes the eternal kingdom of the righteous.

No two descriptions of the coming age of salvation are identical. The term Messiah often does not even occur. When it does occur, Messiah is usually followed by a genitive for example Messiah (= anointed) of the Lord or his Messiah—i.e. the person anointed by the Lord. The key point in all these different writings is that God will finally complete his dealings with his creation and with his people by establishing a radically new era of peace and righteousness. Reread the description of the messianic king in *Psalms of Solomon* 17 or of the messianic priest in *Testament of Levi* 18. They end with peace, joy and praise of God. Though the mythological and poetic imagery varies from text to text, they all share the fundamental conviction that God is about to intervene to establish definitively his righteousness in the world. Given the fluid character of messianic imagery, it is easy to see why there is no uniform description of the messianic role of Jesus in the New Testament either. Judaism had no set picture of the Messiah or the Son of Man to which a person might appeal or which a person might come along and take up as a career. Each author has woven together a vision out of the prophecies and psalms of the Old Testament and out of the traditions that had gone before him to express the hope and confidence that God does rule this world and that he will soon show that rule unambiguously in the new age. The human and angelic agents used by God are not objects of speculation in their own right. Indeed, Jesus himself focused on the key question of the kingdom or rule of God and not on describing his own position in relation to that rule. All the various messianic functions are attributed to him except that of eschatological warrior—imagery he seems to have rejected in his own preaching. The book of Revelation has the angel Michael as heavenly warrior and reuses much of the older Jewish imagery. It is obvious that many of the functions attributed to messianic figures were not literally carried out by Jesus in his lifetime. It was his exaltation into heaven that made it possible for his followers to describe him as eschatological judge, priest like Melchizedek or even eternal king.

Resurrection and Eternal Life

Christians understood Jesus' exaltation as the consequence of his "resurrection". However, resurrection like many of the Jewish concepts we have discussed did not have a fixed meaning. Most of the Old Testament assumes that God rewards the righteous in this life; hence the Sadducees opposed the doctrine of resurrection as without scriptural basis. Only a few passages in the Old Testament say anything about the future state of the righteous. The traditions about the after-life in Judaism are based on the conviction that God is immanently concerned with justice. He has revealed what justice is, and people may expect to be rewarded and punished accordingly. The Bible usually sees reward and punishment as collective: God rewards or punishes the people as a whole, not individuals. However, during Maccabean times, people began to question that picture. Usually Israel's subjection to foreign powers was understood as punishment for her infidelity to the Law. But pious Jews, who sought to keep the Law, saw others, who rejected it and took up pagan customs, prosper while they themselves might even be subject to persecution. Some came to the conclusion that perhaps the people as a whole would not repent and return to keeping God's Law. Only a remnant of God's people would be saved while the others would perish along with the pagan sinners. Various metaphors are used to encourage people to remain faithful despite persecution and ridicule. God would judge evil (cf. Isa 26:19-21) and receive the righteous into heavenly glory. Read Psalm 9. It is a moving meditation on the fate of the wicked and the plight of the righteous.

The persecutions of the Jews under Antiochus IV led to even more descriptions of this type. Wisdom chapters 2-6 describes the attempts of wicked people to prove that God does not care about good and evil; he does not punish; there is no after-life. They see that the life of the righteous person condemns their behavior and so they try to kill him. But a second scene takes place in heaven when they see that the righteous person has been exalted and will live forever. Here is a selection from that scene:

> They (= godless people) will come trembling to the reckoning of their sins and their crimes will accuse them. The virtuous man stands up boldly to face those

who oppressed him; those who thought so little of his suffering. At the sight of him they will shake with cowardly fear, amazed that he should be saved so unexpectedly . . . and say, "This is the man we used to laugh at once, a butt for our sarcasm; his life we regarded as madness; his death, without honor. How has he come to be counted as one of the sons of God? How has he come to be assigned a place among the holy ones?" Yes, the hope of the godless is like the chaff carried on the wind . . . but the virtuous live forever. Their recompense is with the Lord; the Most High takes care of them. So they shall receive a royal crown of splendor.

You should read these chapters of Wisdom carefully. They are frequently alluded to in New Testament descriptions of the death of Jesus. A similar tradition can be found in Daniel 12:1-3 where it is associated with the final judgment. Exaltation to angelic existence in heaven was also part of the belief of the Essenes. The following passage from their hymn book suggests that the righteous person may already experience such exaltation in this life:

Lo, you have taken a spirit distorted by sin,
and purged it of the stain of transgression
and given it a place in the host of the holy ones,
and brought it into communion with the sons of heaven.
You have made mere man to share the lots of the spirits of
    knowledge;
to praise your name in their chorus.

(1 QH iii. 19-21)

Doubtless, you have noticed that these images are more concerned with the exaltation of the righteous into heaven and eternal life with God than they are with questions about the state of the body or the soul after death.

Metaphors that speak explicitly of a bodily resurrection after death seem to have come into use during the Antiochen period when Jews were being martyred for refusing to renounce their faith. Violence against the body would be re-

warded by bodily resurrection. The following statement occurs
in the martyrdom story in 2 Maccabees 7:

> And with his last breath he exclaimed, "Inhuman
> fiend, you may discharge us from the present life, but
> the king of the world will raise us up since it is for his
> laws that we die to live forever." When he neared his
> end, he cried, "Ours is the better choice to meet death
> at man's hands yet relying on God's promise that we
> shall be raised by him, whereas for you there can be no
> resurrection; no new life."

You may have noticed that these texts do not expect resurrection or eternal life for the wicked. The resurrection/exaltation
is itself the reward for righteousness and fidelity. The wicked
are condemned to eternal death/punishment. Here are some
other expressions of the same view:

> The destruction of the sinner is forever, and God will
> not remember him when he visits the righteous. But
> those who fear the Lord will rise to eternal life; and
> their life will be in the light of the Lord and will never
> end (PsSol 3).

> As many as are godly will live again on earth, when
> God gives breath and life and grace to them, the pious
> (SibOr IV).

In these cases resurrection is equivalent to God's vindication of
a person's righteousness. A resurrected person could not be a
sinner. Thus you can begin to see why the resurrection of Jesus
plays such an important role in early Christian preaching. For
them, it confirmed the fact that Jesus had been "from God" and
not a crazy, sinful or misguided person.

Some other Jewish writings treat the resurrection as a
preliminary to the universal judgment of humanity (cf. IV Ezra
7:78-10:1). Early rabbinic writings show that bodily resurrection came to be associated with universal judgment. However,
the majority of our texts from the time of Jesus have treated
resurrection in a positive sense. It is the reward for fidelity to

God in this life. God's justice is vindicated against those who either disregard the Law in general or who persecute the pious. Again the authors of these texts are using metaphorical language. The picture changes from one to another. They are not out to provide precise information about the post-mortem state of the person any more than they provided precise information about how the world would end. These metaphorical descriptions are to encourage the faithful. The texts that describe the final state of the righteous as exaltation into heaven differ as to when that exaltation takes place. For some it seems to be directly after death; for others at or before the judgment. When you read the New Testament, you find a similar diversity of pictures. Bodily resurrection is the dominant metaphor of salvation for Christians because Jesus was raised from the dead. As in the Jewish sources, resurrection is usually used in the positive sense as the reward for fidelity rather than as a neutral prelude to the judgment. Indeed, where the righteous are exalted into God's presence before the judgment they are not judged at all; only the sinners and Gentiles are judged. New Testament authors too may speak of Christians as not being judged but as exalted and participating in judgment like the righteous man in Wisdom 5. St. Paul reflects such a belief in 1 Corinthians 6:2f.

Today we find many people looking for "facts" about life after death. Doctors and psychologists produce books about the experiences of people who have been declared dead and revived. The Bible does not provide facts like that about resurrection and eternal life—which does not mean that people did not think to ask such questions. The Corinthians, for example, had a great many questions about resurrection. It was one of those elements of Christian preaching that did not make sense to many pagans, since they did not have the Jewish background of the earliest Christians. Read 1 Corinthians 15. Paul argues that Christians can be certain about resurrection because Christ has already been raised; they can expect that "resurrected body" will be a glorious one not like a resuscitated corpse. But he cannot give them facts about that state. Indeed, if it represents a complete transformation of bodily reality as we know and experience it, then it cannot be discovered by scientific procedures designed to manipulate the social, psychological and material structures of this world. Rather the Christians should see the resurrection as an image of hope and confidence, so that if they are faithful, their final state will be like that of Christ, himself.

Conclusion

Much of what we have covered in this lengthy excursion into the world of Jesus may have been strange and unfamiliar, but for the first believers it was part of the world in which they lived. You can see that the Old Testament played an important role in people's lives. Many of the later Jewish writings that we have been quoting used Old Testament language and stories as the foundation of their own attempts to understand how God is working in their times. We also see that they used a plurality of images to express their hopes for the salvation that God was to bring to his people. It is not possible to reduce all of this rich imagery to a single, unified concept of Messiah, end of the world or eternal life as many Christians have attempted to do with the New Testament. Rather we must realize that the wealth of images and metaphors illuminates different facets of the believer's experience of God and his salvation—an experience formed and informed by long centuries of tradition embodied in the Old Testament. This plurality of images, hopes and expectation does not diminish the truth about salvation for these authors. The truth lies in God's sovereignty over the world; his fidelity to the covenant and to those who have allied themselves with it over against the various countervailing tendencies toward evil and rejection of God's revelation. Medical facts about life after death can never perform the function of religious hope. They will never encourage people to live lives of love and fidelity to the revelation of God who brought a people out of slavery and who raised Jesus from the dead. Biblical authors do not claim to give us scientific information or facts. They tell stories about God's dealings with people in such a way as to persuade us to base our lives on the Bible's teaching—lives sustained by these various stories and metaphors of hope.

STUDY QUESTIONS

⸰ 1. Why did their subjection to foreign powers constitute a religious problem for pious Jews?
  2. Who were the Maccabees? What was their contribution to Jewish history? What Jewish religious holiday is associated with them?
 ⸰ 3. Describe the origins and beliefs of each of the following groups: Sadduccees, Pharisees, Essenes, zealots.
  4. Explain why descriptions of the end of this world, judgment of sinners and the new age became prominent features of Jewish religious writings around the time of Jesus.
  5. List and identify four major religious feasts in the Jewish calendar.
  6. Why was interpretation of the Law a crucial religious issue for Jews in Jesus' day? How did the Sadducees, Pharisees and Essenes approach that problem?
  7. List five roles that human and/or angelic figures play in Jewish descriptions of the age of salvation. How does each one contribute to the victory of God's law, righteousness, goodness over the forces of evil?
  8. Why do Jewish writers use many different images and metaphors to describe salvation?
 ⸰ 9. What did Jews in Jesus' time believe about resurrection/eternal life?
 10. Why did the resurrection of Jesus become a central feature of early Christian preaching?

Part II

THE MESSIAH, JESUS

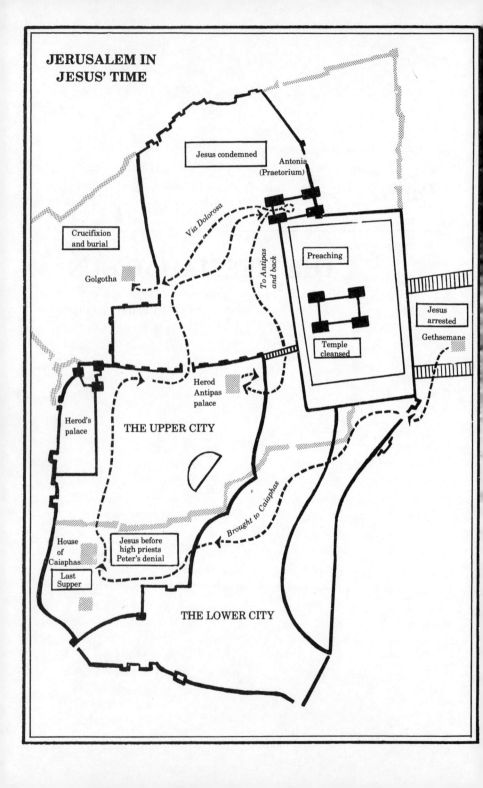

JERUSALEM IN
JESUS' TIME

Jesus condemned

Antonia
(Praetorium)

Via Dolorosa

Crucifixion
and burial

Golgotha

Preaching

To Antipas
and back

Jesus
arrested

Gethsemane

Temple
cleansed

Herod
Antipas
palace

THE UPPER CITY

Herod's
palace

Brought to Caiaphas

House
of
Caiaphas

Jesus before
high priests
Peter's denial

Last
Supper

THE LOWER CITY

Chapter Three

THE LIFE OF JESUS

Recently as I was reading a book about Richard Nixon written before Watergate and his resignation, I couldn't help wondering if the author would still consider him the exponent of political liberalism. Thirty or forty years from now a book about Nixon will probably look even different than it does today. By that time, the long-range effects of his economic policies and his foreign policy initiatives will be known. This example reminds us of some important facts about individual lives. Even with all our reporters, live TV coverage and legions of historians ready to jump in and research an individual who becomes a prominent figure, we still perceive a person's significance differently at different times in his or her career. We also still need to look back on a completed life from the perspective of several decades to see "how it worked out." Further, even with all our documentary skills we may agree on the external details of a person's life and still disagree strongly about that individual's significance.

These observations remind us of some important things about our gospels. They are all written several decades after Jesus' death. Each evangelist has had the opportunity to see how "it worked out" in a different area. Each has a slightly different perspective on the significance of Jesus. They are all looking back on his life from the perspective of a community that believes he is exalted in heaven at God's right hand. These simple observations remind us that the gospels are not simple, factual accounts of Jesus' life. They are attempts by Christians of a later generation—the main apostles had all died before any of the gospels were written—to state the significance of Jesus for Christians of their own time. Thus, they embody the teaching that was still important in Christian communities some 40 to 50 years after Jesus' death. Their understanding of that teaching has been shaped by nearly a half century of living and preaching the Christian message. Although some people may wish we had tapes of Jesus or that the evangelists had been investigative reporters, reflection shows that there are advantages to the present state of affairs. All the gospels indicate that Jesus' contemporaries found him difficult to understand. Even his own followers were not always certain where he was leading them. But from the later perspective of the evangelists, we can see what had influenced people to change their lives. The gospels are as much a story of those first believers as they are of Jesus. They were the ones to perceive the significance of what God had done through him.

Sources and Methods of Research

This realization of the varied perspectives of the gospel writers is the fruit of almost a century of gospel study. At first, people were trying to reconstruct an historical core based on the outline of Mark. Then they realized that Mark is no more an historical record than the other gospels. However, this analysis shaped methods of study that are still part of the backbone of gospel research.

Source Criticism

Source criticism is the oldest of the three methods we will describe. Since antiquity people have known that Matthew, Mark and Luke have much material in common. Some passages are almost identical. Therefore they are called the synoptic gospels. Look carefully at the three versions of the story about plucking grain on the Sabbath:

Chart #1: Source Analysis: PLUCKING GRAIN ON THE SABBATH

Mt 12:1-8	Mk 2:23-28	Lk 6:1-5
At that time Jesus went through the grainfields on the sabbath	One Sabbath he was going through the grainfields and as they made their way	On a sabbath while he was going through the grainfields
his disciples were hungry and they began to pluck ears of grain and to eat.	his disciples began to pluck ears of grain.	his disciples plucked and ate some ears of grain, rubbing them in their hands.
But when the Pharisees saw it, they said to him:	And the Pharisees said to him:	But some of the Pharisees said:
Look, your disciples are doing what is not lawful to do on the sabbath.	Look, why are they doing what is not lawful on the sabbath?	Why are you (pl.) doing what is not lawful to do on the sabbath?
He said to them: Have you not read what David did, when he was hungry, and	And he said to them: Have you never read what David did, when he was in need and was hungry, he and	And Jesus answered: Have you not read what David did, when he was hungry, he and
those who were with him: how he entered the house of God	those who were with him: how he entered the house of God,	those who were with him: how he entered the house of God,
	when Abiathar was high priest	
and ate the bread of the Presence, which it was not	and ate the bread of the	and took and ate the bread of the
(continued on next page)	*(continued on next page)*	*(continued on next page)*

Mt 12:1-8 (continued)	Mk 2:23-28 (continued)	Lk 6:1-5 (continued)
lawful for him to eat, nor for those who were with him, but only for the priests?	Presence, which it is not lawful for any but the priests to eat, and also gave it to those who were with him?	Presence, which it is not lawful for any but the priests to eat, and also gave it to those with him?
Only in Matthew Or have you not read in the law how on the sabbath the priests in the temple profane the sabbath and are guiltless? I tell you something greater than the temple is here. And if you had known what this means, "I desire mercy, and not sacrifice," you would not have condemned the guiltless.	And then he said to them: The sabbath was made for man not man for the sabbath, so the son of man is lord even of the sabbath.	And he said to them:
For the son of man is Lord of the sabbath.		The son of man is lord of the sabbath.

We have underlined all the words common to the three versions and put dashes under those unique to each one. You can
easily see that all the versions are different. You can also see
that Matthew has more material in Jesus' defense than the
other versions. Matthew and Luke both have smoother intro-
ductions to the story than Mark does. Source criticism makes
detailed comparison of these sorts of parallels. Source critics
found that most of Mark is reproduced in Matthew and/or
Luke. They also found that where one departs from the order of
events in Mark, the other usually retains the Markan order.
Therefore, they concluded that Matthew and Luke each used
Mark as a source when composing his own gospel. However,
that observation does not solve all the problems of relationships between the synoptics. A large section of Mark (Mk
6:45-8:10) is not reflected anywhere in Luke. Some people suppose that Luke's version of Mark may have been different from
Matthew's.

We can find other relationships between Matthew and
Luke that are independent of Mark. The Sermon on the Mount
(Mt 5—7) is probably the most famous piece of Christian literature in the world. It contains the beatitudes (Mt 5:3-12) and
the Lord's Prayer (6:9-13). You will not find either of these
anywhere in Mark. Now look up Luke's Sermon on the Plain
(6:17-49). You will find some of the beatitudes there as well as
some other parallels to the Sermon on the Mount. But you did
not find the Lord's Prayer there. Keep reading and you will
come to Luke's version of the prayer in 11:1-4. Comparisons of
this sort led scholars to another hypothesis: the sayings and
parables of Jesus had been written down in a collection used by
both Matthew and Luke. They designated that collection "Q"
from the German word for source, "Quelle." We assume that
when Matthew and Luke have almost identical sayings or
stories that they came from Q. Perhaps Q contained other parables or sayings that neither or only one evangelist used. We
may suppose that each evangelist arranged the material from
Q in his own way as Matthew has done with the Sermon on the
Mount and Luke with chapter 11 on prayer—though many

scholars think that Luke sticks closer to the original order of material in Q than Matthew. Unlike Mark, Q is an hypothetical source; we do not have any copies of such a collection to compare with Matthew and Luke. But our confidence in the existence of such collections was considerably strengthened when a 2nd century collection of sayings and parables of Jesus, the *Gospel of Thomas*, was found in Egypt. We only have the complete gospel in a Coptic translation, but fragments of the work in Greek have also been found. As it stands, the Coptic gospel of Thomas—and we suspect the Greek original—shows the influence of a 2nd-century heretical movement known as Gnosticism. But it also contains parables and sayings known to us from the synoptic tradition. Some of them were previously only found in the gospel of Luke. This discovery at least confirms the hypothesis that collections of the sayings and parables of Jesus were circulated in early Christianity and makes it likely that there was more in Q than we can reconstruct on the basis of material used in both Matthew and Luke. In fact, recent analyses of the beatitudes have suggested that Luke and Matthew probably used slightly different versions of Q.

Source analysis, then, helps us understand the relationships between the synoptic gospels. It also suggests that material about Jesus was circulated in a written form prior to the composition of the gospels. It was relatively easy to do source analysis of Matthew and Luke because they could be compared with Mark and with each other. But today scholars are asking another question: what about Mark? Lack of comparative material makes the question harder to answer. Scholars analyze the language and style of Mark carefully to see if they can detect signs that he is using an earlier source. While we are much less certain of such results, two suggestions are widely accepted: first, that there was a pre-Marken account of Jesus' trial and death perhaps composed for liturgical purposes; second, that Mark used earlier collections of Jesus' miracles in chapters 2—5. However, as far as we know he was the first person to write an account that combined incidents from the life of Jesus, his teaching and miracles with an account of his trial and death to create the literary form that we know as "gospel."

Form Criticism

Source criticism points to literary stages in the composition of the gospels, but that still does not help us assess those written sources. After World War I, a new discipline came into gospel study called "form criticism." It is founded on the very basic observation that much biblical material—form criticism was used on the Old Testament much earlier—was handed on by word of mouth. Folklorists and anthropologists who have studied oral cultures help us understand that process of transmission. While no two versions of a story even by the same reciter ever are identical, stories are cast into set language and patterns in order to make them easy to recall. Form criticism studies the patterns into which biblical material has been cast. It also looks for analogies in other writings of the time. Understanding of these patterns helps us identify stories that have been combined, truncated or expanded once they were written down and it was no longer necessary to preserve the conventions of the oral form. It has played an important role in source analysis of the Markan miracle stories. But there is more: form critics suggested that oral tradition itself is not neutral reporting but that stories took shapes that made them suitable for use within the Christian community. Go back to the incident about plucking grain on the Sabbath in the previous section. It is an example of a controversy story or of the more general type known as a "pronouncement story." Such stories were commonly circulated about wise people in antiquity. Their general form is very simple. An incident or an opponent poses a difficulty or question for the teacher. Often that question is a difficult one that he is not expected to solve, but the teacher responds with a wise saying that cuts through the difficulties and resolves the dilemma. Here is an example of such a story. It was told about the Greek philosopher Diogenes:

On reaching Athens, Diogenes followed Antisthenes although the latter turned him away because he never took pupils. Diogenes wore him out by his sheer persistence. Once when Antisthenes raised his staff to hit him, Diogenes offered his head saying, "Strike, for you will not find any wood hard enough to keep me away as long as I think you have something to say."

Now look at the story about plucking grain on the Sabbath. It is more complicated because Jesus gives two answers. First, there is the example of David from the Old Testament (Mk 2:25f.). That in itself might justify the disciples' action. But there are two additional sayings in Mark 2:27f. Matthew and Luke only preserve the second: the Son of Man is Lord of the Sabbath. These additional sayings may have been added as the story was used in Christian preaching. The initial story concerned violation of the Sabbath by Jesus' disciples. The next story in Mark (3:1-6) has Jesus himself violate the Sabbath. Jesus' teaching is characterized by freedom with regard to the Old Testament Law and by objection to the way it was being interpreted by others in his day. A story that ended with an Old Testament quote would set Jesus' authority as interpreter of the Old Testament against that of others like the Pharisees. The additional sayings take the policy further. They do not deal with particular instances of Sabbath-breaking but seek to establish a general principle: the Sabbath was made for man; not man for the Sabbath or the Son of Man is Lord of the Sabbath. Those assertions fit in with a general policy of freedom vis-à-vis Sabbath observance. We know that such a policy was characteristic of some part of the Christian community from the time of Paul. But the dispute over the question in some of Paul's Churches suggests that it was not universally the case and hence probably not a general principle enunciated by Jesus himself. What happened then was that a story that told of a particular instance in which Jesus condoned relaxation of the Sabbath rule was adapted by adding other sayings of Jesus about the Sabbath to be an explanation of Christian freedom from those religious obligations. The saying that concludes the whole grounds that freedom in Jesus' authority as Son of Man. You can see in Paul's letters (e.g. Gal 4:10; Col

2:16f.) that not all Christians were sure that Jesus had freed them from the obligations of Jewish religious law. (There are even groups of Christians today who follow Jewish religious laws because they do not think that the mainline Christian tradition of freedom from those obligations is in line with the teaching of Jesus.) Stories like this one may have played an important part not only in controversy with the Jews but within the Christian community itself as an explanation for their departure from Jewish ritual observance. This example, then, shows how a story was reformulated to fit the needs of the community that preserved it.

Now look again at the opening of the story in each gospel. It shows us more about how stories differ when they are handed on orally. Mark's opening does not give any reason for plucking the grain; nor is it clear that merely plucking an ear would violate the Sabbath any more than picking a flower would. The Old Testament justification mentioned that David and his men were hungry. That motif occurs in Matthew 12:1 as the motivation for the disciples' action. In both Matthew and Luke the disciples pluck the grain to eat. The Lukan version does not stress the hunger motif but has the disciples rub the grain together in their hands thus explaining what it was they did that would constitute "work." You can see then that not only have the versions in Matthew and Luke smoothed out the introduction to the story but they have also given fuller explanations of the actions that take place in the story. Such examples are frequent in New Testament stories.

When the form critic does this sort of analysis, he or she is really trying to trace out a history of the tradition. How was a story or saying passed on or modified? What function did telling that story have within the Christian community? This example makes it clear that the earliest Christians did not treat the sayings and stories handed on to them from Jesus as "dead weight." They were living sayings and stories. They were told and retold; modified and combined so that Christians could hear what Jesus was saying to them. The form critic is not simply interested in finding some "earliest version" of a story or saying—that may be impossible as the folklorists tell us—but he or she wants to "listen in on" the early Church. The variety of life-settings (called by the technical term "setting in life," *Sitz im Leben*) of the stories and sayings account for the shapes of the Church's oral tradition. Early Christian teaching, preaching and worship are closely related. We also find stories that have been shaped by controversies with outsiders, Jews and Gentiles. Finally, stories and sayings of Jesus are used to provide the early community with rules for organization and discipline.

Classification of various forms and study of their general features still continues. That study is aided by other discoveries of popular writing at the time of Jesus. Two main divisions are between sayings material and narrative. Three main types of sayings material are easily distinguished:

(1) *Pronouncement stories* like the one we just read are considered "sayings" rather than narrative because the focus of the whole incident is on the saying or sayings with which it concludes.

(2) *Short sayings* without any story leading up to them. Some of these short sayings like "No person can serve two masters for either he will hate the one and be devoted to the other or he will be devoted to the one and despise the other" (Mt 6:24), are proverbial. Proverbs are an ubiquitous form of folklore. The Old Testament has an entire book of them and New Testament writings like James are heavily indebted to Jewish proverbial wisdom. Other sayings are called "judgment sayings." They declare what will happen to a person if he or she does not follow the teaching of Jesus, for example Mark 8:38 or Matthew 7:1f. Notice that these sayings contain a passive verb. We call it a "theological passive" because it was used as a circumlocution for saying that God would do what is described. Jews had a variety of circumlocutions by which they avoided using the holy divine name. The beatitudes may be viewed as eschatological judgment sayings. They are not simply proverbs because they do not describe the way human affairs as we know them turn out.

You may have noticed in reading the Sermon on the Mount that sayings tend to come in groups or at least in pairs. The most common way of grouping sayings is around a common theme or catchword. Very often paired sayings are antitheses of one another. Sometimes—as in the two versions of the beatitudes—the order or content of a block of sayings will vary from one version to another. Thus the grouping of sayings of Jesus seems to have varied within the oral tradition. The early Christian preachers may have even added proverbs and judgment oracles from elsewhere to fill out a particular collection. An anthropologist once told me how proverbs were used in the legal procedures of an African tribe. A case would be presented before the chief, who would then retire into his hut. When he came out to render his decision, he would do so by quoting proverbs. The wisdom of the chief did not lie in his ability to make up new proverbs but in his ability to apply the traditional ones to a particular case. A similar approach to proverbial material seems to characterize Jesus and his contemporaries. Sometimes when we run up against a proverb in the New Testament it is difficult to tell what point is being made because we do not have examples of how that particular saying was commonly used in Jesus' time.

(3) *Parables* are the most characteristic form of the teaching of Jesus. The Hebrew term for parable, *mashal*, covers a wide variety of riddles, analogies and stories. It seems to have been one of the most characteristic features of Jesus' preaching. He would make a point by telling a story or using a comparison focused on a commonplace incident from life or on a metaphor well-known to his audience from the Old Testament. Usually that story or metaphor contained peculiar exaggerations or an unexpected result. The key to Jesus' message then lies in these peculiar turns given the commonplace. As parables were handed on by audiences not familiar with the Old Testament metaphors or with the day to day life of people in Palestine, they were often turned into elaborate allegories or supplied with allegorical interpretations at the end. Like the pronouncement story that we studied, other sayings of Jesus

were sometimes added on to the end of a parable to explain how it was interpreted within the Christian community. Many of Jesus' parables ended with a question that threw the burden of interpretation onto his audience and invites such additions. Sometimes a parable that was originally addressed to a Jewish audience has been modified to apply to Christians. There is a great deal of activity in parable study today. People are not only searching out the historical background behind the parables but also analyzing the literary techniques by which they are constructed.

The narrative material is not as easy to analyze. The miracle story and its sub-type, the exorcism, are the clearest units of oral tradition. Miracle stories were a popular form of religious propaganda in antiquity. Here are two examples. The first is an exorcism by a Syrian (Gentile) healer from Palestine:

> Everyone has heard of the Syrian from Palestine, an expert at such things. Whatever moonstruck—rolling their eyes and filling their mouths with foam—people come, they arise and he dispatches them away healthy, when they are free from the terror and for a large fee. When he stands by them as they are lying there he asks from whence they came into the body. The sick man is silent, but the demon answers in Greek or some other barbarian tongue. The Syrian levels oaths at him but if the demon is not persuaded, he threatens and expels the demon.

The second is a Jewish story about a famous rabbi:

> Once the son of R. Gamaliel fell ill. He sent two scholars to R. Hanina b. Dosa to ask him to pray for him. When he saw them he went to an upper chamber and prayed. When he came down he said, "Go, the fever has left him." They asked, "Are you a prophet?" He replied, "I am neither a prophet nor the son of a prophet, but I have learned from experience that if my prayer is fluent in my mouth, I know that it is accepted; but if it is not, I know that it is rejected." They sat down and made an exact note of the moment. When they came to R. Gamaliel, he said to them, "By

the temple service! You have not been a moment too
soon or too late but it happened that way, at that very
moment the fever left him and he asked for water to
drink."

The basic pattern of a miracle story is clear: the illness is
described; the healer takes action—in exorcisms of all cultures
that action involves a shouted exchange between the healer
and the demon—then there is evidence of the cure. Notice that
the Jewish story stresses the piety of the rabbi and his prayer
to God; not he but God is the source of the miracle. While the
miracles of Jesus are not always as elaborately tied to prayer,
they do show a similar reticence about Jesus' power and often
stress the belief of the recipient. Perhaps that emphasis on
faith developed as Christian missionaries used these stories in
their preaching. Other stories about Jesus are less easily clas-
sified; perhaps they did not circulate in formally defined collections as the miracle stories seem to have done.

Redaction Criticism

Form criticism had tended to treat the evangelists as mere
compilers of earlier traditions. But after World War II another
type of inquiry called redaction criticism gained prominence.
People observed that there was often a definite pattern to the
variations in arrangement and story telling between the
evangelists. They began to look for the unique perspective that
each one sought to present. Two types of analysis are involved
in redaction criticism. First, an evangelist may be compared
with his sources to see where a consistent pattern of changes
can be detected. For example, Luke loves to show Jesus praying. Here are two versions of the opening of the story of the call
of the twelve disciples:

A. And he went up into the hills and called to him
those whom he desired, and they came to him. And
he appointed twelve to be with him and to be sent
out to preach and have authority to cast out demons, Simon . . .

> B. In those days, he went out into the hills to pray, and all night he continued in prayer to God. And when it was day he called his disciples and chose from them twelve whom he named apostles: Simon ...

Which one is by Luke? You could easily pick out B because Jesus spends the night in prayer before he makes his choice. The other version is from Mark, the one Luke used as a source. Or, go back once again to the story about plucking grain on the Sabbath. You will notice that Matthew's version has a special section where Jesus gives more arguments from the Old Testament. We will see that that fits in with Matthew's picture of Jesus as the true teacher of the Law; one whose primary concern is with mercy.

The second procedure is to analyze how each evangelist has arranged his material. Matthew, for example, organizes the teaching of Jesus in five discourses. Again we see the motif of Jesus as teacher being brought to the fore. Or, read Luke chapters 1-2. Count the number of times there are references to prayer or examples of people praying. There are many more than in the similar chapters of Matthew. Thus you can see that Luke's interest in prayer played a role even in the way he describes the birth of Jesus.

Redaction critics are particularly interested in those features of an evangelist's work that show what his theological insights were. As a result of their work—which is really only in its infancy compared to the other disciplines of gospel research—the synoptic gospel writers are taking their place alongside Paul and John as Christian theologians, as people who had a unique vision of Jesus and Christian life.

Quest for the Historical Jesus

All our methods of gospel research have shown us that the traditions about Jesus were shaped and reformulated by generations of Christians. Some people might conclude that it is impossible to know anything about Jesus himself. In one sense that situation only reminds us of an important fact about our faith: it depends upon that of the first disciples. They have left us their vision of Jesus' significance as a heritage. No one can prove to someone that he or she should believe in Jesus on purely historical grounds. We can, then, distinguish three types of statement about Jesus:

(1) Purely historical statements could be agreed upon by any student of antiquity even if he or she thought that Jesus and his movement deserved to be rejected.

(2) What are sometimes called "historic" statements about Jesus, that is, statements that indicated that Jesus—and those who wrote about him for that matter—was a significant religious thinker in Western culture and that his thinking has abiding relevance for humanity. Someone like Gandhi who could be inspired by the teaching of the Sermon on the Mount and yet not be a Christian would be an example of someone who made historic statements about Jesus. Such a view of Jesus claims that his teaching should still influence thinking men and women; that he is not a dead figure from the past. A person could of course say the same thing about Buddha, Socrates or Marx.

(3) Faith statements about Jesus can only be made by those who are professed Christians. They go further than historic statements by claiming that Jesus is Son of God, savior of the world, the final revelation of God. Historical knowledge about Jesus might inform the content of statements in the other two categories. It may even correct some false images of him that believers have formulated, but of itself it can never lead logically to faith or even to historic claims about Jesus.

However, believers realize that it is important to have as accurate a picture of Jesus and his times as possible so that they can have a better understanding of the teaching of Jesus and the earliest apostles. At the same time they are always aware that the New Testament writers are speaking as Christians to other Christians and trying to help them understand what their faith is.

In their desire to glean historical knowledge about Jesus from the faith tradition embodied in the New Testament, modern scholars assess each story or saying by a stringent set of criteria. First, they use form critical analysis, source criticism and redaction criticism to get back to the earliest pre-gospel version(s) of a story or saying. Then they ask whether that story or saying could have originated with Jesus or whether it seems to be the product of the later Church. To qualify as authentic, a story or saying must fit in with our knowledge of Palestine in the time of Jesus. It must occur in early stages of the tradition. If a saying or story occurs in several versions or layers of tradition, then it is felt to be more likely authentic than one that occurs only once. Then there is a strict criterion of dissimilarity. Some things in the Jesus tradition are unique: they are unlike what contemporary Jews were saying and they are unlike what the early Christians later said or did. Such sayings or stories have great likelihood of being the authentic teaching of Jesus. Although the criterion of dissimilarity is too harsh in that it weeds out places where Jesus agreed with his contemporaries, it provides an historically defensible reconstruction of the teaching of Jesus. Scholars can then use what they call the criterion of coherence to expand our picture of Jesus. Whatever occurs in the early tradition and fits in with the picture of Jesus gained from strict application of the criterion of dissimilarity is also likely to be authentic Jesus material. Thus while the gospels are testaments of faith and not historical records, they can still be used as sources for an understanding of the historical Jesus.

Trial and Death

We have very little information about the life of Jesus in the biographical sense. Mark does not begin until Jesus' public ministry. It is an undoubted historical fact—though I do meet people who have been given the idea that Jesus might never have existed—that there was a Jewish teacher from Galilee, Jesus, who was executed in Jerusalem under the Roman prefect, Pontius Pilate. Jewish religious authorities seem to have been involved in bringing him before Pilate after an incident in the temple in which Jesus challenged their authority. However, most legal historians agree that they could not have put a person to death unless that person were a Gentile who had violated the sanctuary of the temple. Crucifixion was a Roman form of execution. We know that Pilate never hesitated to execute people—even to slaughter demonstrators—if he thought that they might be stirring up trouble against Roman rule, the grounds on which Jesus was executed. He was not known for patient and fair investigation of the grievances of his subjects.

Roman legal historians also tell us that the trial narrative in Matthew/Mark fits what we know of legal proceedings in the provinces. Someone had to bring the case before the prefect or procurator. Roman officials usually began business at dawn or earlier so as to be finished by mid-day. The prefect could proceed with the trial pretty much as he chose. Almost anyone brought into court under those circumstances could expect to be beaten. Even someone cleared of charges might be given a light beating as a warning. One of the curious features about the trial of Jesus is his failure to make a defense. There was no 5th amendment in Roman Law. Someone who failed to speak in his own defense was automatically guilty. One cannot help but be reminded of Jesus' own teaching about not defending oneself against evil even when dragged into court (Mt 5:38-48). Thus we can see even from an historical point of view that Jesus chose to be condemned rather than resist evil. Pilate was required to condemn someone who would not defend himself. He could, of course, have let Jesus off with a beating, but his tendency to ruthless execution was well-known. One could even claim that Jesus chose death by refusing to defend himself. In sum, we have a picture of a Galilean religious teacher whose preaching drew enough attention to get him into trouble with the religious authorities in Jerusalem. He is brought before the prefect where he chooses not to defend himself and thus die rather than resist, and he is executed by a Roman squad. That much the historian can tell us. How one assesses the death of Jesus depends upon one's faith. An historian can treat it as a "fact" or perhaps find Jesus a bit odd for not offering a defense. A Jewish rabbi once remarked to me that he could see

Jesus as one of many pious Jews who were executed in the time
of Pilate when they refused to compromise their faith in God. A
Christian on the other hand will see that death as something
more, as a key to the reconciliation of humanity and God.

STUDY QUESTIONS

1. Why is it difficult to write a biography of Jesus on the basis
   of the synoptic gospels?
2. What is source criticism? What has it shown us about how
   the synoptic gospels were composed?
3. Where is the Lord's Prayer in Matthew? Where is it found in
   Luke? Why is it found in different places in each gospel?
4. What is a pronouncement story? Find two pronouncement
   stories in Matthew Chs. 17 and 18. Identify the main features of each one.
5. What are the principle features of a miracle story? Of an
   exorcism? Find one miracle story and one exorcism in Mark
   2-5. Identify the main parts to each story.
6. What are the two types of analysis used in redaction criticism?
7. How has redaction criticsm changed our understanding of
   the synoptic evangelists as authors?
8. What is the difference between historical statements about
   Jesus and faith statements about him?

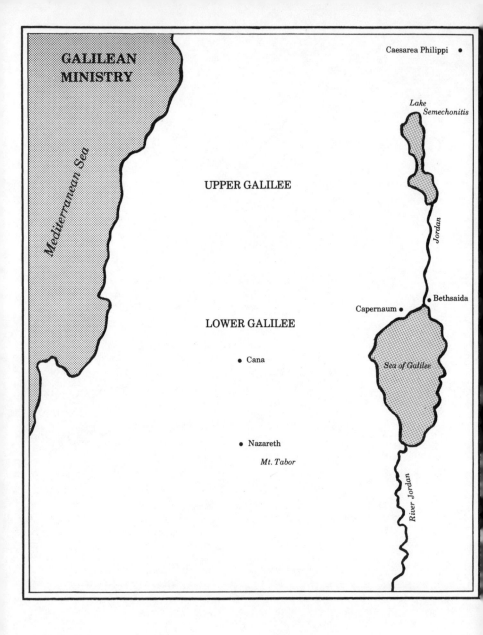

Chapter Four

THE PREACHING OF JESUS

What we know of Jesus' preaching comes from the three synoptic gospels. The fourth gospel reflects on the tradition from the perspective of the resurrected and exalted Jesus and rarely provides any historical information. The other writings of the New Testament rarely quote sayings of Jesus. They focus on the life and problems of the earliest church. We have seen that since the synoptics were written 40 to 60 years after the death of Jesus, scholars have to analyze them carefully in order to reconstruct the teaching of the historical Jesus. But do not think that the necessity for such scholarly research makes it impossible for the average person to improve his or her reading of the Bible. Basic rules that anyone can learn to apply have emerged from all the research. You may not be able to reconstruct the history of a particular story in the synoptic tradition but you can already identify some of the basic types of story and their main features. You can also learn what to look out for in making your own interpretations or in evaluating those you hear from other people. Then you will be able to tell if their claims are reasonable or not.

How To Interpret Miracles

We have already seen that religions at the time of Jesus told various miracle stories. They were a form of religious propaganda. Sometimes the miracle story is simply told to glorify a given wonder-worker. It showed that he personally possessed extraordinary powers. Read the humorous story of Simon Magus in Acts 8:9-24. It shows how such a person might appear to outsiders. We have also seen that Judaism avoided such hero worship by stressing the fact that God worked the miracle in response to prayer by a pious rabbi. The miracle is a sign of the rabbi's piety and of God's power. The individual does not take personal credit for it. As you read the miracles of Jesus ask yourself where they fit in. Is the author simply showing off Jesus as a powerful wonder-worker, a "divine-man"? Or is he using the miracles to tell us something about God and Jesus' relationship to him? Sometimes a miracle is used to introduce a point of teaching as in the healing of the man with the paralyzed hand (Mk 3:1-5), part of a cycle of sabbath controversy stories. In others, the faith of the recipient is stressed (e.g., Mk 9:24). Often stories in which faith is stressed have the recipient be a person whose disease or occupation makes him or her an outcast or a non-Jew requests the miracle (Mk 4:25-34). In those cases, the miracle shows that God accepts such people as well as the righteous.

We have further indications of how Jesus' miracles were understood in Mk 3:23-27 (Mt 12:25-29; Lk 11:17-22). Some people had been claiming that he worked miracles through "magic"—like Simon in the Acts story. Such a charge was a serious one in antiquity. We have cases of people being brought into court on the charge of practicing magic. Jesus argues that his miracles are a sign of something else: they are a sign that Satan's hold on this world is being broken up. Evil no longer has the tight hold on the world that many people attributed to it. We saw in our discussion of apocalyptic that many people thought that the hold of evil over the world was so great that only a cosmic catastrophe could break it. Jesus says, "No." God still rules the world and in the ministry of Jesus, that rule is being demonstrated by the defeat of powers of evil in sickness, sin and death.

Thus when you read the miracles of Jesus you should realize that they are not magic feats to be duplicated. Nor are they promises that every Christian will be spared suffering, sickness or death if he or she prays enough. After all, Jesus did not spare himself. Rather they are meant to be signs to us about God. He loves and accepts the outcast and the sinner. He is greater and more powerful than all the evils that seem to rule the world. Even with the modern medicine and science that have replaced the healers of antiquity, we still need signs of these truths about God.

Interpreting Parables

We have already pointed out that parables are the most characteristic feature of the teaching of Jesus. We saw that they are metaphors, stories or analogies and not allegories. Nor can they be reduced to single sentence morals. Here are some basic points to remember when you read a parable:

(1) They depend upon audience for their impact. Some listeners, the rich, the powerful, the religious establishment may be offended. Others, the poor, the dispossessed may be amused or enjoy the discomfort of some of the principal characters.

(2) Although the parables are often spoken of as life-like because they draw on everyday events, the characters in them are not exactly "real people", they are often more like comic or TV stereotypes of real people.

(3) The parables often contain elements of surprise, of departure from everyday life either in the outcome or in what the characters say and do.

(4) The parables are part of Jesus' statement about God and humanity. They are often a critique of peoples' views and attitudes. But they are not just ways of transmitting some doctrines about God and man. Jesus wants his hearers to share those stories by coming to adopt and live the vision embodied in them.

When you read a parable, then, observe the following rules:

(1) Since they are stories and not allegories, every detail does not have a meaning beyond what it contributes to the story. The stories want to give us a new vision, not a series of ethical points or new doctrine.

(2) Jesus frequently ended with a question that forced the listeners to decide the answer on the basis of how they felt about the story. Where is the question? How would you answer?

(3) The sayings and interpretations that follow the parables in the New Testament were added on later. They tell us how the parables were used in the preaching of the early Church.

(4) Look for the points of exaggeration or the places where Jesus has changed an Old Testament story line or image. They are the clues to what was unique about Jesus' vision of God and of how people should live in the presence of that God.

Remember that there are good and bad interpretations of a parable; but because they are stories they may have more than one good interpretation. In many cases a person's interpretation of Jesus' words would have varied with his or her background: was he or she Jew or Samaritan or Gentile; a landowner or a tenant farmer or a slave. Try reading the parables from such different points of view and see what new light is shed on them.

Interpreting Sayings

We have already pointed out that there are different kinds of sayings in the New Testament and that they are often arranged in groups. Many are proverbial. If people interpret the sayings of Jesus as statements of fact or principle, they will find them boring and repetitive. Remember that Jesus did all his teaching orally and so did most of the early Christians. Each person had to remember what he or she heard. They could not look it up in a Bible. Therefore, parallelism and repetition were very important. Not only does repetition aid the memory, it has other functions as well. On the most primary level, repetition is basic to the human organism's way of adapting to its environment. It has elements of incantation, song and poetry. Repetition also has its effect on the feeling level. A single sentence is enough to give us information but repetition works on a different level.

Advertising in our society is the most obvious example of people trying to use repetition to influence our behavior. Repetition can also help us "catch" what is being said. Every good teacher knows that new ideas should be presented several times from slightly different angles so that those who did not "get it" one way may have a chance with another version. Those who "got it" the first time may be helped by the new examples to see other applications of what has been presented.

Finally, such a mode of generalization is open-ended. Every possible application has not been surveyed but enough examples have been given so that a person should be able to extend the series for himself or herself. The sayings of Jesus have all of these characteristics. They are persuasive examples that ask us to look at the world and ourselves in a new light. They are not abstract principles or laws.

Read the passage about the lilies of the field from Matthew 6:25-33:

Life, Food, Clothing
Therefore I tell you, do not be anxious about your life, what you shall eat, or what you shall drink, Nor about your body, what you shall put on. Is not life more than food? And the body more than clothing?

Food
Look at the birds of the air: they neither sow nor reap nor gather into barns, and yet your heavenly Father feeds them. Are you not of more value than they? And which of you by being anxious can add to his span of life?

Clothing
And why are you anxious about clothing? Consider the lilies of the field, how they grow: They neither toil nor spin, yet I tell you, even Solomon in all his glory was not arrayed like one of these. But if God so clothes the grass of the field, which is alive today and thrown into the oven tomorrow, will he not much more clothe you, O men of little faith?

Life
Therefore do not be anxious, saying, What shall we

eat or what shall we drink or what shall we wear? For
the Gentiles seek all these things. Your heavenly
Father knows that you need them all. But first seek
His kingdom and His righteousness, and all these
things will be yours as well.

Notice how carefully the parallelism in the passage has
been constructed. Jesus wants to coax us out of a certain anxiety
about the progress of our lives. We all have tendencies that
want to see around every corner in the future; to have everything planned. Young people today are particularly worried
about their economic future. I know college students who are
majoring in business or pre-med even though they dislike the
fields; they are so worried about having a job that they cannot
study what really interests them. Jesus' answer to that kind of
anxiety is not to try to reason us out of it; nor is he commanding us not to worry. Rather this string of sayings sets worry in
a context that makes it look ridiculous. The great King
Solomon—renowned for his wealth and splendor—is compared to lilies in a field and is found wanting! The metaphor is
using a technique that is common in both the sayings and
parables of Jesus: if something is true in this unimportant case
(birds, lilies, grass) then it must be even more true in a more
serious case (peoples' lives).

Here are some rules for analyzing sayings:

(1) They are not statements of fact or general principles to
be rigidly applied. They are metaphors to be lived. We are
supposed to apply them by analogy.

(2) Look for the key words (we have supplied headings for
you) and parallels. What things is Jesus comparing?

(3) Then ask yourself what other types of situation this
comparison might be applied to. Perhaps you can even think of
some modern analogies.

The Kingdom of God and a New Chosen People
The expression "kingdom of God" occurs frequently in the
teaching of Jesus. The most famous Christian prayer, the

Lord's Prayer, is a prayer for the coming of the kingdom. What does the expression mean? The word frequently translated "kingdom" does not mean territory. It means the activity of ruling. Therefore, the NAB usually translates this expression as "reign of God." What is referred to in this expression then is whether or how God rules the world. We have seen that this question was central in the minds of many Jews in Jesus' day even though they did not sum it up with the expression "kingdom of God" as Jesus did. The triumph of people, who did not worship the God of Israel, over the pious would seem to deny that the God of Abraham, Isaac and Moses was really the creator of this world. The picture of God as king, creator and judge, as the one who upholds the order of the universe and society is central to Old Testament piety. Turn to your Old Testament and read psalm 82. God is pictured as sitting in judgment in heaven while the psalmist cries out to him to destroy the wicked and rescue the needy (vv 2-5). God pronounces sentence against the princes of the world (v 6). This psalm is not predicting literal events. But it teaches those who recite it that God does rule the world and not foreign gods or powers. Many of the psalms are pleas to God to vindicate the righteous and deliver them from evil. Others, like psalm 93, praise him as the eternal creator and ruler of the universe. The psalmists could see enough of God's activity in creation and history to confess that belief in the world.

But we have already learned that many people in Jesus' day were more pessimistic. Evil had such a hold on this creation that there would have to be a cosmic judgment and a new creation. Only then would the kingdom of God appear. (Go back to pp. 39-41 for quotations from some of their writings.)

Many people who came to hear Jesus talk about the kingdom of God probably expected a sermon about the impending end of all things and perhaps a call to repent before the judgment such as that issued by John the Baptist. That is where they would get their first surprise. Sometimes Jesus spoke about the approaching rule of God, but at other times, he spoke of the rule of God as something that people could already experience—not as a big cataclysm at all. In that respect, his attitudes may be more in line with our examples from the psalm than with some of his contemporaries. When we discussed the miracles, we saw that Jesus considered his own healing activity to be an indication of the presence of God's rule and the break up of the power of evil (cf. Lk 11:20). When some people asked for *signs* that the reign of God was coming—they were still thinking in apocalyptic terms—Jesus told them that the reign of God was right within reach (Lk 17:20f.). David Flusser, a Jewish New Testament scholar, once remarked that Jesus is "the only Jew known to us from ancient times who proclaimed that the new age of salvation had already begun." Recent studies of the beatitudes have suggested that they are not just future promises but that they are proclaiming the presence of everything people had hoped to receive from God.

Many of Jesus' parables are descriptions of what God's rule is like. There we find some striking contrasts with the apocalyptic metaphors of Jesus' time. Jesus almost never describes God as a cosmic warrior or king. Instead we get stories about landlords and tenants. Nor does Jesus dwell on the wrath that God is supposed to direct at sinners. Instead he tells stories of compassion and acceptance.

Read Matthew 20:1-14, for example. Here the master takes up the obviously absurd labor policy of paying all the workers the same wage and even goes out of his way to arrange the payments so that those who had labored all day would find out that the others received the same pay that they had. You know what would happen if someone tried that today. The grape pickers' union would be up in arms against him.

Read Matthew 13:24-30. No farmer would have acted the way this one does. Obviously Jesus does not think that the righteous are in any danger from living in a world full of evil people, the weeds. We have seen that that attitude is quite different from that of the Pharisees or the even more extreme Essenes who thought that the righteous had to avoid contamination by evil people as much as possible. We know that Jesus was often accused of spending too much time with sinners.

Many people looked forward to the destruction of sinners in the messianic age. Jews did believe that God was merciful and would accept someone who repented, but the primary emphasis in much of the apocalyptic language is on *exclusion*. One must exclude everyone and everything that is defiled or sinful from one's midst. That is the way in which God's people are to become holy.

Non-Jews, the Gentiles, were sinners by definition. People were divided over whether or not there might be righteous Gentiles who would be saved in the age to come. There were also some Jews whose occupations made them like Gentile sinners and meant that they lost all rights in the chosen people. They were dice-players, money lenders, those who bought or sold produce grown in the sabbatical year when the land was supposed to lie fallow, tax collectors, shepherds and swine herds, and revenue farmers. The pious Jew was not to allow such people in his house. The Law said, ". . . a tax collector defiles everything in the house by entering as does a Gentile."

Now read Jesus' parable of the prodigal son (Lk 15:11-32). You can see how extravagant—even unjust?—the father's reception of the younger son is. Or reread the famous section on love of enemies (Mt 5:43-48). Notice that Jesus uses another of his nature analogies from the lesser case to the greater (cf. p. 89): "God gives all people the same weather, therefore . . ." The section ends with a definition of what God's perfection is. It does not depend upon excluding the sinner, but on equal love for everyone. We often think of loving enemies as loving those we or society would admit are "good people" but whom we do not happen to like. Jesus' examples are more radical. They include those whom most people would consider "bad." As long as people divide good and evil in that way, they cannot see the rule of God; it looks to them as though sinners predominate or "get away with it." They cannot conceive God's love for the sinner. Jesus' perspective on the true nature of divine perfection also makes it clear that he could not accept the exclusivism of the Pharisees or Essenes. The righteous are not contaminated by living with evil people any more than God is contaminated by their presence in his creation.

Jesus does expect some manifestation of God's rule in the future. The Lord's Prayer asks for the coming of the kingdom. Many people do not even know what they are praying for when they recite it. The shorter version is in Luke 11:2-4, but we use the version from Matthew 6 that seems to have been elaborated for Christian liturgical use. It has two sets of three petitions. The first three have God as their subject. They are petitions for the manifestation of his rule:

(1) The expression, "may your name be sanctified," is asking God to manifest his rule in such a way that all people will bless his name. Look at the Jewish descriptions of the messianic age on pages 39 and 52. You can see that they conclude with all people praising and blessing God.

(2) The second petition asks for the coming of God's rule.

(3) The expression "thy will be done on earth as it is in heaven" uses the theological passive again. God is the subject; not people. He is being asked to do his will on earth as in heaven.

The next three petitions refer to the disciple:

(4) The request for bread is not for food in general but for the bread of the messianic banquet (Mt 8:11; Lk 13:28f.). The Lord's Prayer occurs in a eucharistic liturgy from the end of the 1st century that says the eucharist is an anticipation of that banquet.

(5) Forgiveness of debts is a common theme in the preaching of Jesus. It is picked up in the sayings that follow the Lord's Prayer in Matthew and in many of the parables (Mt 18:23-25; Lk 7:41-43).

(6) The final petition is not for deliverance from personal temptation. The Greek word *peirasmos* is used to refer to *the trial*, that is, the horrors before the end of the world in which Satan will make his final effort to lead people astray. No one wants to live in that time—and so far, we have been spared it.

This prayer for the kingdom shows that Jesus did not think that everything had arrived in his ministry or that giving people a new perspective on God's perfection and justice answered all the hopes and aspirations people had for the future. He knew that his followers would have to preserve their vision of God's rule in the face of evil and testing, but he expects his followers to be able to live out that vision in the world even as they pray for the coming of God's rule.

The Ethics of Jesus: God and Righteousness

It is a common mistake to reduce all of Jesus' ethical teaching to the command of love for enemies. While that is an important part of his teaching, love is not the main topic in the teaching of Jesus, the rule of God is. Perhaps because people today do not think much about God as ruler of the world, as having some plan for his creation and as active in its history, they tend to focus only on more subjective and individualistic language like that of love. The question of the rule of God embraces a wider set of issues than individual moral attitudes. All facets of justice are involved. One could say that Jesus' ethical teaching is an indication of how we are to deal with one another in light of his central realization about the perfection of God and his rule. Unless we accept the truth of Jesus' vision of God, we will have a very hard time responding positively to the type of behavior his teaching suggests.

Our discussions of proverbs and sayings point out some important features of Jesus' ethical teaching. It is not systematic or philosophical. He does not lay down general rules or a code of law. He teaches by specific examples, which must be treated as analogies for how a person who believes that God's rule is present and active in this world will behave. Jesus presupposes much of the ethical teaching of the Old Testament, though he sometimes lashes out at how his contemporaries interpreted the Old Testament.

We saw that Jesus views God as the all-inclusive, loving, creator. That picture of God was used to validate Jesus' teaching on love of enemies—a teaching he admits runs contrary to ordinary human behavior. Look at his criticism of some Jewish teaching on divorce in Mark 10:2-9. Jesus appeals beyond the tradition of Moses to God's will in creating man and woman. Just as today, people debated the grounds for divorce. Pagan law made it easy for either husband or wife to obtain a divorce. Jewish law was stricter and more one-sided. A husband could write a bill of divorce and have it witnessed by two men; though such bills frequently went through a court, they did not have to. The wife did not have a clearly defined right to divorce her husband. She could ask him to give her a divorce and might in some cases be able to get a court to force him to give her a divorce, but she could not technically divorce him. People argued over the meaning of the Old Testament passage that allowed a husband to divorce his wife. Some said that it referred only to cases of adultery; others, that a husband could divorce his wife for anything that consistently displeased him—like frequently burning his dinner! Jesus clearly sided with the more conservative view and felt that even that exception ran counter to the will of God in creation. Students today often find that teaching extremely unfair. They always have to be reminded that Jesus' ethical teaching is part of his whole vision of how a person can live in light of the rule of God. It includes the sayings on love and not resisting evil but no sayings on "what's fair" by our standards. If husband and wife were both trying to live according to that teaching, the usual arguments in favor of a liberalized teaching on divorce would hardly apply.

The real difficulty with Jesus' ethical vision is that it seems to be saying to us, "Change human nature." Look at what Jesus says about anger in Matthew 5:21-26 or adultery in 5:27-31. Of course, one cannot command a person not to be angry or to lust, but these sayings indicate that the inner dispositions of a person are the real issue. They are what lie behind the deeds prohibited in the Law. We know from the various traditions of religious asceticism that people can attain such universal compassion that anger and lust do not arise. The prophet Jeremiah had taught that the only way humanity would follow God's Law would be if he created a "new heart" within people (Jer 31:31-34). Jesus does not seem to have been that kind of moral pessimist. Again, notice how the sayings progress: rooting out lust is surely a lesser thing than tearing out an eye or cutting off a hand. Or, if I have not gained control of my temper or my tendency to insult others, I can surely manage to be reconciled with the person I have offended.

Not only are we to seek reconciliation, we are not to resist evil. Look at Matthew 5:38-42. Jesus is not overthrowing a crude type of vengeance code when he rejects "eye for an eye and tooth for a tooth." That principle is basic to any legal structure. A person is entitled to just compensation for an injury received. In our society that compensation takes the form of monetary damages. A 19th-century English jurist who realized what is at stake here, remarked that the ethical teaching of Jesus is "not only pernicious but unjust." All of the examples of not resisting evil were live issues in Jesus' day. A person was protected against seizure of necessary clothing in a lawsuit (v 40) and against being conscripted to carry loads for more than a mile (v 41). Christians are told not to defend themselves against evil either physically or legally, nor are they to protect their self-interest by refusing requests for gifts or loans. The Christian takes injury on himself or herself and does not demand that others accept such injury from himself or herself. We saw in the last chapter that Jesus apparently carried out this principle when he refused to defend himself before Pilate.

Needless to say, this ethical vision has made people nervous throughout the centuries. If you read books on the ethics of Jesus, you will probably find a variety of explanations given for why his teaching seems so extreme. Here are some of the types of explanation you would find:

(1) Take it *literally in every detail*. Many saints, like Francis of Assisi, have been inspired to do just that.

(2) Take it as a *perfectionist ethic*, that is, Jesus knew that people would not be able to attain the ideal he set up. But by presenting it he expected people to exert themselves more strenuously than they would with an easier goal. That way they would attain at least some part of the ideal and would realize that salvation is an extremely serious matter.

(3) Take it as an *impossible ideal* that has been set up to shatter human pride. We may look down on the murderer and the adulterer from a position of righteous self-esteem because we would not do something like that. But when we measure ourselves against these ideals, we realize that we, too, are sinners and must rely on the mercy and graciousness of God.

(4) Take it as suited to Jesus' time but argue that it *must be up-dated* to fit the ethical awareness of our own time and in light of contemporary psychoanalytic theories about human nature.

(5) Take it as an *interim ethic* that was only intended to apply for a short period between the ministry of Jesus and the coming of the new age. The major objection to this view is that there is no indication that Jesus considered these suggestions dependent upon the nearness of the messianic ages or that he thought they were only temporary. Rather, the references to judgment are used to underline the seriousness with which he speaks.

(6) Take it as *completely irrelevant* for people today. This view is usually based on analyses such as those suggested in Nos. 4 and 5 and then reach the conclusion that such an historically conditioned ethic cannot have any relevance for people today.

(7) *Reject* Jesus' ethical view as not only irrelevant but as fundamentally wrong and detrimental to the development of independent creative human persons. Frederich Nietzsche, for example, spoke of the ethic of love and meekness as a slave morality from which humanity needed to be freed.

(8) Finally, there are even attempts to argue that Jesus' vision is *fundamentally a-moral*, that is, that Jesus simply intends to shatter our ordinary ways of looking at the world and our accepted categories. He is not setting himself up as a new moral teacher at all. The first four suggestions do indicate something true about the ethic of Jesus, and it is also true that he wants us to have a new vision that is different from our usual ways of looking at the world and people. But that new vision does not preclude offering serious ethical alternatives to

accepted behavior. The a-moral interpretation smacks too much of 20th-century preoccupations with the absurd and the demise of Western culture to be convincing for a 1st-century Jewish cultural milieu.

The real difficulty in interpreting any of the teaching of Jesus is its open-ended character; its persistent use of story, analogy, metaphor and proverb. It cannot be pinned down to a set of declarative sentences, theological propositions or ethical rules. The analogies and chains of examples are not a code of conduct or a set of principles. They have to be applied by finding the situations in our own lives that would fit the case or continue the chain. The teaching in the parables about what the rule of God is like is much the same way; it is as though Jesus tossed us some examples and said, "Now you find the rule of God."

STUDY QUESTIONS

1. How should we understand the miracles of Jesus?
2. Give four rules for interpreting parables. How would you apply them to the parable of the Prodigal Son (Lk 15:11-32)?
3. What are the three rules for interpreting sayings? Apply them to Matthew 5:21-31.
4. How is Jesus' teaching about the rule of God different from that of other people in his day?
5. Explain what each of the petitions in the Lord's Prayer means.
6. How would you describe Jesus' ethical teaching? Suppose someone said to you that the Sermon on the Mount is impossible to follow. How would you answer him or her?
7. What is Jesus' view of the perfection of God?
8. What do you think is the hardest teaching to follow in the Sermon on the Mount? Why? How would you go about trying to put it into practice?

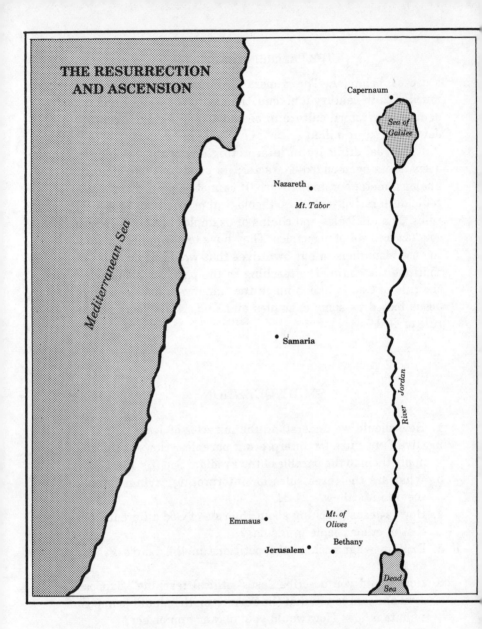

THE RESURRECTION
AND ASCENSION

Capernaum

Sea of Galilee

Mediterranean Sea

Nazareth

Mt. Tabor

• **Samaria**

River Jordan

Emmaus •

Mt. of Olives

Jerusalem • • Bethany

Dead Sea

Chapter Five

THE RISEN CHRIST: BEGINNINGS OF CHRISTOLOGY

We all know that for most Christians Jesus is more than a Jewish teacher from the past; he is the Messiah and Son of God, the unique and definitive revelation of the Father. You probably noticed that there were no specific claims about Jesus himself in the chapters on his life and teaching. It is very difficult to draw any conclusions about Jesus' own self-image from works that were written decades after the fact and by people who believed him to be Son of God. Most scholars agree that Jesus was extremely reticent about making any specific claims for himself. It is also clear that his life did not fit into any of the images people had of the Messiah. Instead, Jesus seems to have concentrated on proclaiming the rule of God. His proclamation linked the realization of that rule with his ministry. We saw that interpretation when we saw that his miracles were to be viewed as signs that the power of Satan was being broken up. Jesus' claim to teach with authority about God, whom he taught his followers to call Father, also implies that he considered himself to have a peculiar place in God's dealings with His people. He may have avoided claiming any particular role for himself lest he be misunderstood. Thus, people today have come to speak of "implicit Christology." What Jesus said and did implied a special relationship between himself and God. Some of his followers may have expected Jesus to be the type of Messiah who would free Israel from foreign domination. But none of the Jewish pictures of the Messiah expect that he will die the kind of death Jesus did. Thus, his followers were scattered and dismayed when he was suddenly executed. Read Luke 24:13-27. Verses 19-21 give a clear picture of the reaction of the early disciples.

Resurrection and the Beginning of the Church

That section from Luke 24 also shows us that it was appearances of the risen Jesus that restored the disciples' confidence. Go back to our discussion of resurrection in Judaism. Resurrection was predominantly conceived of as a reward for the righteous. Those who had suffered for their fidelity to God would be rewarded by resurrection or by exaltation to an angelic existence in heaven. Frequently that exaltation is part of the messianic age, the judgment and the manifestation of the rule of God. What is peculiar about the resurrection of Jesus, then, is that the judgment and the end of the world did not come. There was no universal vindication of all the righteous who had suffered. This peculiarity explains both the difficulty and the importance of the apostles' preaching about the resurrection.

Anyone who believed that Jesus had been raised from the dead would probably feel that God has exalted him in a way that he had not done for any other prophet or righteous person. But imagine the first disciples going out and telling other people that God had raised Jesus of Nazareth, a man crucified by Pilate, and had exalted him in heaven. People might well look at them and say, "That's ridiculous!" After all, none of the other messianic promises had been carried out. The world was still going on as it had before Jesus was even born. He hadn't done anything to change the external circumstances of his people; he was no more widely followed than other religious teachers of the time. At best, they might be willing to agree that Jesus was a good man; maybe even that he was right in

some of his criticisms of prevailing interpretations of the Law
and their concomitant picture of God, but as for resurrection,
he'd have to wait his turn along with all the other suffering
righteous. You can see why St. Paul switched from persecuting
the early Church to preaching about the risen Lord after his
vision of the resurrected Jesus. It proved to him that God had
indeed done something unique in and through that person. You
can also see why resurrection, which is a relatively minor belief in Judaism, became a central feature of Christian belief
and preaching.

The Gift of the Spirit

Their belief that Jesus had been raised and exalted, led
early Christians to re-think their assumptions about the Messiah. Such favor from God surely suggested that Jesus was the
Messiah. Another experience undoubtedly confirmed their
conviction. They experienced a new outpouring of God's
spirit—something that had been predicted for the messianic
age in the Old Testament and that we know from the evidence
of the Qumran scrolls was part of peoples' hope for the future.

There are several references to the gift of the Spirit in the
New Testament. The most famous is the Pentecost story in
Acts 2:1-21. That story associates the gift of the Spirit with the
missionary activity of the Church. Other New Testament passages point to the Spirit as the mode in which the risen Lord
continued to be present in his Church. Many, if not most,
Christians assumed that Jesus, who had been exalted into
heaven, would soon return, judge the world and destroy evil as
everyone had expected the Messiah to do. They used the Son of
Man metaphor from Daniel 7 to describe Jesus as the coming
judge (see Stephen's vision of the exalted Jesus as Son of Man
in Acts 7:55-56). Given the unparalleled experiences they had
had, it is easy to see how people came to that conclusion, but it
was a conclusion based on earlier messianic images and expectations. One which time would show them had not yet taken
full account of the new definition of Messiah given in the life,
death and resurrection of Jesus.

The New Age: Radical Discipleship

The resurrection of Jesus and the gift of the Spirit did suggest that the new age was even closer than people thought. Such a conviction was not merely a matter of calculating time tables. Indeed, the timing question was probably less important than the renewed confidence it gave those who believed that God was present and active in the world. He had really begun to break up the stranglehold of evil and offer people the salvation they had been waiting for. The outpouring of the Spirit and the defeat of evil also meant hope for the individual that his or her life could be lived in that new spirit. Just as Jesus' preaching of the rule of God had called upon them to live according to the new age, so their experience of the Spirit called the earliest Christians to discipleship along the road Jesus had shown them. Of course, that did not mean that people were becoming saints overnight. The early communities had plenty of problems maintaining their original fervor and living in the Spirit as they found themselves called to do.

Preaching Christ to the Nations

Acts 2 tied the gift of the Spirit to the missionary effort of the disciples. If you look at the resurrection stories at the end of Matthew, Luke and John, you will see that Jesus always commissions the disciples to go out and preach. But they did not simply repeat the things that Jesus had told them about the rule of God. They began to speak about what God had done in and through Jesus. While Jesus himself had preached almost exclusively to Jews, they also began to attract Gentile converts. Paul, one of the most famous converts from Judaism, will become the missionary to the Gentiles. You may wonder then how a Jewish religious movement could appeal to non-Jews. First of all, we know that Judaism itself had some missionary zeal in this period. Its monotheism and ethical standards appealed to people. Some would attend the synagogues but would not take the steps such as circumcision required to become converts to Judaism. They were called "god-fearers." Secondly, many of the Jewish messianic texts claim that in the messianic age "the nations," that is, the Gentiles, will come to revere the God of Israel. The mission to the Gentiles, then, could be seen as another sign that Jesus' enthronement in heaven had inaugurated the new age. Some Jewish scholars have even written of Christianity as the means by which God made it possible for Gentiles to come to know him.

Of course, this intense missionary drive and change of audience from Jews to Gentiles also left its mark on the traditions about Jesus as they were handed down. Old Testament quotations were found that predicted what had happened in Jesus. They were used to help prove that Jesus was indeed the Messiah. Sometimes such Old Testament quotes are even used to supply details in a story about Jesus. The miracles were collected for use in missionary preaching. Collections of sayings and parables were made. But even more important, Christians began to look back on Jesus from their new perspective. The question, Who is Jesus? had to be answered differently after the resurrection than before. Before the resurrection many were probably content to assume that he was just a good man, a prophet, maybe even the messianic deliverer of Israel. Afterward, the concept of a Messiah was retained but had to be revised to fit what had happened in Jesus. The question, Why did Jesus die? returns in a new way. The resurrection does not answer that question. People could have seen his death as another in a long line of righteous people who died because they obeyed God rather than men. In Jesus' time, such a person might well have expected God to vindicate him at the judgment. But Jesus is seen to have already received that favor. Why then did God allow him to be killed? Who was he anyway? Why did his death/resurrection inaugurate the new age?

Jesus as Savior or Lord was the most general confession made by early Christians. Other titles like Messiah, Son of God or Son of Man are all peculiarly Jewish and require some Jewish background in order to be understood. But Lord and Savior could be understood by both Jewish and Gentile converts. Both had used such titles to refer to their respective gods. New Testament scholars suggest several stages by which people came to speak of Jesus not only as human but also as divine. Today some people are claiming that it is no longer necessary for Christians to continue proclaiming the divinity of Jesus—that language, they claim, belonged to the myth and metaphor of earlier ages. Most Christian theologians would argue that the confession of Jesus' divinity, properly understood, is the only way of making sense of the Christian understanding of salvation as it is tied to the life and ministry of Jesus of Nazareth. The steps by which an insight into his divinity was reached will show you why that belief is central to the Christian faith.

(1) *Jesus is coming as Messiah.* The earliest response to the resurrection seems to have been that Jesus would return soon as Son of Man and judge the world.

(2) *Jesus as Messiah Reigning in heaven.* If Jesus has been exalted into heaven as Son of Man, then it is not surprising that people came to believe that he must have been made Lord over the cosmos just as the Messiah had been pictured as King over all the nations of the earth. The resurrection and the coming of the Spirit were signs that the Messiah now rules.

(3) *Jesus Must Have Been Different, of Divine or Heavenly Origin.* The earliest confessions that Jesus is God refer to this conviction. It develops to explain why what happened in Jesus could inaugurate the new age and a way of salvation for all of humanity. Early Christian hymns were the earliest expressions of this belief. Paul quotes our earliest example in Philippians 2:6-11:

Who (= Jesus) being in the form of God
    did not consider being like God something to take advantage of,
But emptied himself,
    taking the form of a slave.

Being in human likeness,
    and being found in human shape,
He humbled himself,
    being obedient unto death.

Therefore, God exalted him,
    and gave him the name above every name,
So that at the name of Jesus every knee might bend,
    and every tongue confess:
Jesus Christ is Lord.

(Our translation represents a reconstruction of the original hymn behind the Philippians passage and recent studies of the contemporary meaning of some of its language.) The most recent exegetical study of this hymn has pointed out that it is drawing on the tradition about the righteous person in Widsom 2—6 and the servant songs of Isaiah 53. The righteous person was thought to be "like God." Wisdom speaks of him as "son of God" and immortal—unlike the wicked who will die. What this hymn is saying, then, is that Jesus was "like God," that is, perfectly righteous, not a sinner. But he did not take advantage of the immortality to which he would have been entitled. Instead, he willingly took on the lot of sinful humanity and passed through death. If you look back at Wisdom, you will see that the reward Jesus receives here is greater than that promised the righteous there. They are exalted in heaven as "sons of God," but God is the one who is Lord over them forever (Wisd 3:8). Here, on the other hand, the extraordinary nature of Jesus' humility and obedience has been rewarded with an exaltation even beyond theirs: he now has the name Lord.

It is a very short step from this hymn to account for the unique character of Jesus' righteousness and obedience, by reflecting on his identity with the divine Word or wisdom through which God had created the world. See the hymns in Colossians 1:15-20 and John 1:1-16 for examples of this transition. Once that step had been made, people began to read this hymn in Philippians in the same way. But initially, these hymns are really telling us about Jesus' heavenly exaltation as the result of his extraordinary obedience and humility. They want us to see why Jesus has been Savior of the world. They are not independent speculation about the nature of Jesus.

(4) *Jesus as Divine Man.* Finally, people began to tell the

life of Jesus in such a way as to make it clear that even then he was not so humiliated as to be without the messianic and divine glory that he now possesses in heaven.

Christians had formulated all of these perspectives on Jesus before any of the New Testament was written. We will see how each presented the significance of Jesus and his ministry in God's plan for the salvation of humanity. But you should always remember that even the most divine portraits of Jesus in the New Testament do not set him up as an independent deity. He would not have any glory or exaltation without the Father to whom he was obedient. People today often think of Jesus as "god" as though he were an independent divinity and forget that the divinity of Jesus depends on his relationship to God the Father. The New Testament authors never lose the Jewish perspective that God the Father is the one who is ultimately glorified and praised for the salvation he has extended to humanity through his Messiah.

STUDY QUESTIONS

1. Why do theologians speak of Christology as "implied" in the ministry of Jesus?
2. Why would Jesus' contemporaries have thought the claim that God had raised him from the dead an unlikely one?
3. What is the relationship between the resurrection of Jesus and the missionary activity of the disciples?
4. How did the early Christians reach the conclusion that Jesus was of divine origin?
5. How does the early Christian hymn in Philippians 2:6-11 describe the relationship between Jesus and God?
6. Why didn't those who knew Jesus during his lifetime realize that he was divine?

Part III

PAUL, MISSIONARY
TO THE GENTILES

Chapter Six

Great problems encountered by christians.

THE WORLD OF PAUL

Christianity came into being at a time when the world was undergoing great changes. Individual native city states had been destroyed, swallowed up by imperial expansion from the West. First, Alexander the Great; then some three centuries later, Rome. No one was immune to these changes. The conquerors changed as much as the peoples they subjected. People, goods and ideas traveled from one end of the empire to the other. The popular novels or "romances" of the period focused on the separation and wanderings of the heroes. Popular lives of Alexander told fantastic stories of his visits to the East as did the lives of another famous wise man and itinerant wonder-worker, Apollonius of Tyana.

The Spread of Religious Cults

Religions traveled, too, and as they did so they changed. For a long time scholars were only interested in classical religion and philosophy. Everything that occurred in our period was neglected, but recent years have seen growing interest in Graeco-Roman religious movements. We need to understand the growth of religious traditions in this period in order to understand the spread of Christianity.

There seem to have been two conflicting pressures on religious traditions. In their native countries, Palestine for Judaism or Egypt for the very popular cult of the goddess Isis,

111

say, the traditional religion was a focus of resistance to Graeco-Roman imperialism and culture. National pride, languages and traditions were retained in the cult, which could then become a focus for national Messianism. But people also traveled, and as they moved to new cities, those from a given area might set up a small group to worship the gods of their homeland. For the second and third generation immigrants as well as any others who might join the group, the deities had no homeland. Sacred texts might be translated into Greek and the cult interpreted according to common Hellenistic ideals. Thus the religion was freed from nationalistic associations and dependence upon particular sacred places. The gods were no longer concerned with guaranteeing national prosperity but with the salvation of individuals wherever they might be.

Hellenistic Judaism

Judaism was also affected by this process. Its sacred writings were translated into Greek. Fragments of a Greek Old Testament have even been found at Qumran. Jewish philosophers, like the older contemporary of Jesus, Philo of Alexandria, interpreted the Old Testament in such a way that its teaching fitted in with popular philosophy. Philo hints that some Jews in Alexandria may have even adopted forms of worship more like the pagan mystery cults. Jews wrote histories and other books to show that their cultural heritage was as good as—or even the source of—that of the Greeks. Plato was called "Moses speaking Greek." One author sought to turn the history of Israel into an epic poem. Some Jews were actively engaged in missionary activity. They stressed Jewish monotheism and ethical values. Abraham was invoked as father of all the nations. Converts to Judaism could become sons of Abraham.

This is the Judaism into which Paul of Tarsus was born. He came from a large, important city. Like many such Jews, he had two forms of his name, the Semitic one, Saul, and the Greek, Paul. Presumably he came from an important family since he was a Roman citizen—probably inherited from his father, who might have been granted citizenship for some service he performed. Although Paul became famous as a Christian missionary to the Gentiles, he may have engaged in missionary activity as a Pharisee before his conversion. Perhaps that was the context in which he first encountered and began to persecute Christianity.

Pagan Philosophies, Religions, Astrology and Magic

The breakup of old certainties was accompanied by a more individualized search for salvation. People were increasingly obsessed by Fate. Astrology had only come into the Greek world after Alexander, but by the 1st century it was so widespread that we have even found horoscopes among the texts from Qumran. Astrology fit in with the increasing pessimism of the age, since the stars were thought to control everything according to inflexible laws. This period has also been characterized as one in which rationalism, confidence in the power of reasoned inquiry to guide human affairs, was on the decline. Many felt that revelations and oracles were better guides to truth than human intelligence. The widespread picture of the unbending rule of fate over the universe was also symptomatic of the individual's feeling of powerlessness with regard to his or her own life. At the same time it provided some assurance that there was order in the universe. Astrology, the popular manifestation of this belief in the rule of fate, cut across all social class lines. All the Roman emperors believed in it, though they sometimes took measures to have astrologers expelled from Rome and made it a capital offense to cast the emperor's horoscope—measures aimed at discouraging those who might seek to overthrow the empire.

Just as has happened in our own day, the growing belief in astrology was accompanied by growing concern with demonic powers and the spread of magic. Most of the magical formulae that have been recovered are for prosaic purposes: success in love, the victory of a favorite horse, or the destruction of an enemy. It was thought that a person could obtain a familiar spirit who would work for him. Many of the texts require lengthy oaths and sacred names. Here is a love spell by a pagan magician that includes sacred names of the Jewish god:

> I abjure you, demonic spirit, who rests here, by the sacred names Aoth; Abaoth; by the god of Abraam and the Iao of Jahu; the Iao, Aoth, Abath; the god of Israma: hearken to the glorious and fearful and great name, and hasten to Urbanus whom Urbana bore and bring him Domitiana, whom Candida bore, so that he, loving, frantic, sleepless with love and desire for her, may beg her to return to his house and become his wife. I abjure you by the great god, the eternal and almighty, who is exalted above the exalted gods . . . (the passage continues with more oaths and repetition of the request formula) . . . Make it so that he, loving shall obey her like a slave and desire no other wife nor maiden, but have Domitiana alone, whom Candida bore, as his spouse for the whole of their life, at once, at once! Quick, quick!

Astrology will tell you what fate has in store; magic is a means to get around that fate.

But magic was not the only means. This period saw the rise of a number of "mystery religions." The Egyptian goddess Isis was a particularly popular figure. Such cults had two sides. The public side involved processions in honor of the goddess; the yearly reenactment of the myth; ceremonies in the temple. Frescos from Roman houses at Pompey and Herculaneum show ceremonies taking place before the temple of Isis. Archaeologists have also found coins that show the temple of Isis in Rome (built in A.D. 38), with the cult statue visible through the door. The Iseum there also had a granite carving of Isis' consort, Osiris, that had been imported from Egypt. Inscriptions praising the goddess could be found on various stele. The educated might also read about them in the history of Diodorus of Sicily (*Hist.* I.27, 3-6; written in the 1st century B.C.). Here is an example of such a list of praises found in Asia Minor (from 2nd century A.D.):

> I am Isis, mistress of every land. I was taught by

Hermes, and with Hermes I devised letters both the sacred (hieroglyphs) and the demotic (= the alphabet in which ordinary Egyptian was written), so that everything might not be written with the same letters.

I gave and established laws for men which no one can change,

I am the oldest daughter of Kronos.

I am the wife and sister of king Osiris.

I am the one who finds fruit for men.

I am the mother of king Horus.

I am the one who rises in the Dog Star.

I am the one called goddess by women.

I divided the earth from the heaven.

I showed the paths of the stars.

I set up the course of the sun and the moon.

I devised business in the sea.

I made the right strong.

I brought together woman and man.

I established that women would bear their babies in the tenth month (= lunar month).

I ordained that parents be loved by their children.

I laid punishment on those without natural affection for their parents.

I and my brother Osiris made an end to the eating of men.

I revealed mysteries to men.

I taught them to honor images of the gods.

I consecrated the precincts of the gods.

I broke down the governments of tyrants.

I put an end to murders.

I caused women to be loved by men.

I made right stronger than gold and silver.

I ordained that what is true should be thought good.

I established marriage contracts.

I assigned their languages to Greeks and barbarians.

I made the beautiful and shameful distinguishable by nature.

I ordained that nothing should be more feared than an oath.

I deliver the one who plots evil against others into the hands of those he plots against.

I established penalties for those who are unjust.

I decreed mercy to suppliants.
I protect righteous guards.
The right prevails with me.
I am Queen of rivers, winds and sea.
No one is honored without my knowledge.
I am Queen of war.
I am Queen of the thunderbolt.
I stir up the sea, and I calm it.
I am in the rays of the sun.
I inspect the courses of the sun.
With me everything is reasonable.
I free the captives.
I am Queen of seamanship.
When it pleases me, I make the navigable un-
navigable.
I created walled cities.
I am called Lawgiver.
I brought islands up out of the depths into the
light.
I am Lord of rainstorms.
I overcome Fate.
Fate listens to me.
Hail, O Egypt, that nourished me!

Notice that Isis is the source of cosmic order, law and culture—including the various religions by which people worship. She is mistress of the entire world and is superior to Fate, since she is the one who established the course of the sun, moon and stars. Both this inscription and the reference to the "great god . . . exalted above the exalted gods" in the magical incantation that we just read show another religious tendency of the period that some scholars have called a tendency toward monotheism. The plethora of deities is seen as subordinate to one divine principle or one divinity, which is the true source of cosmic order. Such public inscriptions, processions and ceremonies constituted all that most people would know about the worship of the goddess—or of other deities whose cults were organized in a similar manner.

However, there was another, more private side to the religion, which is what most people think of when they refer to the "mystery religions." Individuals could be initiated into the mysteries of a particular god or goddess. Since secrecy was enjoined on the members, we do not know as much as we would like about these initiations. However, the last book of a 2nd-century A.D. novel, *The Golden Ass*, describes the initiation of its hero, Lucius, into the mysteries of Isis and Osiris. (The author of the book, Apuleius, was himself an initiate.) The novel recounts the adventures Lucius had suffered, since being turned into an ass by drinking the wrong potion—one of the hazards of magic. (Apuleius himself was tried on a charge of magic, and the speech he gave in his own defense survives.) The goddess appears to him in a dream vision and tells Lucius that she can save him from *blind Fortune*:

> Behold, Lucius, I have come, moved by your prayers! I, nature's mother, mistress of the elements, first off-spring of the ages, mightiest of the divine powers, Queen of the dead, chief of those who dwell in the heavens, the one in whose features are combined those of all the gods and goddesses. By my nod, I rule the shining heights of heaven, the wholesome winds of the sea and the mournful silences of the underworld. The whole world honors my sole deity under various forms, with varied rites, and by many names . . . (a list of the names under which the goddess is honored in different countries and languages follows) . . . and the Egyptians mighty in ancient lore, honoring me with my own rites, call me by my true name Isis the Queen.
>
> I have come out of pity for your woes. I have come propitious and ready to help. Cease your weeping and lamentation, and lay aside your sorrow. By my providence, the day of salvation is dawning for you! Therefore turn your afflicted spirit to heed what I command.

Lucius first goes to a public procession in honor of Isis. The priest there tells him—once he has been restored to human shape—that Isis has saved him from Fortune:

> O Lucius, after enduring so many labors and es-caping so many storms of Fortune, you have finally

reached the port and haven of rest and mercy! Neither your noble birth, nor your high rank, nor your great learning did anything for you; but because you turned to servile pleasures, by some youthful folly, you won the grim reward of your unfortunate curiosity. And yet, though Fortune's blindness tormented you with various dangers, by her very malice, she has brought you to this state of religious blessedness. Let Fortune go elsewhere and rage in her wild fury, and find someone else to torment. For Fortune has no power over those who have devoted themselves to serving the majesty of our goddess. For all your afflictions— robbers, wild beasts, slavery, burdensome and useless journeys that ended where they began, and daily fear of death—all were of no advantage to Fortune. Now you are safe under the protection of a fortune who is not blind but who can see, who by her light enlightens the other gods. Therefore rejoice and put on a cheerful expression matching your white robe and follow the procession of this Savior goddess with joyful steps.

The events of Lucius' initiation into the mysteries of Isis began with a ritual washing and presentation in the temple. After that he had to abstain from meat and wine for ten days. The initiation ceremony itself took place at night in the innermost part of the sanctuary. Lucius does not reveal what was done, but he does say:

Hear then and believe, for I tell you the truth. I drew near to the confines of death, treading the very threshold of Proserpine. I was borne through all the elements and returned to earth again. At the dead of night, I saw the sunshining brightly. I approached the gods above and the gods below, and worshipped them face to face. . . . As soon as it was morning and the solemn rites had been completed, I came forth in the twelve gowns that are worn by the initiate, most holy apparel that no sacred ban forbids me to speak about since many saw me wearing it. For in the middle of the holy shrine, before the statue of the goddess, I was directed to stand on a wooden platform, arrayed in a linen robe so richly embroidered that I was something to behold. The precious cape which hung from my

shoulders down to the ground was adorned wherever
you looked with the figures of animals in various colors ... This cape the initiates call Olympian. In my
right hand I carried a flaming torch, and my head was
decorated with a crown made of white palm leaves,
spread out to stand up like rays. After I had been
adorned like the sun and set up like an image of a god,
the curtains were suddenly drawn and people crowded
around to gaze at me.

He says of the day of his initiation, "I celebrated this most
joyful birthday of my initiation." Later Lucius receives two
further initiations into the mysteries of Osiris, Isis' consort,
and god of the underworld. He claims to have spoken directly
with Osiris in a dream and that Osiris furthered his career as a
lawyer.

We have gone into the story of Lucius at some length because it may help eradicate some of the typical misconceptions
about pagan religiosity. The gods and goddesses were not
thought to be in the statues. Both Isis and Osiris appear to
their followers quite independently of such representations.
Marketplaces, houses and temples were full of statues and
other representations of the gods so people expected to see
them in specific humanoid forms. It is also clear from this story
that the relationship between the goddess and her worshippers
could be an intensely personal one. Isis personally guided the
progress of Lucius' initiations by dream revelations both to
himself and to the various priests and officials involved. (Note
that the Spirit uses similar modes of guiding early Christians
in Acts where dream visions play an important role in peoples'
decisions. See, for example, the story of Paul's conversion in
Acts 9 and the Cornelius story in Acts 10.)
    The salvation that Lucius experiences is not just "other-
worldly" though he has gained immortality through his initiation. But the "this worldly" side of salvation is even more important. His life is no longer ruled by the blind powers of Fate
but is under the personal care and protection of the goddess
herself. The very practical consequence of that protection was

prosperity in this life. You might also notice that the Isis cult does not demand that a person renounce earlier gods, follow a particular ethical code, or have a particular set of doctrinal beliefs beside that in the saving power of Isis. The author, Apuleius, was not only an initiate of Isis and Osiris but also a priest of Asclepius, the god of medicine. Such ancient cults, then, were not based on doctrine but on personal allegiance and right practice. A person could participate in as many as time, inclination and financial resources permitted.

Someone might not choose either magic or religion as the way to be delivered from the hazards and uncertainties of this life. The various philosophical schools also promised to deliver one from the fears and uncertainties of life. From Socrates on, some of the greatest martyrs and heroes of antiquity were philosophers. Unlike the religious cults, the various philosophies offered a comprehensive picture of the origin and structure of the universe. Such doctrines were not formulated in the interests of pure science but to explain man's place and destiny in the universe and how he might best conduct his life. Wandering philosophers went from city to city preaching and calling upon people to abandon the illusions, superstitions and concerns with material pleasure that cause them pain and distress. Philosophy claimed to heal the soul, to turn people to a life that would bring them as much happiness as possible for human beings.

A whole body of philosophic literature grew up, which included letters, sermons, summaries of the lives of famous philosophers and handbooks. (As a youth, St. Augustine was inspired to reform his life by reading such a handbook by Cicero.) Ethics played an important role in philosophical teaching. We do not need to go into the details of the various schools and doctrines here, since they do not play the major role in the formation of New Testament thought that they do in that of the later Church Fathers. But we may look briefly at the three major pictures of salvation offered by the philosophical traditions:

(1) Epicureanism held that *rational analysis* of the uni-

verse in terms of atoms and void would deliver a person from the three pervasive human fears:

(a) *Death:* because he or she would realize that once the atoms constituting a human person have come apart, there is nothing more to experience.

(b) *the gods:* because immortal beings are made out of their own peculiar element and are concerned with their own happiness; not with the affairs of mortal humans.

(c) *Misfortune:* since everything is determined by the random motions and interactions of atoms, the only thing the individual can do is try to arrange his or her life to be as tranquil and pleasant as possible.

(2) Platonism was more metaphysical. *Contemplation of the divine* realm of perfection and the pure forms of which this physical world is only a poor copy could lead the soul to mystic union with the divine. The various forms of Platonism all located value and goodness in the divine realm and frequently used the image of the soul fleeing its prison in this material realm (the body) to return to its true divine home.

(3) Stoicism was probably the most popular philosophical option. Stoic physics explained that everything in the universe was formed out of the divine spirit. (One recent author has referred to it as a "good and wise gas.") That Spirit guarantees the divine order or reason behind everything in the universe. The cosmos is pictured as a vast body in which everything is ultimately connected with everything else. This view enabled the Stoics to speak of people not simply as citizens of this or that city but as citizens of the cosmos. They also held that the universe was involved in a cyclic process. A great conflagration would return everything back to the original spirit/fire, and the evolution of the universe would start over again.

The main attraction of Stoicism was its ethical ideal of *apatheia,* passionlessness. A wise person could face any situation with complete self-control and equanimity because he or she was not attached to this life. The philosopher truly conquers fate by not being moved by the external circumstances of

life. They used the image of a dog tied to a cart. When the cart
(= fate) begins to move, the dog has to go along. If the dog lies
down and resists, it will be dragged down the street. The dog
who gets up and runs alongside the cart will wind up in the
same place as the one who is dragged but without injury.
Human beings cannot control the circumstances of their lives,
but they can control how they react to them. Here is a passage
from one of the most famous Stoic philosophers, the slave Epic-
tetus (b. *ca.* A.D. 50):

> Keep this thought ready for use at dawn, by day and
> at night. There is but one way to serenity, and that is
> to give up all claim to things that lie outside the
> sphere of moral purpose; to regard nothing as your
> own possession; to surrender everything to the Deity,
> to Fortune; to yield everything to the supervision of
> those whom Zeus has made supervisors; and to devote
> yourself to one thing only, that which is your own . . .
> that is why I cannot yet say that a man is industrious
> until I know for what end he does so . . . For I would
> not have you praise or blame a man for things that
> may be either good or bad, but only for judgments.
> Because these are each man's own possessions, which
> make his actions either base or noble . . . if you have
> gotten rid of or reduced a malignant disposition . . . if
> you are not moved by the things that once moved you,
> at least not to the same degree, then you can celebrate
> day after day . . . How much greater cause for thanks-
> giving is this than a consulship or a governorship!

The language and ideals of Stoicism were widespread. They
would later play an important role in the formulation of the
Christian ascetic tradition. Many scholars hold that Paul owes
his image of the Church as body of Christ to stoic imagery of
the cosmos as a living organism and people as united in a
universal brotherhood. For the Stoic virtue was what united
humanity to the divine, since human reason was the inner
divine spark or spirit.

Emperor Cult

There is much confusion about what the status of the emperor cult was in various parts of the empire at this time. Most Christians have the idea that the first Christians were martyred because they refused to worship the emperor as a god. The actual situation is more complex than that. You must remember that it was possible in antiquity for a human being to claim divine ancestry, since gods and goddesses were thought—at least in the past—to have had human-divine offspring. The emperors might also be honored as divine with sacrifices similar to those offered the gods much as Catholics have masses in honor of certain saints without such honor implying that the individual in question was a god.

Living emperors were closely associated with the goddess Rome. Sacrifices for/to him were symbols of allegiance to the empire not theological statements. Temples were dedicated to the emperor Augustus and to the cult of Rome. There is a small round temple to Augustus on the Acropolis at Athens. Inscriptions also show that a highly formulaic language evolved by which people gave praise to the emperor. Again, that language is a set and stereotyped way of honoring a person; it is not a statement of belief about his divinity. Early Christians picked up some of this language to speak about Christ. Here is a rather lengthy passage from the procounsul to the cities of Asia. Some key expressions have been italicized:

> ... whether the natal day of the most *divine* Caesar Augustus is to be observed most for the joy or the profit of it—a day which one might justly consider equivalent to the beginning of all things, equivalent, I say, if not in reality, at least in the *benefits* it has brought, seeing that there was nothing ruinous or fallen into miserable appearance that he has not restored. He has given another aspect to the universe, which was only too ready to perish, had not Caesar—a blessing to all of mankind—been born. Therefore each individual should look on this day as the beginning of his own life and physical being, because there can be no more of the feeling that life is a burden, now that he has been born ...
> Resolved by the Greeks of the province of Asia, on the proposal of the high priest Apollonius:

> Whereas the *providence* which orders the whole of human life has shown a special concern and zeal and conferred upon life its most perfect ornament by bestowing Augustus, whom it fitted for his *beneficent* work among mankind by filling him with virtue, sending him as a *savior* for us and for those who come after us; one who should cause wars to cease; who should set all things in good order, and whereas Caesar, when he appeared, made the hopes of those who forecast a better future look poor compared with reality, in that he not only *surpassed all previous benefactors* but left no chance for future ones to go beyond him, and the *glad tidings (Gk: euangelia, gospel)* which by his means went forth into the world took its rise in the *birthday of the god*; and
>
> Whereas, after that Asia had passed a resolution, Smyrna under Ludiu Volcacius Tullus . . . conferring a wreath upon the man who should invent the greatest honors to be shown *the god*, Paullus Fabius Maximus, proconsul of the province . . . devised what had hitherto been unknown among the Greeks in honor of Augustus, that *from his birth time should be reckoned* in human affairs.

This language of praise does not suppose that Augustus is god in the same sense as Zeus or the divine Providence which controls the universe. His divine honors are based on the benefits he is said to have conferred on humanity—and usually the community making such a dedication. People at this time often set up dedicatory inscriptions or monuments to gods whom they felt had answered their prayers to thank them for favors as well as to honor individuals. Benefits conferred by a public official might include anything from monetary grants, food, new buildings, public shows and the like to protection in war, new laws or good government. In many cases such inscriptions represent public gratitude for order and stability.

Roman authors such as Tacitus and Cicero recommended that the state cultivate religion among the masses as a means of inducing patriotism and social cohesion—remember the people who are being asked to rejoice in Augustus' birth here are conquered subjects from Asia Minor, not citizens of Rome.

Later emperors followed Augustus' lead in making such use of religious propaganda. Coins at first showed the deceased emperors wearing Jovian crowns symbolic of their post mortem apotheosis. Nero was the first emperor to have himself portrayed in that fashion, but the shift to such visual portrayals of the emperor did not occur until the end of the 2nd century. From the Roman point of view, then, the issue at stake in the emperor cult was less what we would consider a religious one than a political one. Refusal to participate suggested sedition and disloyalty. The educated Roman official would hardly understand why a Christian did not take the same view of the matter that he did: of course the emperor isn't a god, but religion is an important social and political expression of loyalty. Jewish refusal to offer incense before a statue of the emperor was considered part of their well-known obstinacy. But if Christianity was just a religious cult and not a subversive movement, why did it not show the same tolerance as the other cults? People today are often critical of those passages in the New Testament which encourage Christians to be obedient to political authorities, but they should remember that many of those passages were written at a time when Christians could be forced into conflict with those same authorities for their refusal to show loyalty to the empire by offering divine honors to anyone but God—even as a gesture of patriotism.

Religiousness: Jewish and Pagan

This rapid survey of the religious options within pagan society should make it clear that "religion" meant different things to different people. Sometimes Gentile converts to Christianity assimilated it to their earlier religious ideals—a difficulty that seems to have been particularly rampant in the Corinthian church. It should also be clear that the Jewish origins of Christianity provided the movement with some religious beliefs and practices that were not familiar to the average pagan convert. We have set up a rough schema contrasting Jewish and pagan religiousness in the following chart to help you see some of the contrasts involved. When you have finished looking at the chart, you might try filling in your own answers to the various categories. Which view are you closer to?

STUDY QUESTIONS

1. Give two examples of how religions became universal in the Graeco-Roman period.
2. Why were astrology and magic very popular in the 1st century A.D.?
3. Describe the public side of the Isis cult.
4. Give two ways in which an individual might become free from the domination of Fate.
5. What does the story of Lucius show us about the relationship between the individual and the gods/goddesses in paganism?
6. Explain how at least one philosophical movement claimed to save people from their fears and anxieties.
7. Why did pagans offer sacrifice to the emperor? Do you think that the early Christians were right in refusing to do so? Why? Why not? What would you have done?
8. List three differences between Jewish and pagan religiousness. Which feature(s) of Judaism do you think would be most difficult for a pagan to understand? Why?

Chart #2: JEWISH AND PAGAN RELIGIOUSNESS

OPTION:	JEWISH	PAGAN
type of religious leader	priest (till A.D. 70) prophet, teacher of the Law	demi-god (divine man, a person claiming divine powers or ancestry); prophet = oracle; philosopher
proof of authority	speaks for God; interprets Scripture	predictions; miracles; wise teaching
future of world	judgment, new creation	none (eternal cosmos) or cyclic conflagration (Stoic)
future of humanity	belong to the "elect" in new creation; sinners damned to eternal death	none (Epicurean); individual immortality (at least until next conflagration—Stoic) reincarnation (in some circles for those souls that had not attained philosophic or religious enlightenment)
primary religious experience	obedience to the covenant; prophetic word; will of God	ecstatic (mysteries; dream visions); mystical (philosophic contemplation); philosophical asceticism
religious praxis	sacrificial cult limited to Jerusalem temple feasts (Passover) repeat history of Israel; hearing: Scripture	sacrifices to gods; dedications; processions; reenactment of myth; private initiations & ways of attaining ecstasy; metaphysical contemplation; reading esoteric books
modes of revelation	Scripture and its interpretation	individual visions; esoteric books

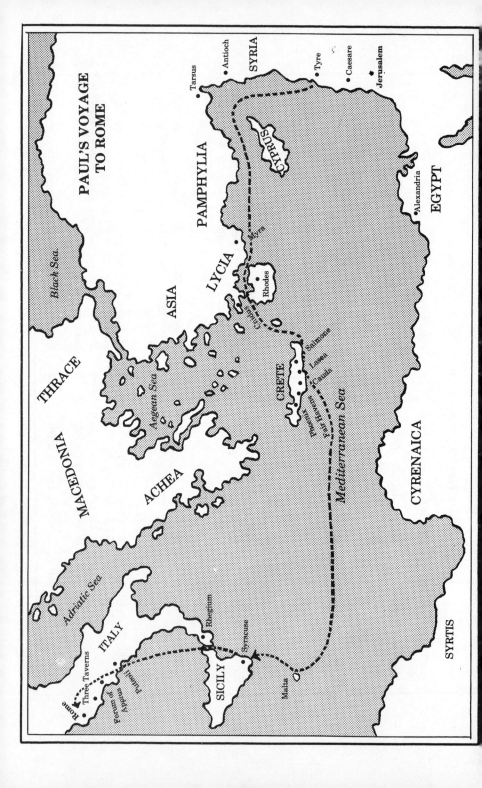

Chapter Seven

THE LIFE OF PAUL

We now turn to one of the most controversial figures in the history of Christianity, the apostle Paul. Some people claim that without him there would have been no Christianity; others, that he totally distorted the teaching of Jesus. Both views show a common tendency to treat Paul as a "loner." Actually, if you read his letters carefully, you will see that Paul was rarely alone. He was surrounded by associates and companions in the ministry. You will also learn that he had persecuted the early Christian movement. That means he probably knew something about it before his conversion. We may even hear arguments he had used against Christians when he speaks of the impossibility of reconciling belief in Christ and obedience to the Law as a way of salvation. We may presume that it was a Christian mission teaching freedom from the Law that first attracted the ire of the apostle.

Read Philippians 3:4-7. Paul describes his zeal for Judaism and its traditions. He tells us that that zeal had led him to persecute the Church. Notice that Paul says that he could fulfill the Law as a Jew. He did not become a Christian because of guilt feelings over the impossibility of fulfilling the demands of the Law as some authors have claimed but because he became convinced that God had indeed raised Jesus and established a way of salvation for all humanity based on faith in him.

Sources and Methods of Research

We do have some firsthand sources for Paul's life. At least
seven of his letters were written by the apostle himself. We
also know from these letters that he wrote others that have not
survived (cf. 1 Cor 5:9; 2 Cor 2:4; Col 4:16). But all these letters
came from the last years of his life. There are additional statements about Paul in the Acts of the Apostles. You may remember from the first chapter that they were written a generation after his death. Scholars find additional difficulties when
the material in Acts is compared with Paul's own remarks
about the same events:

(1) Paul's account of the meeting in Jerusalem in Galatians 2 is quite different from the version in Acts 15. Paul says
that the meeting was only his second visit to Jerusalem (Gal
2:1); Acts, that he had been there twice before. Acts 15:22ff.
reports that they had decreed some basic food legislation for
the Gentile converts. Galatians 2:6 excludes such an agreement. Further, Paul's handling of the problem of eating meat
sacrificed to idols in 1 Corinthians 8-10 directly contradicts it.

(2) Acts has no trace of Paul's own treatment of Christ as
the end of the Law and his justification of a Law-free Gentile
mission. The Gentile mission depends entirely on miraculous
signs given Peter.

(3) Paul's speeches in Acts show no traces of the apostle's
own language or theological arguments (e.g. compare the discussion of paganism in Romans 1:17-32, where it is negatively
assessed with the positive assessment in Acts 17:22-31).

(4) Acts' picture of Paul differs from what he himself tells
us. For Luke, Paul is a successful orator and miracle-worker,
who continued to be a devout Jew all his life. There is no hint of
the severe opposition he encountered from other Christian
missionaries and from his own Churches, an opposition that
pained him much more deeply than his sufferings at the hands
of outsiders.

(5) Paul's version of his conversion (Gal 1:13-17) is much
less elaborate than Acts, which has three different versions of
the story (9:3-19; 22:6-16; 26:12-18). Differences such as these

have convinced scholars of two things: First, Luke cannot have been a close disciple and co-worker of Paul's. Letters written by disciples of Paul in the apostle's name show a much greater familiarity with his language and theology than Luke. Second, Luke probably had a variety of sources for his information about the early apostles. While some scholars would insist that Acts gives us no reliable historical information about Paul, most would use information from Acts where it fits in with the picture we derive from Paul's own letters.

Life of Paul

None of Paul's letters are dated. Those in our list are only guesses arrived at by studying the relationships among the letters and a few chronological hints about Paul's life derived from Acts. These events are:

(1) Removal of Pilate and sending of a new prefect, A.D. 36. The interim is a likely time for the illegal execution of Stephen. If the story that Paul was present is correct—and it might only be a legendary elaboration of the well-known fact that he had been a persecutor of the Church—then he must have been converted in A.D. 36 or 37.

(2) Claudius expelled the Jews from Rome for rioting at the name of Chrestus (= Christ) in A.D. 49. According to Acts 18:2, Aquila and Priscilla had come to Corinth just before Paul's arrival there, which would have been in A.D. 50/51.

(3) Paul's mission in Corinth ended under the proconsulship of Gallio (Ac 18:12). An inscription helps us date that event to either 51/52 A.D. Paul had spent 18 months in Corinth.

(4) Paul was sent to Rome after the change of procurators from Felix to Festus. The date of that change is debated. Some propose an early date, ca. A.D. 55; the chronology followed here uses a later date, ca. A.D. 60. Paul is said to have been in prison for two years before A.D. 60 so that he would have been arrested in A.D. 58.

(5) The exact date of Paul's death, whether he was freed and then executed in Rome after a second trial or killed im-

mediately, is uncertain. Tradition has it that he suffered martyrdom under Nero, which could have been anytime from A.D. 64-67.

These are the external dates that we can derive from the letters, Acts and what we can find out about the history of the time. Acts does give us some further information about Paul's life. According to Acts 22:3, he was born in the town of Tarsus in Cilicia. Tarsus was a prosperous commercial center, the capital of the province. It was also known for its philosophical schools, both Stoic and Epicurean. Paul's letters also show some acquaintance with Greek rhetorical techniques and thus suggest that he had received at least some Greek education.

But he was also a Pharisee and proud of his Jewish heritage (Phil 3:5ff.; Rm 11:1; 2 Cor 11:22; Gal 1:4). Acts 22:3 claims that he had studied in Jerusalem under Gamaliel I (flor. A.D. 20-50). He himself never tells us anything about his teachers. Perhaps he himself was persecuting the Church as an officially recognized teacher.

After his conversion (ca. A.D. 36) Paul spent time in Arabia, probably the Nabatean kingdom in Transjordan (cf Gal 1:13-17). He then spends about three years in Damascus (Gal 1:18) until he was forced out by Jewish opposition (2 Cor 11:32). Around A.D. 40 he made his first visit to Jerusalem. Paul then returned to the regions of Cicilia and Syria, probably working out of his native city of Tarsus.

According to Acts 11:25f. Barnabas brought Paul back to Antioch where he stayed for a year. That sojourn is linked with a prophecy of the widespread famine that affected the Mediterranean world in A.D. 46. For most of the years 46-48, Paul is engaged in missionary work in Greece and Asia Minor along with Barnabas.

But the widespread conversion of the Gentiles led to questions: Did they have to be circumcised and keep the Jewish Law if they wanted to be Christians? Paul—and probably others at the Church in Antioch—said "No." Others were not so sure. A meeting was held at Jerusalem ca. A.D. 49. According to Paul (Gal 2:1-10) and one version in Acts 15:6-12, the subject was simply the circumcision question. Acts 15:13-29 introduces an additional question of dietary laws, probably not discussed at that meeting. Paul insists that the dispute was resolved in his favor.

In the fall of A.D. 49 a painful incident occurred at Antioch between Paul and Peter. We only have Paul's version (Gal 2:11-16). Apparently Jewish and Gentile Christians were accustomed to eat together. Peter came to Antioch and did the same. But when some strict Jewish Christians arrived, the community split in two with Peter, Barnabas and other converts from Judaism eating with the visitors. Paul says that he publicly called Peter a hypocrite for his conduct. (Some scholars think that the decree in Acts 15:13ff. was a response to this problem. In a mixed community, the Gentiles would keep minimum kosher rules so that the two groups could eat together.) Though he does not say so in Galatians it looks as though Paul lost the argument.

After this time, he no longer acts as a missionary from the Antioch Church but has a new set of companions. His letters all come from that later period and suggest that he was operating as an independent missionary. However, he has one item on his agenda that goes back to the Jerusalem Council. He wishes to take up a collection among all the Gentile Churches for the sake of the Jerusalem community (1 Cor 16:1; Rm 15:25f.). If you read 2 Corinthians 8 and 9, you can see examples of letters Paul wrote to different Churches to encourage contributions. Paul considered that collection very important. It symbolized the unity of Gentiles and Jews in one Church just as Jews everywhere in the world contributed to the support of the temple in Jerusalem. For the Gentiles it also meant recognition of their debt to Israel. We know from the end of Romans that Paul was going to take the collection to Jerusalem himself and that afterward he intended to visit Rome on his way to missionary work in Spain. Acts is our only source for what happened to Paul after Romans. The fears expressed in Romans that he might have trouble in Jerusalem, apparently came true though we cannot be certain how accurate all the details in Acts 21-23 are. Jewish hostility led to Paul's arrest; he was kept in jail awaiting trial through the change in prefects, and finally sent to Rome for trial there, a right he enjoyed because of his inherited Roman citizenship. Acts ends with Paul in Rome awaiting trial.

Paul as Missionary and Pastor

This brief sketch of what we know about the apostle's life makes several things clear. He was a Jew, at home in both worlds. He was also a figure of some controversy not only in his own time but throughout Christian history. The Jewish philosopher, Martin Buber, once wrote that Christian history could be divided into periods by the rediscoveries of Pauline thought and the theological revolutions that followed. Paul had had a theological education, but our only records of his thought are not theological tracts, they are responses to practical situations and often written in situations of conflict. This observation has important consequences for the way in which you should read Paul's letters:

(1) Do not expect them to be closely reasoned, abstract theological treatises. Paul may leave many things unsaid because he knew his audience. He sometimes strays from one thought to another.

(2) Look for the practical problems to which Paul is addressing himself. He will very often quote a liturgical phrase or earlier theological formulation to make a practical conclusion. For example, in 2 Corinthians 8:9 Paul says: "For you know that the grace of our Lord Jesus Christ, that though he was rich he became poor, so that by his poverty you might become rich." That statement is not intended to convey information about Jesus but to encourage the readers to give to the collection.

(3) Distinguish between what Paul quotes from the Old Testament and early Christian creeds or liturgy from what he himself writes. The verse just quoted is an example of such a citation. You can identify the quotations that Paul introduces with "For you know . . ." or "It is written . . ." for yourself.

Others are identified by scholars on the basis of language and terminology. Here are some examples: Romans 1:3f. is set up in the parallel structure of an early creed. Romans 3:24-26 also contains an older credal or liturgical statement about the significance of Christ's death. We already saw that Philippians 2:6-11 is an early hymn. Now look at the context of that hymn. Paul is using it to encourage certain specific virtues among the Philippians. What are they?

(4) Remember that Paul is usually trying to persuade people who may not agree with him. That means he uses rhetorical devices. He may, for example, make fun of his opponents or portray the situation as much worse than it was in order to win people over. Always ask yourself what tone Paul is using in a particular passage. Is he pleading? Is he ironic? Is he angry? Then ask how his persuasive intentions have influenced what he is saying. (We make such judgments all the time when we listen to politicians, advertising, editorials, public personalities, etc.)

(5) Look out for the rhetorical devices that Paul likes to use:

A. He likes to set up a problem in terms of antitheses or paradoxes. He will tie a whole section together by use of paired concepts that may be summed up in certain key words, slogans or phrases. Be sure you identify these words and phrases. Then ask what Paul is saying about the paradox.

B. Paul likes to use what is called a *diatribe* style, that is, the speaker addresses an imaginary opponent; gives points the opponent might make and then refutes them. Paul is using this technique in Romans 6:1.

C. Paul often sets passages up in chiastic patterns, i.e. themes are treated in an abc—cba pattern. Keep an eye out for them.

Many people find Paul the hardest reading in the New Testament. His line of argument can be hard to follow; he hardly ever seems to be talking about Jesus, and his personality is often grating and seemingly self-serving. Many of the issues he discusses seem far removed from our own concerns.

There is no way to make reading Paul simple. He requires careful and patient analysis. But if you remember the context of his letters and take the time to work with our basic rules, you will discover that Paul has one of the most versatile and interesting minds in early Christianity.

How Paul Wrote Letters

You can see from our survey of the contents of the New Testament that most of its writings are either letters or treatises in letter form. The letter has continued to be an important literary form in Christian writings up to the present day: bishops write pastoral letters; popes, encyclicals. It is not too much of an exaggeration to say that Paul's letters are responsible for that development. Because of the importance of the letter in the New Testament, scholars have been studying various types of ancient letters in great detail. You may remember being taught how to write a letter when you were in school. You learned the difference between formal and informal letters. If you studied another language, you had to learn how to write letters in that language too. In order to appreciate the uniqueness of Paul's letters, we are first going to learn how to write a letter according to the "school books." Personal letters had four sections:

(1) *Introduction, prescript or salutation:* This included sender, addressee, greetings.

(2) *Thanksgiving, wish for health:* The thanksgiving could be expanded with an additional greeting or a wish for the good health of the addressee.

(3) *Body:* Often introduced by a stereotyped phrase, the body of the letter is where the author states the business that prompts him to write the letter.

(4) *Conclusion:* This is made up of greetings, wishes for other people, a final greeting, wish or prayer and sometimes a date.

Now you are ready for some examples. I have identified

the parts of the first letter for you. Notice that that letter is by a Jew but that he uses the stereotyped pagan greeting "gods." He was writing in Greek.

GREETING: Toubias to Apollonios, greeting.

THANKSGIVING: If you and all your affairs are flourishing, and everything else is as you wish it, many thanks to the gods! I, too, have been well, and have thought of you at all times as was right.

BODY: I have sent you Aineias, bringing a eunuch and four boys, house slaves and of good stock, two of whom are uncircumcised. I append descriptions of the boys for your information.

CONCLUSION: Goodbye. Year 29, Xandikes 10.

Now here are two more letters. The first is a tax receipt; the second deals with the release of a prisoner. See if you can pick out the various sections.

Simon, son of Jazaros, the tax farmer who controls 25% of the fisher's tax for the 28th year, to Mesoeris, greetings. I have received from you as tax for you and your sons in the month of Tybi, 4,000 drachmae in copper, total 4,000. Written by Dellous at the request of Simon because he is illiterate.

(What sections are missing from this letter?) Notice that literacy was not required for public officials, since a scribe could be employed to do the actual writing.

Philon to Zenon, greetings. If you yourself and those whom you wish to be so are in good health, it would be well. I, too, am keeping well. Please make a serious effort to settle the matter about which my brother Ptolemaios has sailed up to see you, in order that he may return to me quickly and that I shall not be prevented from sailing up if I need to, for I must be off from here soon. I wrote to you once before about Her-

mokrates, as I had heard that you were exerting yourself to help him, and had myself informed him of this,
and I really think he will be set free in a few days.
Several others troubled themselves on his behalf but
the most effective was Kaphisophon, son of Philippos,
the physician. The written report of the inquiry,
which acquits him of all charges, is already in the
hands of Dositheos, the memorandum-writer in order
that the king may read it before letting him be re-
leased as this is the regular procedure. For the rest be
prepared to receive a visit from me soon. And of the
things at home, even if it is a bother to you, keep an
eye on my place . . .

Letters written in Aramaic, the language used by Palestinian
Jews in this period, (though some scholars argue that a form of
mishnaic Hebrew was more common in Judea while Galilean
Aramaic and possibly some Greek dominated outlying regions
like Galilee and the coastal plain), follow similar forms. Here
are some basic features of those letters:

(1) For initial greetings we frequently find expressions
using *shalom*, peace, well-being, or the verb *barak*, bless. Here
is a sample greeting from an Aramaic letter written by a non-
Jew: "May all the gods (other letters may have the name of a
particular god) be very much concerned about the well-being of
my lord always."

(2) Sometimes further greetings to individuals other than
the addressee follow. These may also occur further on in the
letter.

(3) The concluding formula is usually a short "be at peace"
or "be well."

(4) Sometimes the name of the scribe who actually wrote
the letter and a date are included.

Having surveyed these basic letter types, let us look at
Paul. One of the clearest differences between his letters and
these examples is the expansion of many of the elements in the
letter. In addition, he usually includes a section of paraenetic
(= ethical exhortation) material. Most Pauline letters have the
following parts:

(1) *Opening:* Both sender and addressee may be qualified with relative clauses. Paul frequently mentions his apostolic authority. The greeting is also much longer than in a conventional letter.

(2) *Thanksgiving:* This section is much more elaborate than in conventional letters. Paul's thanksgivings set the tone of the whole letter and seem to be adapted to the situation of the letter. Sometimes—as in 1 Thessalonians—it is difficult to tell where the thanksgiving ends and the body of the letter begins. Also note that the occasion for thanksgiving is no longer deliverance or health from the gods but it is the faithfulness of the congregation for which Paul writes. The thanksgiving frequently includes prayer of *intercession* for the community and ends with some eschatological reference.

(3) *Body:* The formal opening of this section of the letter can take several forms. Most commonly it opens with a request, an appeal or the expressions, "I want you to know . . ." or "I rejoice that . . ." Just as he ends thanksgiving sections with an eschatological reference, so the body usually has an eschatological conclusion attached. *Travel plans* frequently follow the body of a Pauline letter. They are usually part of the reason Paul has written the letter in the first place.

(4) *Paraenesis:* We mentioned above that Paul consistently includes a section of ethical exhortation. These sections use traditional Hellenistic and Jewish material that Paul has modified to suit the situation of his audience.

(5) *Closing:* This section contains two or three different elements: greetings, doxology and benediction. Now turn to the shortest of Paul's letters, Philemon. Try to analyze it. Here is what you might come up with:

Opening: sender(s) (v 1); Addressee(s) (v 2); greeting (v 3).
Thanksgiving: (vv. 4-7)
Body: (vv 8-22); opening (vv 8-10); travel plans (v 22).
Paraenesis: (v 20f.)?
Closing: Greetings (vv 23f.); benediction (v 25).

Since this is a short, personal letter dealing with the return of a slave this letter is not as elaborate as the others, but it shows that even in a private letter Paul uses many of his characteristic formulae and structural patterns.

Perhaps you noticed in the analysis of Pauline letter form that his letters seem to be very close to preaching. Both the thanksgiving sections and the ethical ones have been compared with liturgical and homiletic practices. Many scholars see the travel sections as part of this development. The letter constitutes the way in which the apostle is present with his Churches when he cannot be there in person. We read a passage in the first chapter that showed that some of Paul's opponents went even further. They accused him of making a strong case by letter but not being much of a preacher: "For they say, 'His letters are weighty and strong but his bodily presence is weak and his speech of no account.' Let such people understand that what we say by letter when absent, we do when present." (2 Cor 10:10f.). Even allowing for the irony and rhetorical exaggeration that goes into Paul's writing in this chapter, the remark shows that Paul's letters were a significant part of his ministry to his congregations.

Philemon

Now let's go back to Philemon. This letter is seldom read because it does not deal with any lofty theological topics. But it shows us a more human side of the apostle, one which is less clear in some of his major writings where he was embroiled in controversy. First look at the greetings at the beginning and the end of the letter. Paul has a large company of fellow workers, he is not a loner. You will also notice that women are regularly included in his greetings to people at specific Churches. We do not know whether they held official offices, but they clearly played an important role in the congregations of the Pauline mission. The thanksgiving is typical of Paul. He has heard that his addressees have been faithful and actively concerned for the Church. He hopes that they will continue to win people to Christ.

The body of the letter deals with a very delicate matter: returning a slave who had run away from his master. The law was hard on such runaways. If a slave did not seek sanctuary in some temple, he tried to go underground in a large city. Some scholars think that Philemon was written while Paul was in prison in Ephesus. The temple of Artemis there was a sanctuary for runaway slaves. This slave, Onesimus, had not only run away from his master but had apparently taken money as well (v 18). Paul has converted Onesimus to Christianity and would like to keep him as an assistant in his mission (vv 10f.), but he returns the slave to his master as is legally required and volunteers to pay any damages. Notice that neither here nor in his other discussion of Christian slaves (1 Cor 7:17-24) does Paul claim that Christians must free slaves or that only free men can be Christians. The Christian slave has the same status in the congregation and before Christ as the apostle himself (vv 15-17). He is just as capable of spreading the gospel as the apostle. Thus, Paul would not support the view held by many people in antiquity that some people are slaves by nature. He always insists that everyone has the same status before God.

Paul and Apocalyptic: 1 and 2 Thessalonians

Some people argue that the reason Paul did not try to change social conditions was his conviction that the world was about to end. In 1 Corinthians 15:51f. he speaks of the resurrection as a transformation he expects to experience while he is still alive. 1 Corinthians 7:25-31 draws practical conclusions about the desirability of remaining single from the conviction that the world is about to end. Romans 8:18-25 interprets the present suffering of Christians as a necessary prelude to future glory (cp. 1 Cor 4:17). Paul's language about the end makes three points:

(1) Suffering in this world is the necessary prelude to glory.

(2) Christians still live in a time of hope even though they have received forgiveness of sins and the spirit in baptism.

(3) Both believer and non-believer are bound together in a common hope for redemption.

In this case, then, Paul's language about the end makes an important statement about the conditions of Christian life in the world. Some of his observations remain valid regardless of when the end of this age comes. Others, like 1 Corinthians 7, are so clearly tied to the conviction that that end is right around the corner, that they would need reevaluation in other contexts. There are other cases in which Paul seems to use language about the coming judgment to reinforce his paraenetic instruction (cf. 1 Cor 6:9f; Gal 5:21). The seriousness of that instruction is not related to when the end might arrive but to the necessity for the Christian to have died to sin and live in the spirit—a conviction which we saw that early Christians associated with the new outpouring of the spirit.

Two short letters to Thessalonica deal with confusions about the end. Many interpreters feel that a student of Paul's wrote 2 Thessalonians because—unlike other Pauline letters—the opening of the two letters is almost identical; the emphasis on apostolic authority in 2 Thessalonians is not against those who oppose Paul but against others who are claiming his authority; and 2 Thessalonians treats eschatology as an independent topic of reflection rather than tying it to the realities of Christian life as Paul usually does. Also the language of 2 Thessalonians is much closer to the apocalyptic language of Qumran or the book of Revelation than to other Pauline apocalyptic passages. Finally, Paul himself always treats suffering in a Christological context, which 2 Thessalonians does not do.

Other scholars have tried to account for these differences by suggesting that 2 Thessalonians is much earlier than the other Pauline letters—perhaps written in the 40's when Caligula was trying to set his image up in the temple. That date seems too early for the Pauline mission to Thessalonica and would not account for the fact that other people are trying to claim Pauline authority. We assume, then, that this letter was written after 1 Thessalonians, possibly by one of Paul's associates. Both 1 and 2 Thessalonians give us important insight into the difficulties apocalyptic language caused for the

Gentile congregation at Thessalonica which had no tradition of such metaphorical language before their conversion and were very uncertain about how to interpret it.

1 Thessalonians

Opening: 1:1

Thanksgiving: 1:2-2:16. As we noted above, this letter is peculiar in that much of the body is also thanksgiving. Some would even continue the thanksgiving section to 3:10. But 2:16 seems to be the eschatological climax of the thanksgiving section.

Body: Delayed travel plans (How often we encounter these in Paul's letters!) 2:17-3:10. Eschatological conclusion, 3:10f.

Paraenesis: 4:1-5:22. Besides general Christian ethical exhortations, which the Thessalonians had already heard and were obeying (v 3f.), this section takes up two points about the coming judgment. First, that Christians who have died will share in the resurrection and second coming (4:13-18, cp. 1 Cor 15:52). Paul bases that assertion on a "word of the Lord" that was apparently being handed down orally among the Christians. Second, that there are no signs of the judgment. The Christian does not need to calculate when the judgment will come anyway. As long as he or she perseveres in the teaching, then he or she is not liable to judgment. Christians are to encourage one another confident that they are saved from the wrath that is to come on non-believers and those who persecute the Church (1:16).

Conclusion: Benediction, 5:23f.; greetings, vv 26-29.

Some commentators have suggested that this letter represents the type of message Paul preached to Gentiles when he began converting them. Ethical and eschatological perspectives dominate the letter. Vv 9b.-10 are very probably a pre-Pauline formula expressing what the conversion of the Gentiles meant: ". . . you turned to God from idols, to serve a living and true God, and to wait for his Son from heaven, whom he raised from the dead, Jesus who delivers us from the wrath to come." The resurrection of Jesus is seen as establishing him as the judge who will deliver those who remain faithful to his teaching.

At the same time, this letter also exhibits another motif that runs throughout the Pauline letters (cf. even Phlm 8): the true character of Paul's apostleship. We will consistently hear him defend himself against charges of personal gain or desire to please people. Every wandering preacher or teacher had to make some such defense. There were religious frauds in antiquity just as there are today. Paul made a particular point of working to support himself rather than to take a fee for his preaching (2:9). Thus, he could avoid the charge of "being in it for the money." But that policy also backfired when some people argued that Paul did not charge because he had nothing worthwhile to give (cf 1 Cor 9:1-18). Paul always points out that his apostleship was not his by choice but a mission given him by God (2:4). He considers suffering a key factor both in his own apostleship and in the present life of Christians who must wait steadfastly for the coming of Jesus (2:14-16). For Paul, that suffering takes two forms: the persecution he suffered from fellow Jews and the hindrance to his plans for visiting the Church (3:1-5). That change of plans seems to have been a major reason for the epistle. Both types of affliction plagued Paul throughout his career. But this letter also illustrates the deep personal concern that Paul had for the Churches he founded. His own destiny at the judgment is linked to their fidelity (1 Thess 2:19).

2 Thessalonians

We have already discussed the reasons for thinking that a disciple of Paul's wrote this letter. You can see the contrast with 1 Thessalonians easily. All the details of personal care and concern, the warm relationship between Paul and this Church, are missing. When suffering is mentioned, it is not tied to the suffering of Christ. The usual discussions of apostleship and travel plans are missing. There is little ethical exhortation, and the letter itself is awkwardly fitted into the Pauline

letter form. A disciple may have composed this letter to protect
genuine Pauline teaching. We are told of false Pauline letters
claiming that the Parousia had already come (2:2; 3:17). This
problem is unlike the direct attacks against Paul in some of the
other letters. Here people are claiming to give Pauline teaching but are distorting it. If Paul is still alive at this point, he is
not in a position to return to the Church in the future and back
up what he says with a visit or, apparently, to send a close
associate. This letter must bear the full weight of defending the
apostle's teaching (3:14f.) and of keeping the community faithful to it (2:15).

Its author may have used an earlier apocalypse for the
scenario that makes up the body of the letter (2:3-14). Here
that revelation takes on a function quite unlike that of the
usual apocalypse. The usual apocalypse reveals to people how
close the end is. They are being told that they will only have to
endure evil a little longer. This revelation, on the contrary, is
to show how many things have yet to come. Its message: the
end is not yet. The practical problem created by false teaching
about the end is suggested in 3:6-12: some people have given up
work. We have witnessed similar phenomena today. Every few
years another group abandons homes and occupations to go
wait for beings from outer space who will rescue them from the
impending collapse of civilization on this planet. (Such an
event predicted for July 4, 1977 did not, obviously, occur.) The
author of this epistle is presenting what Paul might say to
them as much as to the people in Thessalonica in the 1st century: the world is not ending yet. The Christian must continue
living and working in this world just as the apostle Paul did
and not gear his or her life around some calculation of times.
Paul had already pointed out in the first letter to the Thessalonians that Christians who remained faithful to their calling
were "saved from the wrath to come"; they have no need to
worry about it.

These short letters show what a vital role the Pauline
letter played in the missionary effort that occupied the concluding years of the apostle's life. Indeed, he seems to have

created his own style of letter-writing so that the letter could serve as a vehicle of apostolic presence and preaching when he could not visit the Churches in person. They also show us the care and concern for all his churches which the apostle carried with him throughout his travels. In some of his other letters we will see that same concern issue in stern warnings to his converts.

STUDY QUESTIONS

1. What are our sources for the life of Paul? Why do we have to be careful in using Acts as a source?
2. Describe two or three of the major events in the life of Paul. Indicate how we arrive at dates for those events and where in Paul's letters or Acts we find information about them.
3. Give an example of Paul's solution to a practical problem. Do you agree or disagree with his approach? Why?
4. Write a short letter to Paul using the conventional 1st-century letter format.
5. Give two examples of how Paul's letters differ from ordinary 1st-century letters. Explain how those differences make Paul's letters more suitable for his missionary work.
6. What do you think that Philemon said in response to Paul's letter? Do you think that he let Paul continue to use Onesimus in his work?
7. On the basis of 1 and 2 Thessalonians, how would you characterize the relationship between Paul and the Churches he founded?

Chapter Eight

CHRISTIANS: JEW AND GENTILE

A recent TV interview show quizzed people who had converted from Judaism to Catholicism or vice versa. It was clear that people considered the two quite separate religions—as indeed they are today. But people often read the same situation back into Paul's time. They think of him as converting from one religion to another. While that may have been the experience of Gentile converts, Paul and other early Jewish converts did not feel that way. For Paul, his vocation as a Christian missionary was the fulfillment of the destiny God had given him from before his birth. Read Galatians 1:12-15. You can see that Paul views his whole life as under the direction of the one God whom he had served from his youth. Those Christians who maintained Jewish customs after they became Christians probably felt even less discontinuity between their past and present religious life.

Christianity and Judaism

Today the relationship between Christianity and Judaism is being reevaluated as part of the ecumenical movement and the efforts of the various Christian bodies to eradicate the anti-Semitism that has characterized so much of Christian history. From the Jewish side, one finds new attempts to assess the place of Christianity and especially Jesus within Jewish history. It is very difficult to avoid reading New Testament statements about Judaism in the light of later developments. One increasingly finds Jews who take the position that Jesus was an acceptable—if eccentric and not very successful— liberal teacher, like the Pharisees of the Hillel school. Paul is then held responsible for the theological and practical developments that made Christianity a non-Jewish religion. We have already seen that that view is too simplistic, since as a zealous Pharisee Paul had already found the Christian movement unacceptable from the Jewish side. Belief in Jesus as Messiah would not of itself have constituted grounds of persecution, but criticism of Jewish traditions such as that in Stephen's speech in Acts 7:2-53 might well have. Recent studies of Paul's pre-Christian persecutions of the Church remind us of the following points:

(1) From the Jewish side, Christianity was still considered subject to its disciplinary authorities. As a Christian Paul himself would be tried and punished by the synagogues and courts of the diaspora (2 Cor 11:24).

(2) Although Christianity was a messianic movement centered around Jesus, it was different from other such movements in that (a) Jesus had been tried and condemned with the approval of Jewish authorities; he had suffered a form of death considered a curse, and yet Christians claimed that he had been exalted to God's right hand; (b) Christians proclaimed that the new age had been inaugurated and that fidelity to the God of Israel/Torah was determined positively or negatively by one's belief in Jesus; (c) Christians pronounced judgment against fellow Jews for rejecting God's Messiah. Thus the zealous missionary activity of the Church seems to have provoked ad hoc disciplinary action by Jewish authorities. Flogging and imprisonment were punishments that could be administered by a local court of three judges. Their intent was to get Christians to stop their preaching. If you look back at 1 Thessalonians 2:14-16, you will see that such opposition did not involve trying to put a person to death—the martyrdom of Stephen seems to have been an illegal mob action. Paul says that he

was driven out of Judea and that the Jews displeased God by
trying to prevent him from preaching to the Gentiles. You
should always remember that much of the anti-Jewish language in the New Testament—for example, the curse in 1
Thessalonians 2:16—refers to those who were trying to stop
the Christian mission. It is not a general statement about Jews
or Judaism.

Freedom for the Gentiles

We pointed out in our earlier discussions of the messianic
expectations of Judaism that in that age (1) God's revelation in
the Torah would be followed by all; (2) the Gentiles would come
to acknowledge the God of Israel. Christians preached that the
Messiah had come. Two questions would then present themselves: (1) What is the status of the Torah? (2) What is the
relationship between Jews (including Christian Jews) and
Gentiles? Christians did not always answer these questions in
the same way. Some, including Paul's opponents, would argue
that the coming of the Messiah and the gift of the spirit meant
that a more perfect obedience to the Torah could be expected.
Such a viewpoint could be—and apparently was—linked with
missionary activity among the Gentiles. Their conversion implied that God was carrying out his call to them through that
missionary activity. They were now being brought into the
chosen people. Those who joined would be saved in the judgment along with the righteous; the rest would be condemned.
For such Christians there could be no sense in speaking about
Christians *and* Jews. There is only one chosen people. The
difference between Christians and other Jews is that their
faith in Jesus as Messiah has let them in on the true interpretation of the Torah that will be the standard by which he
judges the world. But others—for whom Paul will become the
leading spokesman—argued that through the coming of Jesus
God had provided a new way of righteousness, one which both
Jew and Gentile had to adopt and one which did not require
that the Gentiles become strictly observant Jews.

Salvation in Christ

At least one pre-Pauline understanding of this new salvation associated it with the death of Christ. Christians often suppose that Christ's death "for sins" represents a simple transfer of Old Testament animal sacrifices to a human being. But such a transfer was and is repugnant to Jewish thought and hence unlikely from converts of Jewish origin. At a recent Catholic-Jewish dialogue on Jesus, a Jewish scholar remarked that the most offensive feature of Christian doctrine to him as a devout Jew was its application of sacrificial language to the death of a human being; not the claim that Jesus is Messiah and exalted in heaven. Jews have never done that. Neither the suffering servant of Isaiah 53 nor the suffering righteous of Wisdom 2 are ever seen as redemptive figures. At best, God might choose to heal the sinfulness of his people after the righteous have suffered out of fidelity to the Law. In other words God does not require the sacrifice of the righteous, that sacrifice does not *cause* a change in the relationship between God and his people. But God hears the prayer implied in the faithful suffering of the righteous, and, although all of Israel has not repented, turns to his people and rescues them from oppression. That view of suffering is expressed in the stories of the Maccabean martyrs and also in the treatment of Christian martyrs in Revelation (see Rev 6:9-11).

How then did the redemptive significance of the death of Jesus come to be expressed in sacrificial language in Christianity? We can understand this process if we look at an early pre-Pauline formula that scholars have identified in Romans 3:25f. The pre-Pauline expression ran something like this:

> . . . God set forth (Jesus Christ) as a sin-offering—on account of his fidelity—at the cost of his blood; as a demonstration of his (= God's) righteousness, on account of his (= God) letting their (= Gentiles) previous sins go unpunished due to God's restraint; as a sign of the righteousness of him who is righteous and makes righteous the person of Jesus' faith.

This formula originated in the Gentile mission. It is not speaking about the Jews but about how God has made Gentiles righteous. We know that because the language about God passing over sins was used in 1st-century Judaism in a negative sense to explain why God always punished his people when they sinned but let the Gentiles go unpunished. The idea was that God's punishment of his own people was an act of mercy, since it would save them from the terrible judgment that awaited the wicked. Here is an explanation of that concept from 2 Maccabees 6:12-17:

> So I beg those who read this book not to be discouraged by such misfortunes but to remember that these punishments were not intended to destroy our people but to correct them. For it is a sign of great benevolence not to let the impious alone for a long time but to punish them promptly. For in the case of other nations, the Master is long-suffering and waits until they have reached the full measure of sins before he punishes them; but in our case he has decided differently, so that he would not take vengeance on us afterwards when our sins have reached their height. So he never withdraws his mercy from us, and although he disciplines us with misfortune, he does not abandon his own people.

The second concept that you have to keep clearly in mind in order to understand our passage is that of "righteousness." You can already see from the Romans passage that righteousness is primarily an attribute of God. He gives righteousness to his chosen people. A few passages from the Essene writings will help clarify this concept. Their hymns explain that God is the one who makes people righteous:

> Only through your (= God) goodness can one be righteous (I QH 13:16-17).

> (Man is) guilty of unfaithfulness from his mother's womb until old age. And I have recognized that man

has no righteousness and the son of man is always
imperfect (I QH 4:29-31).

For I rely on the favor and the great mercy you have
shown. For you to forgive sins; to cleanse man from
guilt by your righteousness (I QH 4:36-37).

Similar expressions may be found elsewhere in the Essene
writings. Being righteous before God is equivalent to salvation. Notice that man's constant unfaithfulness is the reason
he must rely on God's mercy and gift of righteousness. The
Romans formula points to Jesus as an exception to that generalization about humanity. He was faithful to the end (cp the
sacrificial understanding of Jesus' death in Hebrews 5:7-10).
Of course the Essenes thought that God's gift of righteousness
and his spirit had to be coupled with obedience to the Torah;
there would be no righteousness at all without it.

Now we are ready to have a look at our formula. Instead of
planning some terrible destruction for the Gentiles when their
sins had reached the full measure, this passage claims that
God has provided a way for them to be made righteous. He has
given them Jesus, the one faithful person, as a sin-offering.
You can see that this passage represents a clear consistent
interpretation of the significance of Jesus' death. It is not
yet—as in Paul—understood as necessary for Jews to obtain
righteousness—God had not been neglecting their sinfulness!
But it is understood as the plan God had all along (implied by
the verb "set forth") to deal with the Gentiles. He would not
condemn them—or most of them—to terrible punishment at
the hands of the Messiah but would provide them with forgiveness by regarding the death of Jesus as their sin-offering. They
can now become righteous through the "faith of Jesus." (It is
not clear whether this expression referred to Jesus' fidelity or
to the believer's faith in Jesus.)

Now read the surrounding verses in Romans 3 and you can
see what Paul has done with this insight. He claims that not
only the Gentiles but also the Jews must find the righteousness
of God in Jesus. This modification provides the context for

Paul's doctrine of righteousness (= justification) by faith. Now take out a concordance and look up the word "righteousness" and the verb "to justify/make righteous." You can see that most of the uses of these words are in Romans, Galatians and Philippians—all letters in which the relationship between Christianity and Judaism is at issue. Galatians and Philippians warn Gentile converts against taking up Jewish customs. Romans is written to a Gentile Church in the realization that Christianity is rapidly becoming a Gentile movement. Paul wishes to justify inclusion of the Gentiles in the people of God and to explain the relationship between Gentile Christians and Jews (not Jewish converts to Christianity).

Galatians

If you remember the basic structure of the Pauline letter, you will notice something very unusual about Galatians; there is no thanksgiving at all! Paul usually follows his greetings with some thanksgiving for the faith of the Church to which he writes. (That Church may not have even been very faithful lately, see 1 and 2 Corinthians!) Here he jumps right to the issue: some people (traveling Christian missionaries) were presenting a different gospel, a different message about salvation in Jesus than Paul had preached. They were probably also attacking Paul's credibility as an apostle, since Paul first gives an account/defense of his career and apostleship (1:11-2:14). They may have used Paul's controversy with Peter at Antioch and the fact that he had not been one of the original disciples of Jesus but a persecutor of the Church as arguments against him. Perhaps one of Paul's Gentile converts, Titus, had been circumcised. (Galatians 2:3 only says that he was not forced to be circumcised.) The point at issue does not become clear immediately. In Galatians 6:12 we learn that these people are compelling the Galatians to be circumcised. Paul also refers to those who think they can become righteous "through works of the Law," but he does not make it clear whether these missionaries were asking the Gentile converts to keep the whole Jewish Law or only demanding that they be circumcised—

according to Jews a sign of belonging to the covenant—and to keep some minimal set of regulations like those in Acts 15:13ff.

Some interpreters suggest that Paul himself was not well informed about the situation. He does not send any greetings from or to associates and has no immediate plans to travel there. (You will notice, however, that travel plans are so much a part of his letters that he has a surrogate for them when he interrupts the argument at 4:12-20 to detail his earlier visit and express his desire to be with the Galatians.)

When you sit down to read the actual argument in this letter, one of the most confusing things is the way Paul keeps switching back and forth between the situation of the Jews and that of the Gentiles. The letter is dominated by paired antitheses. Here is a list of some major ones; you can probably add more to it.

Opponents' (=Merely Human)	**Paul's (= God's)**
gospel: pleases men	gospel: please God (= be persecuted by men)
flesh	spirit
Moses	Abraham
circumcision/uncircumcision division of humanity	new creation (= Israel of God) neither Jew nor Gentile
slavery to Law pagan gods	freedom
works of Law	faith in Christ
Christ as "cursed"	Christ crucified
slave/son as child	free/son as heir
works of Law/walk according to flesh	Law of love/walk according to spirit
earthly Jerusalem	Jerusalem above

Remember Paul is making a rhetorical argument in Galatians. He is not trying to give a fair, objective representation of the opposing position. Once he has set up this antithetical structure, Paul can advance much of his argument against them by implication. The negative or positive characteristics that apply to one member of the set are carried over to the others even if they would not logically apply in that case. Now let us run through the argument as he presents it.

Galatians 2:15-21: Paul opens his case by speaking about Jews. *Even they* must find righteousness in Christ and not in works of the Law. If the Law does the Jews no good, then *a fortiori* it will not help the Gentiles either.

Galatians 3:1-5: Gentiles received the spirit through faith. Therefore they should not end "in the flesh"—note how Paul is using his antitheses here!

Galatians 3:6-9: God always intended to make the Gentiles righteous through faith. That salvation was predicted in the promise that all nations (= expression used for Gentiles by 1st-century Jews) would be blessed in Abraham. (Abraham appears in Jewish missionary preaching as father of the Gentiles, though Jews did not expect their gentile converts to be free from the Law.)

Galatians 3:10-13: Those who rely on the Law (= Jews) are under a curse from which Christ has set them free.

Galatians 3:14: Consequences of Christ's death for Gentiles are that they receive the blessings of Abraham; the spirit through faith. (This verse returns to the opening of this section of the argument.)

Galatians 3:15-29: The promise to Christ (= Abraham's offspring) comes through faith.

Galatians 3:15-18: God did not annul the promise to Abraham when he gave the Law to Moses.

Galatians 3:19-22: The Law consigns all things to sin until the promise is fulfilled.

Galatians 3:23-25: We Jews had the Law as a custodian until Christ and justification by faith.

Galatians 3:26-29: Through faith *you Gentiles* are just as much heirs to the promise as Jews.

Galatians 4:1-31: Both Jews and Gentiles were "slaves" before the coming of Christ.

Galatians 4:1-7: Jews were like children, subject to household slaves until Christ.

Galatians 4:8-11: Gentiles were slaves to false gods and the powers of the universe (notice that Christianity might also appeal to a person as a way to become free from fate and the powers of the cosmos).

Galatians 4:9: Don't go back to slavery corresponds to 3:5, don't end in the flesh.

Galatians 4:12-20: Excurses, pseudo-travelogue in which the apostle makes a personal appeal to the Galatians by recalling the beginning of their association.

Galatians 4:21-31: Allegory of Sarah and Hagar to prove on the basis of the Law that no one should wish to be under it. The antithesis slave/free binds this section to the one before it.

Galatians 5:1-12: Final appeal to the Gentiles not to go into slavery under the Law but to remain in the freedom of Christ.

Galatians 5:13-6:10: The concluding paraenesis, which Paul has tied to what precedes by contrasting freedom and being led by the spirit with "desires of the flesh." The flesh/spirit contrast from the earlier discussion of law/faith is now applied to ethical exhortation. The use of flesh/spirit in paraenetic contexts is common in Jewish circles. Qumran texts, for example, can speak of sinful behavior as being led astray by the flesh.

Galatians 6:11-16: These verses make a final plea for Paul's case by pulling together flesh, circumcision, not keeping the Law and human glory into one set that is opposed to glorying in the Cross of Christ and the new creation. Notice that verse 16 identifies the Christians as the "Israel of God." What Paul has been arguing in effect is that the chosen people are and always have been those made righteous by faith in Christ.

Philippians

This letter, written while Paul was in prison, presents us

with a phenomenon common in the Pauline correspondence, the combination of more than one letter from the apostle. When they collected Paul's letters, early Christians sometimes put more than one together if they were addressed to the same Church. We mentioned earlier that 2 Corinthians 8 and 9 are separate letters by Paul seeking collection monies from different Churches in the area. Scholars identify such combination letters on the basis of sharp breaks in language and content and disorganized Pauline letter structure. In this case you can do some detective work yourself. All you have to do is remember what we learned about how to write a Pauline letter. Okay now, let's begin identifying the sections of Philippians:

Opening: 1:1-2

Thanksgiving: 1:3-11. Notice the topic of the letter that is introduced here: the Philippians are sharers in the grace of Paul's imprisonment and testimony to the gospel.

Body: 1:12-26. The topic of the letter is now formally introduced. Paul wishes to explain to the Philippians that his imprisonment has really helped rather than hurt the missionary effort because others have been inspired to preach more vigorously. The eschatological climax concerns Paul's own destiny: will he die and be with Christ or—as he expects—be set free and return to Philippi.

Paraenesis: 1:27-2:18. The practical exhortation that Paul now has to give the Church is to remain steadfast in persecution even though Paul is not there. Again notice the close connection Paul makes between the success of his communities and his own status at the judgment.

Travel Plans: 2:19-30. Plans for himself (?), Timothy and Epaphroditus, a member of the Philippian community follow the paraenesis.

Conclusion: Begins at 3:1a but is suddenly interrupted and not picked up again until 4:4-9. You might notice that two women are mentioned as having labored side by side with Paul in spreading the gospel.

Fragments of two separate letters have been attached to the main letter. Presumably the main letter was the last one that he wrote to them, as his case is finally coming to a head.

Notice that he tells his readers that Epaphroditus had been sick for a long while after bringing the Philippians' gift to Paul (2:26-28). Now read 4:10-23. There Paul has written to the Philippians thanking them for their gift, which has just been delivered by Epaphroditus. Therefore, scholars think that this section comes from a thank-you note written soon after Epaphroditus had arrived.

Philippians 3:1b-4:3: This section is in a very different tone from the rest of the letter. Elsewhere the dominant motif is rejoicing. Here Paul is pleading—even weeping—as he warns the Philippians against those who might lead them astray (v 18). The issue here is not enduring persecution but the specific problem we have already met in Galatians: Gentile Christians who seek to adopt Jewish religious practices. The argument is much less elaborate than in Galatians—perhaps because Paul is in closer personal contact with Philippi—but uses some of the same antitheses found there:

Opponents	Paul (gospel)
circumcision in flesh	true circumcision/ worship in spirit
righteousness under the Law	righteousness through faith
(knowledge of the Law)	knowledge of Christ/ willingness to share his sufferings
earthly things	heavenly ones

The body of this letter against Judaizing is found in 3:2-16. Its eschatological climax in vv 12-16 has the same tone as that in the main letter, Paul's reflection on his own fate. Verses 17-21 pick up the eschatological tone of the previous verses by speaking of Christ's coming in judgment, but they are being used as paraenesis. Paul is exhorting the Philippians to imitate him. Philippians 4:1-3 may be the conclusion to this letter or—as other interpreters think—part of the conclusion to the main letter. Paul's focus on Jesus in heaven suggests that this polemical letter was written before the main letter at a time when he did not expect to be freed. Obviously from the main letter the threat being posed to the Philippians' faith was not serious; they continued to be faithful to the teaching of the apostle.

You can also see that this correspondence presupposes that Paul is in jail where he can be in constant contact with Philippi. People used to think that the reference to the Praetorian guard meant that Paul was writing from Rome. Such a location, however, is 4 to 5 weeks journey from Rome. Inscriptions from the area of Ephesus have shown us that *praetoriani* were stationed there on lands belonging to Augustus. Other inscriptions show that people belonging to the *familia Caesaris* managed the imperial bank in Asia. These inscriptions have made it possible to understand the references to the praetorium (1:13) and Caesar's household (4:22). Paul himself tells us that he faced death in Asia (1 Cor 15:30-32; 2 Cor 1:8-10). 1 Corinthians 15:32 mentions facing beasts in Ephesus and 2 Corinthians 8 says that he despaired of life itself. These references fit in with the kind of imprisonment reflected in the Philippian correspondence. Therefore, many scholars now hold that Philippians was written while Paul was in prison in Ephesus sometime before he wrote 1 Corinthians.

Romans

We turn from these letters written early in the last stage of Paul's life to a letter many think was the last one that he wrote. This time Paul is writing to a community he has never visited but which he hopes to visit after he has taken the collection to Jerusalem. Like Philippians, Romans may also have part of another letter added to the end. Romans 16:1-23 refers to many people Paul had known at Corinth and Ephesus. Verses 17-20 show particular knowledge of the community's problems and deliver a warning similar to that in Philippians 3. Therefore, many interpreters think that this chapter is part of another letter that Paul wrote from Corinth at the same time as he wrote Romans. They suggest that it is a farewell to the Church at Ephesus (cp. Ac 20:17-38 where Paul gives a farewell address to the Ephesian elders). Romans 15:22-24 makes it clear that Paul did not intend to return to the East after he had delivered the collection. Some even suggest that Paul sent a copy of Romans along with the letter in chapter 16.

Romans has been one of the most influential writings in the history of Christianity. Its first eleven chapters address the issue of Judaism, Christianity and salvation. The paraenetic section in chapters 12-15 shows parallels with problems Paul had confronted earlier in Corinth. Therefore, many consider Romans a summary of Paul's earlier preaching. It is not easy to tell what specific details Paul knew about the Roman Church. Two of his close associates from Corinth, Aquila and Priscilla, had been exiled from Rome under Claudius. That expulsion was due to rioting among the Jews over "Chrestus." Therefore, some 8 to 10 years before Romans, unknown Christian missionaries were probably preaching among the large Jewish community in Rome. But it seems from the tenor of his remarks in Romans that Paul is writing to a community that is predominantly Gentile. The concluding chapters of the body of the epistle give Paul's view of how they should consider actual Jews—not Jewish or Judaizing Christians.

Because Romans is a very long and intricate letter, we can only sketch the main outlines of Paul's arguments. Chapters 1-11 are the classic exposition of his doctrine of righteousness through faith. You will remember from our discussion of Paul's use of an earlier formula (Rm 3:24-26) and from Galatians that the difficult thing about Paul's formulation of the doctrine is his claim that it applies to Jews as well as Gentiles. Some Jews and earlier Christian missionaries might have been willing to grant that faith in Christ makes it possible for the Gentiles to be righteous, but they would argue that Jews already knew about righteousness and God through the Law.

Opening: 1:1-7. Verses 3 and 4 are an earlier Christian credal formula.

Thanksgiving: 8-15. Note that the topic introduced in the thanksgiving is Paul's desire to visit Rome; that is the reason Paul has written this letter.

Body: 1:16-3:31. Both Jew and Gentile must have faith in order to be righteous. This section begins much like a typical Jewish sermon. If you look back at the quotation from *The Assumption of Moses* 10 (p. 39), you will discover that the righteousness (= justice) and wrath of God were to be revealed together when he judged the world. People at present may not always be convinced of the righteousness or justice of God. Innocent people seem to suffer and others prosper while flagrantly ignoring the commandments of God. The Jews particularly could look back on the long history of their sufferings and persecution and wonder if God really does care for his chosen people. Thus, when God does punish the wicked and reward the righteous, his justice will also be revealed.

Now you can see that there is something odd about Paul's opening. He says that the righteousness/wrath of God are already revealed to the person who has faith. (Such a statement has parallels to what Jesus himself had said to people worried about when God was going to reveal his rule over the world. He told them that if they changed their lives to fit the rule of God, they could see that he does indeed rule.) Paul sees the death of Jesus as the decisive manifestation of God's righteousness. Because of that death, God makes both Jewish and Gentile believers righteous (3:21-31). God is redeeming all people from their sin and thus manifesting his righteousness. Most of this section is designed to show why people need that redemption.

The first part treats paganism much as any Jewish sermon would. They are lost in idolatry and sin. But the usual Jewish sermon would go on to point out that the one true God in whom the Jews believe has saved them from that sinfulness by giving them the Law. Paul switches that argument by claiming that even with the Law, the Jews fell into sin. He never denies that it is better to be a Jew and to know the true God than to be a pagan sinner. But because the Jews too have been unfaithful, they are as much in need of the salvation in Christ as the Gentiles.

Romans 4 returns to the Abraham story as proof that God always intended to save humanity—Jew and Gentile—through faith. If you compare this version with Galatians 3 and 4, you will find that this passage is much less complex: the awkward argument about progeny and heirs and the Sarah/ Hagar allegory are both gone. Paul is simply claiming that Abraham became the father of nations (= Gentiles) because of his faith. (Jewish sources attribute works to Abraham such as the sacrifice of Isaac or the hospitality he offered the angels.)

Romans 5 turns to the question of the death/resurrection of Christ and salvation from sin. There were two conflicting views about when the Messiah would come. Some thought that he would not come until there was a time of great goodness: all Israel would keep the Law for one day. Others, that he would come at a time of great sinfulness. Paul draws on the latter view. The Messiah did not wait until people were righteous and were keeping the Law, but came when sin prevailed.

The Adam/Christ parallel helps Paul explain how what happens to one person can affect the whole race. Notice that Paul does not hold a doctrine of inherited original sin. Rather, he says that through Adam death and sinfulness became part of the human condition. Individuals all die, and they all manifest sinfulness in different ways (5:14). That caveat is necessary because the death of Christ did not bring salvation to everyone automatically. It brought a free gift of grace by which reconciliation and righteousness could come to reign in human life. Notice also that Paul insists that just as death and sin are universal so acquittal and life are for all people.

Romans 6 uses the diatribe technique to introduce a possible misunderstanding of what Paul has been saying. If God has reached out and made sinners righteous, then why not sin? Paul has already made the case that all people do sin. Here he introduces the key answer to such an objection. You remember that in Galatians he told people to walk according to the Spirit.

Here he returns to that early Christian ethical position. The Christian is free from sin. In other words, he or she is not in the same situation with respect to sin as the non-Christian, Jew or Gentile. One might expect such an assertion in light of the doctrine that the Messiah was to free people from sin and that much early Christian paraenesis sees the new outpouring of the Spirit as making it possible to live according to the Spirit. Here Paul goes further and takes baptism as the sign that a Christian died to sin and its wages, death. He or she is to now live in the Spirit and so reap eternal life.

Romans 7 and 8 follow the same pattern. But they do not begin with the general situation of human sinfulness. Instead they turn to the particular situation of the Jew living under the Law. Doubtless you will notice the neat structure of chapters 1-8. Chapter 1 begins with the thesis that the wrath/righteousness of God have been revealed in Christ and goes on to treat first humanity in general (= pagans) and then the situation of the Jews. Chapter 3 concludes the subsection by applying righteousness through faith in Christ to both groups. Chapter 4 argues that the promise of salvation to Abraham comes to all peoples in Christ. Chapters 5 and 6 take up the situation of humanity in general; chapters 7 and 8, that of the Jews. Both come to similar conclusions:

Romans 6:22-23	Romans 8:37-39
But now that you have been set free from sin and have become slaves of God, the return you get is sanctification, and its end eternal life. For the wages of sin is death, but the free gift of God is eternal life in Christ Jesus our Lord.	No, in all these things we are more than conquerors through him who loved us. For I am sure that neither death nor life; nor angels nor principalities; nor things present, nor things to come; nor powers, nor height nor depth, nor anything else in creation shall be able to separate us from the love of God in Christ Jesus our Lord.

Both praise the glorious salvation that has been granted the believer in Christ.

When Paul is speaking about the Law in chapter 7, do not make the mistake of thinking that he is talking about Law in general. He is talking about the Torah, the Law of Moses; God's revelation in the Old Testament. As the Law of a people it deals with all facets of human life just as any law would have to do. But the reason life under the Law is a problem is not because living under law in general is psychologically problematic for human beings—as some psychologizing interpretations would claim—but because as the revealed will of God, the Law defined what was good and just in his sight, and the salvation of the people depended upon their obedience.

This chapter says much the same thing as the previous one. Applied to the Jew, death to sin in Christian baptism also means death to the Law (= written code). The difficulty with Paul's parallel here is that it seems to equate law and sin and thus to violate the fundamental Jewish perception that the Law is good and holy; it is humanity's guide to what is right and just, and saves them from the idolatry of the Gentiles. Paul takes up the objection that he is making the Law sin by trying to specify the relationship between the Law, sin and death and the human situation in such a way as to maintain the goodness of the Law. He does this by almost personifying sin as an independent power. (Though he does not go as far as the Essenes and some other Jews did and speak of a good and evil spirit at war within the individual.) The power of sin is such that the Law cannot fulfill its good purpose. Although Paul is speaking in the first person for rhetorical effect, he is really talking as he has been throughout about the experience of the whole Jewish people as they have tried to live under the Law. (One may wonder whether Paul has not lost his case about the Law when he draws the concluding antitheses: law of sin, flesh/law of God, mind.)

Romans 8 elaborates that concluding set of antitheses from the perspective of redemption. The affirmation of Christ's liberating work in verses 2f, rearranges the same antitheses

that Paul has been using throughout. The practical consequence of that liberation for the believer is that he or she is no
longer subject to the deadly combination of sin, flesh and law
but lives in the spirit confident of his or her complete redemption in the future.

Romans 9-11 turns to a question that would logically follow from Paul's exposition: the status of Israel as a chosen
people. After all, if the Law was so weakened by sin that it
could not function as it was supposed to, wasn't God unfair?
The Jews thought that they were the chosen people on the
basis of the Law. Did God cheat them by establishing a new
standard of righteousness and letting the Gentiles, who had
not been his people, in? Paul answers "No" on two grounds.
Once again, the Abraham story is used to make the case that
the righteousness pleasing to God has been the same all along
and that the Gentiles have been included in God's plan from
the beginning. At the same time, he insists that God will never
abandon Israel. Her current rejection of Christ has the positive
consequence that the Gentiles are coming to worship the God of
Israel. At the same time, he warns the Gentiles not to boast
that they have received what by rights belongs to the Jews.
They must always remember that they would have nothing
without the long history of the Jewish people and their attempts to live according to the Law of God. Paul is confident
that God will not abandon the Jews but will eventually help
them to see the salvation He offers in Christ. The present disobedience of Israel has only made it possible for the Gentiles to
obtain the mercy God is to extend to all, Jew and Gentile.

Romans 12:1-15:12 give a compendium of Pauline ethical
teaching. Scholars are sharply divided as to whether this advice is merely a summary of Paul's preaching—note the many
parallels to the Corinthian correspondence—or whether Paul
had enough information about the Roman community to tailor
his advice to particular problems that they were having. The
eschatological conclusion to this paraenetic section (15:7-13)
picks up on the virtue of hospitality to return to a major point
in the epistle, in the messianic age the Gentiles will come to

(now, have come to) hope in the God of Israel.

Romans 15:14-33 ends the epistle with the expected discussion of Paul's travel plans.

Students often find the theological arguments of Galatians, Romans and Philippians difficult, dry and uninteresting. In the end, the perspective of Pauline Christianity prevailed; after the 1st century Jewish Christianity has only been a marginal option in the history of Christianity. But something much deeper is at stake in these arguments: the ground and universality of salvation. In effect, if Gentiles do not have to become Jews to be saved through faith in Christ, then Africans or Indians do not have to become Western Europeans. The chosen people is not a people with its own language, tradition, history and culture, but all of humanity. For Paul, Jesus is not Savior because he taught the true interpretation of the Law as the teacher of righteousness from Qumran claimed to do, but because God accepted his death as sin-offering for all humanity, making them righteous through faith in him. The Christian Churches today still have a long way to go in order to realize the implications of God's universal saving act in Christ.

STUDY QUESTIONS

1. Why is it incorrect to speak of Paul as converting from one religion to another?
2. Give two points about early Christian missionary preaching that a Jew might find objectionable, and explain what his or her objections would be.
3. Give a brief description of how Jews in the 1st century viewed Gentiles. What would a Gentile have to do in order to be considered good or righteous?
4. Why did Jews consider it an act of mercy that God punished his people for their disobedience quickly?
5. How does the pre-Pauline formula in Romans 3:24-26 ex-

plain the saving effect of Jesus' death? How does Paul use that formula in Romans 3?

6. What were Paul's Judaizing opponents in Galatia and Philippi trying to get Gentile converts to do? Why does Paul attack them so vehemently?

7. What is Paul's view of the significance of the Abraham story? How might a Jew disagree with his interpretation?

8. Give three or four of the antitheses that Paul uses in Galatians. How do these antitheses contribute to the argument he is making?

9. Why does Paul follow his discussions of righteousness through faith in Galatians and Romans with descriptions of the Christian's new life in the spirit?

10. How does Paul understand his suffering and imprisonment?

11. What is the structure of Romans 1-8? How does it tell us what the overall point of these chapters is?

12. How would you explain the significance of Paul's teaching on righteousness through faith to someone today?

13. Explain either (a) why Philippians is thought to be made up of several letters or (b) why we think that Paul was in prison in Ephesus when he wrote Philippians.

14. What does Romans 9-11 tell us about the relationship between Christians and Jews?

Chapter Nine

THE GENTILES INTERPRET CHRISTIANITY

Although the letters we have been reading were to predominantly Gentile Churches, they dealt with problems derived from the Jewish heritage of Christianity. We have already seen that Jewish and pagan patterns of religious experience, while having points of contact, were widely divergent. The Corinthian Church presents us with an example of what happened when the two views came into conflict. Many of their problems were born of the attempt to understand Christianity in terms suited to the pagan model.

Paul had, as you remember, a very warm relationship with his Churches in Thessalonica and Philippi. His troubles with the Corinthian community pain him deeply because they run so counter to that ideal. As in the case of Philippians, the Corinthian correspondence also represents combinations of letters. By sorting them out and by using the information that we have gleaned from Acts, we have a more extended picture of Paul's relationship with Corinth than with any other Church. Here are some key pegs in that history:

50/52   Paul is in Corinth 18 months. Founded the Church there. Expelled under Gallio.

52/53   "Previous letter" referred to in 1 Corinthians 5:9, which has not survived.

53   1 Corinthians

54   2 Corinthians 2:14-7:4 written from Ephesus as a prelude to a visit to Corinth.

        Visit that ended disastrously.

        2 Corinthians 10-13 part of the "tearful letter" mentioned in 2 Corinthians 2:4 and 7:8, written after the disastrous visit.

54/55   Some scholars think that Paul's Ephesian imprisonment and Philippians and Philemon came at this point in his career)

55   2 Corinthians 1:1-2:13; 7:5-16, part of a letter of reconciliation with the Corinthians.

        2 Corinthians 8 a letter for Titus to take to Corinth to encourage the collection.

        2 Corinthians 9 a general letter concerning the collection to all Pauline congregations in the area.

55/56   Paul visits Corinth again. Romans written.

You realize by now that all of these dates are hypothetical reconstructions, since none of the Pauline letters are dated.

Paul's Corinth was a young city, founded by the Romans in 44 B.C. Because it straddled the narrow isthmus, Corinth was a center for trade going from east to west. Other missionaries like Peter and Apollos (1 Cor 1:12; 3:5-9; Ac 19:1) passed through the city. New ideas and religious cults frequently spread along the trade routes of the Mediterranean world and Christianity was no exception.

The Corinthian Church was a varied lot: the merchants and tradesmen who frequented such ports (1:26f.); Paul who supported himself as a tentmaker while he preached in Corinth; Jews and Gentiles; freedmen and slaves (7:17-24). People today are often interested in this community because they were concerned with "spiritual gifts"—prophecy, speaking in tongues and inspired preaching. The contemporary enthusiasm for charismatic prayer groups among Christians leads them to have some interest in the Corinthian Church— and, one may hope, to learn from their example! Such experiences provide people with a conviction about the reality of the spirit. Positively, such conviction can help them change their lives. We know from the last chapter that where Paul speaks of life in the spirit, he expects it to make that kind of transformation possible. But sometimes people interpret these experiences of the Spirit as indications of their own immortality and spiritual perfection. Many of the practical problems that beset the Corinthian community have been problems in such groups throughout history.

Paul does not reject speaking in tongues, healings, prophecy and visions as modes of religious experience. But he does reject the religious enthusiasm run wild that we find at Corinth. He does not think that Christians should use such experiences to claim superiority over other Christians. He does not think that they are the goal of Christian life. What he wants to argue in 1 Corinthians is that God only gives the Spirit to the Church for one purpose: to build up an harmonious community, one which is unified in love for all the members. One of the striking features of 1 Corinthians is the use Paul has made of a stoic metaphor of the whole cosmos as a body. Paul now applies that idea to the Christian community. But even before he comes to that point, he uses language that deals with the body. Most of the ethical problems raised by the Corinthians were related to how Christians should view their bodily existence. In order to understand some of these problems it is necessary to remember that Hellenistic people often divided a human being into three parts:

(1) The spirit or mind—that is the immortal, divine part of the person.

(2) The soul—that is mortal; it is the life principle of the

body and is responsible for such things as breathing and heartbeat.

(3) The material body—often considered a prison that kept the mind from realizing its true divinity.

Popular philosophic asceticism often taught that a person had to realize inner divinity by becoming detached from the body and contemplating the divine realm. They would preach that only such a detached person could be called "rich" and "king"—not a material ruler or wealthy person.

Now look at 1 Corinthians 4:8 and you can see what has happened. The Corinthians thought that the gifts of the spirit in the Christian community proved the immortality of the spirit/mind of the possessor, so they used this philosophical lingo—which they might have heard from wandering philosophic preachers in the marketplace—to say, "See, Christianity makes us 'wise,' 'rich,' 'kings'—and without the arduous asceticism and philosophic contemplation required by the philosophers!" They also concluded that whatever a person did with his or her body was of no importance. Paul points to his own sufferings as an apostle to show that they are wrong. Throughout he insists that the Christian is still waiting for the redemption of the body; that Christianity is foolishness compared to philosophy, and that the true mark of the spiritual person is not indifference to the material body—which in some cases was apparently manifested in immorality—but a willingness to bear bodily suffering for Christ.

1 Corinthians: The Body of Christ, the Limits of Christian Freedom

You can see from our chronological chart that this letter was not the first one Paul had written since he had left Corinth. Paul is answering some questions raised in the Corinthians' reply and also responding to things that he had heard from others about the Corinthian community.

1 Corinthians 1:1-9: Greetings and thanksgiving. The thanksgiving introduces spiritual gifts, the major issue treated in the letter. Since the problems in the Corinthian community are practical and ethical, it is impossible to separate the body and the paraenetic sections of this letter.

1 Corinthians 1-4 attack the divisions that have grown up among the Corinthians. Apparently some argued over which apostle had conveyed the most spiritual power, Paul, Peter or Apollos. Paul insists on the unity of the apostolic effort. The Corinthians should not boast about their spiritual powers or about the eloquence of various preachers. All powers are gifts of God. Further, the message of salvation through the crucified Christ is not something that rhetorical eloquence can bring either Jew or pagan to accept. It does not fit the categories of ancient wisdom (1 Cor 1:18-25). Finally, he reminds the Corinthians of their own lowly origins (1:26-30). He contrasts their boasting with the lowliness and suffering of the apostle (4:8-13). That apostolic testimony is the real way in which Christ is represented in the world.

1 Corinthians 5-6 deal with various moral abuses that have been reported to exist among the Corinthians. Paul introduces them to further cut down the Corinthians' claim to boast in spiritual powers. Some of the things described seem unimaginable to most people. They warn us that the kind of eloquence and spiritual experiences prized by the Corinthians do not necessarily make someone an ethically good person. Paul appears to be quoting a slogan used by the Corinthians at 6:12, "All things are lawful for me." Some interpreters think that they may even have derived that slogan from Paul's own preaching if he spoke about freedom from the Law. They might have interpreted him to mean freedom from any kind of restraint.

Chapter 5 takes up a particularly serious case, incest. The Corinthians are tolerating a person who is flagrantly violating the moral code by living with his stepmother. Paul insists that they take formal proceedings to excommunicate the man. (The community rules from Qumran list a number of offenses for which a person might be put out of the community.) But notice one thing. Unlike some who might not only throw the man out but also assume that he would be condemned to hell, Paul thinks that if the man is punished now he may be saved in the end. (Compare this with Jewish views about God's mercy in punishing his people now rather than condemning them with the Gentile sinners at the judgment.)

1 Corinthians 6:1-11 deals with the problem of Christians taking each other to court. You notice that it reflects the teaching of Jesus in reminding them that the ideal is to suffer wrong rather than to do it. But granting that people will not live up to that ideal, Paul gives a practical solution: Christians are to settle disputes in their own courts—as Jews did—rather than go before pagan magistrates.

1 Corinthians 6:12-20 turns to another sexual offense, prostitution. Notice how Paul begins to introduce the question of the right relationship between Christians and their bodies by referring to the resurrection. Because Christians believe they are to be rewarded with a transformed, glorious body like that of the risen Christ, they cannot abuse this one. It prefigures the resurrected body by being a temple of the Holy Spirit. He also alludes to the fact that Christians are members of Christ's body, a metaphor that he will build upon and expand until the letter reaches a dramatic eschatological climax with the discussion of the resurrection in 1 Corinthians 15. (Paul's image of the body as temple for the spirit is in sharp contrast with the Hellenistic image of the body as prison for the immortal spirit.)

1 Corinthians 7 deals with questions of marriage, celibacy and divorce. Paul takes the teaching of Jesus on divorce, that is, there should be none among believers, and modifies it in a situation that Jesus had not said anything about. What happens when a person converts to Christianity and finds that his or her spouse is unwilling to live with a Christian? Is he or she to be prevented from remarrying? Paul says no because the Christian party did not insist on the separation. The Christian is not to divorce a pagan spouse who is willing to continue the marriage, just because that spouse is not Christian, however. Later in the chapter (7:17-24) Paul expands that principle to cover all Christians: they should not try to change the outward circumstances of their lives because they convert.

His teaching as applied to the slaves who were members of the Church may seem especially harsh today but remember—as in the case with his preference for celibacy (vv 25ff.)—he is legislating Christian behavior for what he thinks will be a very short time until the end of the world. Notice throughout that Paul stresses mutual responsibility and the willingness of the Christian to do a bit extra for the sake of other people. That principle confronts us again and again in this letter.

1 Corinthians 8 takes up another of the Corinthians' slogans, "All of us possess knowledge." Paul sets a Christian principle of concern for the weaker brother against that principle. The problem was whether or not Christians could eat meat that had been sacrificed to idols. Some claimed that because Christians knew that the pagan idols had no reality, they could eat anything. Others felt that such meat should be avoided. (Paul will continue discussion on the problem in 1 Corinthians 10.) Notice that Paul does not try to reform the Christian of weak conscience. He attacks the strong Christians for offending the weaker. Even if such eating is a matter of indifference, it would be wrong to do so at a time that a weak brother would be offended. The strong Christian sins against Christ in offending the weak.

Two separate issues are involved. Much of the meat sold in the markets came from animals that had been sacrificed at the city's numerous temples. Could the Christian buy such meat? What if he was invited to a banquet at a pagan friend's house and such meat were served? Paul agrees with "the strong" that the Christian has no need to worry about such things (10:25-27). But, he says, if someone makes an issue of it by telling you that the meat is from a sacrifice to a pagan god, then you should not eat it out of respect for the conscience of the person who told you.

The second problem requires a somewhat stricter line. Suppose your friend had decided to offer a sacrifice to one of the gods. He might not just take the animal to the appropriate temple for sacrifice and sell what was left after the temple priests had received their portions. He might invite his friends to help eat the animal afterward at a banquet in honor of the god. (Many people in antiquity only ate meat on such festal occasions.) Archaeologists have discovered invitations to such banquets and the remains of dining rooms attached to temples in Corinth. What should a Christian do if he received such an invitation? Some of the Corinthians were apparently accepting and going to such banquets in pagan temples. Paul grants that the pagan idols have no reality, but he does not think that Christians should attend feasts in their honor. He interprets the Christian meal as a participation in the body of Christ. That participation excludes the possibility of sharing a ritual meal in honor of a pagan deity.

1 Corinthians 9 gives a moving insight into Paul's view of himself as an apostle. He did not exercise some of the rights that the other apostles did. Peter and the others had wives who went with them; Paul did not (1 Cor 9:4). Paul worked for his living—as was Jewish rabbinic custom—rather than be dependent upon his congregation as other apostles and wandering teachers of philosophy did. He does not deny that preachers should be paid for their labor. He even has a saying of Jesus to quote in support of that policy (1 Cor 9:14). But he tells his congregation that he wanted to preach the gospel "for free" even though that meant more hard work and suffering for him.

1 Corinthians 11-14 turns to a number of liturgical matters. Some of this advice seems rather haphazard.

1 Corinthians 11:5 presupposes that women are praying and prophecying in community services while 14:33b-36 invokes the Jewish view that they should be silent at public services. Many pagan cults had women as religious functionaries. Judaism, on the other hand, had always been male oriented. Women were not thought capable of studying the Law. Paul concludes by promising to give more instructions when he comes.

1 Corinthians 11:17-36 deals with a second problem concerning the eucharist. Apparently the Corinthians had a meal followed by blessed bread and wine. Abuses had crept in at the meal. Some people were getting drunk while others went hungry. Perhaps they were treating the Christian meal like a pagan temple banquet. Paul reprimands the Corinthians for not discerning the body of Christ. Such behavior and lack of fraternal charity cannot characterize the body of Christ.

A variety of instructions about prophecy and speaking in tongues follow. Again Paul uses his metaphor of the Church as body. This time it is to argue that a variety of gifts are necessary for the community. People should not boast or compare themselves with each other on the basis of which gifts they have. Besides, none of the things the Corinthians are so proud of are eternal. The Corinthians deceive themselves if they think that the gifts of the spirit are proof of salvation or immortality. The only eternal gifts are possessed by all Christians faith, hope and charity. Paul describes these in one of his most lyrical chapters, the description of love in 1 Corinthians 13. He goes on to encourage the Corinthians to show such love in their dealings with one another.

1 Corinthians 15 brings the various body metaphors to a climax. They culminate in the doctrine of the resurrection. Paul first quotes an early creed attesting Christian belief in the resurrection (15:1-11) reminding the Corinthians that he had taught them this tradition. We have already seen that this belief might be difficult for pagans to understand. The Corinthians may have thought of Christianity as guaranteeing some sort of spiritual immortality and not of bodily resurrection. Paul makes three main points against their view:

(1) The resurrection of Jesus shows that Jewish belief in the resurrection is the destiny of all. Paul's preaching would be in vain if Christ had not been raised (vv 12-20).

(2) The Christ/Adam analogy is then used to portray Christ as the firstfruit of a new creation that will reach its culmination when all creation is renewed and subjected to its God and creator (vv 20-28). Notice that Paul is consistently monotheistic: all is for the glory of the Father.

(3) He refers to a strange custom of being baptized on behalf of the dead. Perhaps that action was thought to spare them from the judgment. Paul thinks that the confidence be-

hind that action should apply to Christians as well. He alludes to his own willingness to suffer as a sign of his confidence in the future that Christians are promised and quotes pagan poets to make his argument.

1 Corinthians 15:35-58 describe the final victory of Christ and the resurrected state of the believer. Paul wants to make it clear that the resurrected body will not be like this earthly one. He cannot say anything more concrete about it, since the resurrected body belongs to the new creation. He portrays the Christian hope of immortality as an eschatological victory over death. That is what the Corinthians should be looking forward to.

1 Corinthians 16 takes up the practical matters of Paul's travel plans and the collection. Read what Paul says about the collection in 2 Corinthians 8 and 9 as well. When Paul closes this letter with a final blessing, he picks up two important themes: the early Christian prayer for the coming of the Lord, and the final eschatological victory, and love.

2 Corinthians: The True Apostle

We have seen that this letter is really a composite of several letters. But even that observation does not solve all the problems in interpreting it. Paul is clearly responding to a variety of events and charges about which we do not have much information. The following sequence of events seems to have occurred. After Timothy's visit (1 Cor 4:17; 16:10), Paul changed his plans (1 Cor 16:3-9) and sent Titus to Corinth to work on the collection (2 Cor 8:5). Sometime after that, other Christian missionaries—apparently of Jewish origin—came to Corinth and began using that community as a base of operation. We saw in 1 Corinthians 9 that Paul defended himself against other styles of apostleship. Paul wrote 2 Corinthians 2:14-7:4 to the Church and followed it up with a visit. But that visit was a disaster. Paul was attacked by one of the members of the Church (2:5; 7:12). Afterward Paul wrote the highly emotional and ironic "letter of tears" (2 Cor 10—13). He sarcastically mocks the "pseudo-apostles" who have made such an impact on the Corinthian Church. Titus went to Corinth again (2:12f.; 7:5-7) while Paul was in jail (? 1:8-11). Upon his release, Paul hurried to Macedonia to meet Titus and learned that the situation in Corinth had changed (7:15f.). Paul still has to explain what should be done about the person who had insulted him and why he had not visited Corinth himself. The letter of reconciliation (2 Cor 1:1-2:13; 7:5-16) deals with these problems.

Paul's opponents apparently also claimed to be apostles but maintained strong ties to Old Testament interpretation in their preaching. Their criticism of Paul suggests that they placed great store by demonstrations of the Spirit in eloquent preaching; inspired interpretation of Scripture; healing and even visions. They carried around testimonial letters (3:1-3) and received recommendations for their ministry (11:7-15; 12:13-18). Paul refuses to engage in such practices. We have already seen that he considers his Churches his crown in the judgment. He tells the Corinthians that they are his testimonial letter. He had already explained why he did not support himself by preaching, but that explanation was apparently not sufficient (11:7-15; 12:13-18). Perhaps his opponents used that refusal to bolster their attacks on the worth of his preaching and apostleship.

2 Corinthians 2:14-7:4: The Corinthians were probably attracted to the emphasis these new apostles put on the Spirit. At the same time their concern with the Old Testament may have seemed to put them securely in contact with the tradition that Paul was encouraging them to uphold. It is difficult to reconstruct their viewpoint from Paul's argument in these chapters. Paul clearly is at pains to deny their validity as Christian missionaries. He calls them "peddlers of the Word" (2:17)—a reference to the pay they received for their preaching? He claims that they practiced cunning and tampered with the Word (4:2), and accuses them of corrupting and taking advantage of others (7:2). They take pride in a person's position (5:12)—something we know was a weakness of the Corinthians from 1 Corinthians. Just as he has done elsewhere Paul points to his hardships and sufferings as the signs that God has made him a minister of the new covenant (4:7-12; 6:3-10). Why? Because those sufferings are like the death of Jesus. Paul even suggests that the sufferings of the true apostle are the source of life for his congregations (4:11f.). Though sinless, Christ was "made sin" for our sake (5:21). The apostle, his ambassador, can at least accept suffering as he continues that great work of reconciliation (5:16-21).

Paul works these appeals into a larger homiletic context that contrasts what is earthly with what is of the Spirit. We saw in Galatians that Paul uses such paired sets of antitheses as a rhetorical way of condemning his opponents. Just look at chapter 3 in 2 Corinthians. Here is a table of antitheses packed into that chapter:

Earthly:	Heavenly:
letters of recommendation	congregation as letter
ink	spirit
tablets of stone	human hearts
human claims to sufficiency	sufficiency given by God
written code (Law)	new covenant
death	life
fading splendor of Moses	eternal glory of the Lord
condemnation	righteousness
veiled face of Moses	unveiling by Christ
veiled heart (understanding) of those who believe in him	unveiled face of Christians
hardened minds	being changed into the likeness and glory of the Lord

These antitheses suggest that one of the ways in which the opponents demonstrated their spiritual power and insight was by allegorical (= spiritual, the "unveiling") interpretation of the Old Testament. They may even have used some of the antitheses Paul sets up here. What he seems to have done is to take over some of those categories and put them into the negative set by beginning with physical letters of recommendation = tablets of stone = Mosaic Law = hardened minds. (Perhaps the opponents also had a more positive picture of Moses than Paul does in his writings.)

Paul follows up this set of antitheses with a description of his own role as apostle. As you read 2 Corinthians 4, you can pick out the phrases about veiling, blindness, light, glory, death/life that come from the previous discussion. They continue into chapter 5. There Paul makes the culminating point in his argument: the real transformation into the glory of Christ does not take place until the resurrection and the new creation. The Spirit received in this life is only a guarantee of future transformation, not that transformation. It does not prove that that person has achieved glory. (Does this line of reasoning sound familiar? It should. Paul used it in 1 Corinthians.) In this life the Christian must live in suffering and faith with his or her treasure in a clay pot. Paul concludes with a moving appeal to the Corinthians to be reconciled to him, reminding them of his love and affection for them. Unfortunately, this appeal does not seem to have been successful. Paul's visit to Corinth ended in disaster.

2 Corinthians 10-13: This section of the letter Paul wrote after that painful visit is one of the most passionate and sarcastic in the entire corpus. Many people are turned off by the sarcasm and irony of Paul's "boasting" in these chapters so it is important to remember the context in which they were written. Put yourself in Paul's shoes. You know the deep personal feeling and love that Paul had for each of his Churches. Now it seems that these "super apostles" (11:6) have succeeded in turning this Church against Paul. They have even attacked his letters, claiming that while they are impressive, Paul's personal presence is not—perhaps that charge refers to the disastrous incident that had occurred during his visit (10:9f.). They have accused him of failing to carry out what he said in his last letter (10:11). How would you react? Would you say to hell with the Corinthians and go elsewhere?

Paul tries once again. He condemns the opponents as people who seek their own glory; people who preach another Jesus (glorious, not crucified) and a different spirit (11:4f.). He agrees that he was not a great orator (11:6)—though that claim may be ironic. It was customary for people defending themselves in law courts to claim that they were not trained in speaking. But Paul will never deny his love for the Corinthians or drop his understanding of the gospel. So he gives an ironical boast for himself as an apostle. He drops hints that he has had as many spiritual experiences as anyone else but will only boast about his weaknesses. Why? Because weakness is the true sign that the power of God is at work in the apostle (12:9). He even cites an oracle from God to support his point, though we know that this picture of the apostolate runs through all of Paul's thought. Miracles, tongues, inspired preaching and interpretation of Scripture, visions—none of these are proof of apostolic authority, only God's ability to use the weak, rejected and despised shows his power. Paul even suggests sarcastically that perhaps the real difficulty was his failure to demand that the Corinthians support him (12:13).

Finally, he reminds them that to reject the power of God in weakness would be to reject Christ himself. He did not come with great displays of power. (The opponents may have emphasized Christ's miraculous power.) He was not an eloquent preacher. He came to be crucified in weakness. Nor does he possess independent power and glory now. The power of God is what raised him from the dead—the same power that shows itself in the mission of the suffering apostle.

2 Corinthians 1:1-2:13; 7:5-16: Fortunately, Titus is able to bring back good news. The Church has been reconciled to Paul (7:5-16), thanks to the tearful letter he had written them. He still must explain that his failure to visit was not out of fear of doing so but out of desire to spare them any more painful incidents. You should also notice that Paul does not even demand an apology from the person(s) who had insulted him. Instead he instructs the Corinthians to comfort him and assures them of his forgiveness (2 Cor 2:5-11; 7:8-12). We may ask ourselves if we would be so charitable in that situation.

People are often amazed by the story of the Corinthian Church because they tend to think that the early communities must have been near perfect—after all, the Corinthians had the advantage of having Paul as their founder and of having Apollos and even Peter work among them. So people find it difficult to imagine the first Christians falling into the strife, moral confusion and competition reflected in these letters. But perhaps this saga should serve to make the early Church more accessible to us. The first Christians and the apostles had as many difficulties as we do today, and perhaps more; they had to work out traditions that we take for granted. Yet they managed to work through the difficulties. Perhaps today as much as ever we need to remember Paul's standards for apostleship. The gospel is not well served if the Church looks to popularity polls or other secular signs of success as criteria for how well or how badly she is carrying out her mission.

Colossians and Ephesians: The Universal Church

We have already pointed out that both these letters have a style and turns of phrase not characteristic of the apostle. Further, Ephesians seems to have copied from Colossians. Therefore, increasing numbers of scholars hold the view that both were written by disciples of the apostle. They expand metaphors used by the apostle, most notably that of the Church as the body of Christ. When Paul first used the expression, he was speaking about a local Church, the group that gathered to celebrate the eucharist. Colossians and Ephesians apply the same metaphor to the universal Church (Col 1:18; Eph 1:23). Both letters speak of the body of Christ, with Christ as head and source of everything that comes to the body. Paul usually speaks of God or the spirit as the source of everything that comes to the Church. Colossians 1:22 contrasts the "body of Christ = Church" with his physical body, his "body of flesh." He takes the philosophical metaphor of the cosmos as body to imply that the risen Lord rules the cosmos through his body the Church.

You will also notice the reverence for the apostle that comes through in both these letters. He is the revered minister of the Church whose sufferings complete those of Christ (Col

1:24-26; Eph 3:7-13). He is the one with true insight into the mysterious plan of God that is now being revealed in the Church (cf. Col 1:26-29; Eph 2:8-12). You can see that this way of speaking about Paul's apostolate is quite different from that in the letters the apostle himself writes. The departure in Ephesians is particularly striking because apostolic suffering paralleled with that of Christ is not placed as central to the mission. Ephesians 2:20 looks upon the apostles as the founders of the universal Church.

Colossians remains fairly close to Pauline letter style. It lacks the eschatological conclusion that Paul adds to the body and paraenetic sections and references to travel plans. Again, Ephesians diverges more from Pauline style than Colossians. It lacks the normal Pauline body. Many interpreters wonder if it was not composed as a general circular letter, since it does not have clear references to a specific Church and its problems. Many manuscripts of Ephesians lack the specific address "to the Ephesians" (omitted in the RSV translation). Both letters contain non-Pauline material that may reflect early liturgical formulae. The hymn quoted in Colossians 1:15-20 has a structure similar to that quoted by Paul in Philippians 2:6-11. Hymnic fragments have also been suggested for Ephesians 2:14-16.

Both these letters move away from the highly apocalyptic vocabulary of the main Pauline letters to a more timeless and cosmic vision of salvation. One manifestation of that universality in Ephesians is the Pauline theme of the reconciliation of Jews and Gentiles in the body of Christ (Eph 2:11-22; 3:6). Paul had used the body of Christ metaphor in 1 Corinthians to correlate the relationship between Christians and their physical bodies; Christians among each other in all phases of their common life and their future eschatological hope of resurrection. Ephesians now uses the metaphor to express the cosmic unity of all in Christ (1:10, 16-23; 2:16). You will notice that the author of Ephesians has picked up another Pauline theme, that a person is not saved by works (2:8f.). He interprets that motif as applying only to Gentiles who now share the heritage of Israel. You notice that where Paul would have spoken of their salvation as righteousness through faith, Ephesians speaks of grace. For the Catholic tradition, the cosmic picture of Church as body of Christ and the discussion of salvation as through the grace of God became the dominant formulations of these key Pauline doctrines.

Detailed study of the language of Ephesians shows that many of its non-Pauline features can be paralleled in the Qumran writings. This observation has led some to suggest that its author was a convert from such a sect to Paul's understanding of the Church as the new Israel including both Jews and Gentiles, and that Ephesians was composed as a circular letter or compendium of Pauline teaching.

Colossians

Colossians is closer to Pauline language and letter style than Ephesians. If Colossae was destroyed by the earthquake under Nero, then the letter would have had to be written during Paul's lifetime even if he himself did not do it. Unlike Ephesians, this letter does address itself to a specific problem, that described in 2:8-23. Earlier commentators—and some modern ones still—thought that this passage was directed against Gnostics. But some discoveries at Qumran have led us to understand this passage against the background of Jewish apocalyptic and mysticism. You can make some comparisons for yourself. First compare the language of this passage with Galatians 4:8-11. You notice that the Galatians are reprimanded for bondage to "elemental spirits" and keeping certain days as well as practicing circumcision. Colossians also insists that Gentiles do not have to be circumcised. It understands baptism not only as the Christian's death to sin—as we saw in Romans—but also as the Christian answer to circumcision. This comparison itself implies that the problem in Colossae is also Christians who wish to follow Jewish religious practices.

Verse 17-19 say that such people even forfeit their membership in the body of Christ. Many interpreters and translators have been mislead by the expression "worship of angels" into thinking that the Colossians were worshipping angels. The expression should be understood to mean "angelic worship," that is the worship that the angels carry on in heaven before the throne of God. You may know that in the Old Testament Isaiah (Isa 6) had a vision of the heavenly throne. The New Testament book of Revelation is full of heavenly liturgy. Paul tells us that he himself had a vision of God in which he heard the heavenly worship (2 Cor 12:1-10). The Essenes believed that their community shared angelic worship. We have already read one passage from their hymn book (I QH iii, 20-22; p.57)' where the living give thanks for being able to sing the praises of God with the angels. Here is a fragment of another work that describes the divine throne chariot:

> ... the ministers of the Glorious face in the abode of the gods of knowledge fall down before him and the cherubim utter blessings. And as they rise up, there is a divine small voice ... and loud praise; there is a divine small voice as they fold their wings.
>
> The cherubim bless the image of the Throne Chariot above the firmament, and they praise the majesty of the fiery firmament beneath the seat of his glory. And between the turning wheels, angels of holiness come and go, as it were a fiery vision of most holy spirits; and about them flow seeming rivulets of fire, like gleaming bronze, a radiance of many gorgeous colors.
>
> The spirits of the living God move perpetually with the glory of the wonderful chariot. The small voice of blessing accompanies the tumult as they depart, and on the path of their return they worship the Holy One. Ascending they rise marvelously; settling they stay still. The sound of joyful praise is silenced and there is a small voice of blessing in all the camp of God. And a voice of praise resounds from the midst of all their divisions in worship of ... and each one in his place and all their numbered ones sing hymns of praise.

Thus, the type of Judaizing being propagated at Colossae

seems to have stressed ascetic practices that would lead to such visions. The author does not deny the reality of such heavenly worship or that people have such visions. But like Paul in Corinthians, he knows that they are not the norm of Christian life, holiness or experience; a person should not seek after them. His answer to the problem comes in chapter 3. There he argues that "being raised up" with Christ does not manifest itself in the ability to join heavenly liturgy. To "seek things above where Christ is" means to live a life of Christian charity in the community. That same life of charity is true asceticism as opposed to those who discipline the body in order to see visions. This solution to the problem is exactly the same thing that Paul had said to the Corinthians when they were carried away with the various manifestations of the spirit in their liturgical life.

This collection of letters shows us how difficult it was for the Gentile Churches to arrive at a genuine sense of community. The spectacular effects of the spirit and the glories of personal religious experience seemed to be more impressive and more adequate modes of religious life and expression. We should not be surprised at their difficulty. We have seen that, at least for the urban population, old community structures and certainties had been breaking down in the wake of imperial expansion. They did not have the tradition of themselves as a separate people of God, which has sustained the Jews through so many centuries of exile. But we cannot help wondering if these letters do not also have something to say to our own situation. We see many people trying to attain visions, mystical experiences and other "highs" whether through drugs, ascetic practices, encounter groups or even prayer groups. The Pauline tradition would caution us against any thought that some form of "enlightenment" could or should be the norm and goal of Christian religious life—which does not mean that experiences of the Spirit are not part of Christianity. The Christian can only "find what is above with Christ" by carrying out his or her responsibilities in this life in the Christian Spirit of charity. Only faith, hope and love abide.

STUDY QUESTIONS

1. List the major episodes in Paul's relationship with the Corinthian Church.
2. Briefly describe the kind of religious experiences valued by the Corinthians.
3. What principles does Paul give the Corinthians to discern true religious experience?
4. Give three examples of Paul's use of the metaphor "body of Christ." What practical problem is he trying to solve in each case?
5. Why do you think that the Corinthian congregation was attracted by the preaching of the "super-apostles" in 2 Corinthians? Do you think they would gain a large following today? What modern methods would they use?
6. What are the signs of the true apostle according to Paul?
7. Describe how the image of the Church as body of Christ has been expanded in Colossians and Ephesians. How does their description differ from that in 1 Corinthians?
8. What is the image of the apostle in Colossians and Ephesians? How does that differ from Paul's description in 2 Corinthians?
9. What type of religious experiences were the Colossians seeking? How does the author of Colossians describe Christian religious experience?

Part IV

THE GOSPELS:
FOUR PORTRAITS OF JESUS

Chapter Ten

MARK: JESUS, HIDDEN AND SUFFERING MESSIAH

We have already seen that a variety of traditions about Jesus circulated in early Christianity. His sayings and miracles were collected; there was probably some account of the passion, and—at least in the formulaic fashion of 1 Corinthians 15:1-7—the resurrection was preached. But as far as we can tell, Mark was the first person to combine such disparate elements into the type of continuous narrative we call a "gospel."

Ancient Lives of Famous Men

We often think of gospels as biographies, but they are not biographies in the sense in which we understand the word. Such documents did not exist in antiquity. The modern biography would have been impossible to write then because people did not preserve the type of written records that we have become accustomed to since the invention of printing. Ancient biographical narrative has four basic characteristics:

(1) *Aim.* The point of telling anything about someone's life was to praise or idealize the subject from a specific viewpoint. Perhaps the person embodied great heroic virtues or was a wise man or had unusual powers, then anything told about his life would be told from that point of view. When you

191

read such an account you always have to ask yourself what the author is trying to teach you by the way in which he presents his hero. You should also remember that if you could have been on the scene, the individuals about whom he writes probably would not have acted exactly as they are portrayed. Authors arranged their accounts so as to present what was believed to be the truth about people: the praise or blame each deserved from posterity. That truth would not be best served by what we might consider objective, factual reporting.

(2) *Rhetoric played an important part in* all of ancient life. We have seen Paul using it in his letters. In a rhetorical culture, truth is not evaluated in terms of scientific objectivity but in terms of value, or praise or blame. The hero is praised; his enemies condemned. Often both activities were carried out in set formulae—like the formulae used in praising the emperors (p.123f). Such formulae were learned in schools. All information about a person or group from antiquity has to be sifted for such rhetorical content.

(3) *Characterization of people* in such accounts is—not surprisingly—quite different from what we are accustomed to. We like to see how someone's personality developed and changed in the course of his or her life. Such an idea is foreign to ancient writers. Whatever stories are told about a person's birth, childhood or youth are meant to show that he displayed his later virtues from his earliest days. Here is a section of the *Life of Moses* by the Hellenistic Jewish philosopher Philo:

> Therefore, the child (= Moses) being now thought worthy of a royal education was not long delighted with toys and objects of laughter and amusement like a mere child ... but he exhibited a modest and dignified deportment in all his words and gestures. He attended diligently to every lesson that could lead to the improvement of his mind. And right away he had all kinds of masters, some from neighboring countries and the different districts of Egypt, and some even from Greece. But in a short time he surpassed all their knowledge, anticipating all their lessons by the excellent natural endowments of his genius; so that every-

thing appeared to be recollecting rather than learning
in his case, while he himself without any teacher understood by his instinctive genius many difficult subjects; for great talent cuts out for itself many new
roads to knowledge.

What does Philo think that Moses' greatest virtue was? You
would not be surprised to learn after reading this passage that
other Hellenistic Jewish writers even claimed that all culture
came from Moses—both the philosophy of the Greeks and the
wisdom of the Egyptians.

(4) *Narrative Style.* The narrative style of ancient biographical accounts fits these concerns. Details of locale, time
and chronology are unimportant and often cannot be established precisely. Sometimes the various episodes in a story are
linked together by the itinerary of a wandering philosopher.
Usually the narrative is made up of short units, episodes, sayings, anecdotes, dialogues, speeches, testaments, death scenes,
court appearances, lists of disciples, letters, or—in the case of a
philosopher—schematic descriptions of his doctrine to show
that he embodied the virtues of an ideal philosopher.

What Is a Gospel?

Many of the features of other ancient lives are found in our
gospels. Scholars have realized for a long time that Mark
created a very general outline or itinerary for the life of Jesus
into which he has fitted independent units of tradition. Some
have even suggested that his model was the ancient popular
biographies of the philosophers. But the life of Jesus in Mark
does not fit that model well not because it ends in death—
antiquity had the example of Socrates as the philosopher
martyr—but because its treatment of suffering is quite different from popular biography. Popular stories emphasized the
hero's ability to triumph over his accusers and enemies. Even if
he is put to death like Socrates, the reader has no doubt about
his moral superiority to those who condemned him. All his
sayings and deeds turn out well and manifest his superiority to
ordinary human beings. Here, for example, is a story in which

the king of India gives his approval to the wisdom of the wandering philosopher Apollonius:

> When Apollonius and the king of India had thus conversed, for by now it was daylight, they went out into the open. Understanding that the king had to give audiences to embassies and such, Apollonius said, "You, O king, must attend to matters of state, but let me go and devote this hour to the sun for I must offer up to him my usual prayer." And the king said, "I pray that he will hear your prayer, for he will bestow his grace on all who find pleasure in your wisdom; but I will wait for you until you return for I have to decide some cases in which your presence will be of great help to me."

The collections of miracles, controversy stories and sayings used by Mark may also have had such triumphant overtones, but the narrative as we have it is shot through with ambiguity, misunderstanding and suffering. Even Jesus' own disciples fail to comprehend what he is telling them.

Mark's emphasis on the hiddenness and suffering of Jesus has led many interpreters to understand Mark's work as a presentation of the life and deeds of Jesus in light of the cross. He may use some of the biographical techniques of his time, but he is not adopting their ideology. For Mark, the true significance of Jesus' actions cannot be understood unless they are seen as the deeds of the Son of Man who came to suffer. This understanding of Mark's purposes is sometimes linked to another interpretation of his opening sentence: "Beginning of the gospel of Jesus Christ, Son of God." We usually do not pay too much attention to that opening because we think that the word "gospel" means book. But you may remember that in Galatians 1:6, 11 Paul is not using the word to mean book. It means preaching. He is objecting to the Galatians turning away from the message about salvation in Christ as he had preached it to them. Mark may be using "gospel" in the same way. He wants to present the "news or preaching" about Jesus Christ.

Redaction Criticism

In our discussion of life of Jesus research, we saw that in the past 20 years people have begun to pay particular attention to the theology of the synoptic evangelists. They ask how each one has rewritten and restructured his material so as to present a particular insight into the significance of Jesus. This task is more difficult in Mark and John than in Matthew and Luke because any sources used must be derived solely from literary analysis of the text. Although there is a strong division between scholars who view Mark as primarily indebted to Hellenistic models and those who see him as still concerned with questions arising from apocalyptic, they all agree that the suffering of Jesus plays a central place in Markan theology. They also agree that one of Mark's sources was a collection or collections of Jesus' miracles that form the basis for the first seven chapters. That collection was not concerned with the suffering of Jesus but with his miraculous power. Such "divine man" portraits of Jesus would be perpetuated in the apocryphal gospels of the following centuries. Here is a story from the Protoevangelium of James (3rd century A.D.).

> When he (= Jesus) was six, his mother gave him a pitcher and sent him to draw water and bring it to the house. But he stumbled in the crowd and the pitcher was broken. Jesus spread out the garment he was wearing, filled it with water and brought it to his mother. And when his mother saw the miracle, she kissed him and kept within herself the mysteries that she had seen him do.

Some people think that it was this divine man picture of Jesus expounded by Paul's opponents in 2 Corinthians. If so, then their interest in miraculous and ecstatic manifestations of the Spirit might have been perceived as merely imitating what Jesus had done. We have already pointed out, however, that it is very difficult to get precise information about a person's opponents in a rhetorical culture. 2 Corinthians is loaded with Hellenistic rhetorical *topoi*. The alternative to such a Hellenistic interpretation of the miracle traditions in Mark is to suggest that they represent an expansion of what may have been Jesus' own understanding of his miracles: the power of Satan is being broken up by the messianic power of God. This cosmic orientation is visible in many of the stories. Jesus has power over the demonic (Mk 1:23-28; 5:1-20); the forces of nature obey him (6:45-51). This collection may have been dominated by the desire to show that Jesus had inaugurated the salvation of the new age.

You may also notice as you read these early chapters of Mark that the miracles are broken up by dialogue, sayings or simple references to Jesus as teacher (e.g., 1:27 even though Jesus has not taught anything yet; 1:39). Another peculiarity of the stories as we have them are commands to silence (e.g. 1:34, why wouldn't Jesus allow the demons to speak?). Sometimes these commands do not even fit in with the rest of the story. Read Mark 1:43-45. The man does not do what Jesus commands at all, but does what most people would do when confronted by a miracle: he goes and tells. These peculiar demands for secrecy seem to have been added by the evangelist. The first example was from what we call a summary passage, which is clearly Mark's own composition. The second example does not fit into its context well. Both Matthew and Luke realized the difficulties, and each tell the story in a different way to avoid them (cf. Mt 8:4; Lk 5:15, the man does not spread the report). Markan scholars call this motif the "messianic secret" because Jesus does not seem to want people to know who he is.

It has also been pointed out that the stories in which Mark adds sayings of Jesus, really give us a message about the gospel. Look at the five stories in 2:1-3:7. These pronouncement stories have been framed by two miracle stories in which Jesus heals a paralytic. The points made in the miracle stories are the same as those made in the pronouncement stories:

(1) The Son of Man has authority on earth to forgive sins (2:10).

(2) Jesus has come to call sinners not the righteous (the NAB incorrectly translates *dikaios*, "just, righteous" as self-righteous). (2:17)

(3) Guests at the wedding cannot fast (2:19)

(4) The Son of Man is Lord of the Sabbath (2:28).

(5) Is it permitted to do good on the Sabbath? (3:4) Thus, Jesus emerges as promised in 1:27 as the one who teaches with authority. The first step in redaction criticism is to collect all such observations about how the evangelist consistently arranges his material and reinterprets his sources. The interpreter must then use these observations to tell us something about the evangelist's view of Jesus. That is the point at which varieties of opinion are most likely to enter.

Literary Structure of Mark

The previous section has already introduced two literary techniques that are important for discussing the structure of the gospel. The first, summary and transitional passages, is common to all the evangelists. These are passages composed by an evangelist either to sum up material he has already presented or to make the transition to new material. Mark 1:32-39 summarizes the activity of Jesus in Galilee. Notice how many typically Markan features are found there: the demons are not permitted to speak; Jesus even seems to avoid the crowds; he is presented as teaching (which we have not yet seen him do) and healing.

A second Markan technique is illustrated by the use of the two cures of paralysis to frame a section of sayings and controversy stories that deal with Jewish customs. Mark seems to choose such frame stories as deliberate comments on the actions that take place between them. Thus, he implies that Jesus' opponents—here, Jewish religious leaders—are like the paralyzed men. Another important set of healings, cures of two blind men (8:22-26; 10:46-52) frames the central section of the gospel where Jesus is trying to instruct the disciples about the divine necessity for his suffering and about the true nature of discipleship. But they do not understand that teaching; they are blind.

A third Markan technique has been called intercalation. It is similar to the framing device we have just discussed. Mark will begin a story; interrupt it with other material or another story, and then continue the story. Read Mark 3:20-35. Jesus' family arrive to get him in v 21 and then are neglected until vv 31ff. Meanwhile a controversy arises between Jesus and some scribes who have just arrived, over the power by which he works his miracles. In chapter 8, the story of the feeding of the 4,000 is interrupted by the Pharisee's request for a sign (8:1-21). Mark 5:21-43 and 11:12-25 are further examples of this technique. Some scholars have suggested that Mark is using this technique to comment on discipleship. The two intercalated stories are meant to comment on one another.

While authors vary in how they outline the gospel of Mark, no one doubts that 8:27ff., Peter's confession, is the pivotal event in the narrative. Before that only the reader and the demons know that Jesus is Son of God. Afterward the disciples know that he is the Messiah, but fail to understand why it is necessary for the Messiah to suffer. The climactic revelation of Jesus as Messiah comes in the trial scene when the High Priest asks if Jesus is the Messiah, Son of God, and he answers, "Yes" (14:61b-62). Of course that climax has negative consequences. Jesus is immediately condemned. The reader knows, however, that Jesus' enigmatic saying about the Son of Man is a judgment oracle against those who condemn Jesus. It says that when Jesus' enemies see the judgment, the Son of Man coming in glory, then he will be vindicated. The earthly Jesus whom they are going to have executed does not fulfill that role. He must follow the path of suffering messiahship that neither they nor his own disciples understand.

The gospel also contains a positive sequence of Son of God—another way of referring to the Messiah—sayings. Besides the demons' knowledge of Jesus' identity, his identity as Son of God is revealed three times in the narrative. First, God speaks at the baptism. As Mark tells the story, Jesus is the only one who hears the voice (1:11). God again reveals his identity when Jesus is transfigured before three of his disciples (9:7). Finally, the Gentile centurion who sees Jesus die declares—without any revelation, that Jesus was Son of God (15:39)—that is the climactic revelation in the gospel. Here is someone who does understand that Jesus' messiahship is revealed in suffering and death; not in glory and power. His confession combines with other motifs in Mark to suggest that his audience was primarily Gentile. Gentiles are frequently commended for their faith (e.g., Mark 5:20, the decapolis were Gentile cities; 7:24-31). Mark often explains Hebrew words and Jewish customs. Thus, there may be an implicit claim behind the story of the centurion: the Gentiles are the ones who have recognized the crucified Jesus as Messiah. The Jews are caught in the paralysis portrayed in chapters 2 and 3.

Major Themes in Mark

We have already touched on several key Markan themes: the miracle-working of Jesus' public ministry; Jesus' authority to annul Jewish Law; the messianic secret; the centrality of Jesus' suffering in defining his role as Messiah; the progressive revelation of his identity as Son of God and the coming of the Son of Man as judge and vindicator of Jesus' message. But there is one theme we have not discussed at all: that of fear and misunderstanding. You may be surprised to see fear as a major motif in a gospel, but Mark has a persistent pattern to his portrayal of the disciples: they do not understand Jesus and they are afraid.

We may begin our study of fear in Mark by turning to the end of the gospel. If you look at the notes in your Bible, you will discover that the end of Mark is a problem. Our earliest manuscripts end at 16:8. Later versions contain other endings, but these are all composites drawn from the other synoptics. Further, Matthew and Luke diverge and are quite different after this point, which suggests that whatever version of Mark they had, it did not contain anything after 16:8. It seems likely then that Mark did not conclude his gospel with an appearance of the risen Lord. We can tell from the way the resurrection stories are told in the other gospels that they circulated independently and were not harmonized with each other. Mark 16:7 suggests that he expected his readers to know the story of an appearance of Jesus to Peter and the others, though he might be referring to a list-type resurrection creed as the one Paul gives in 1 Corinthians 15:5. (Some scholars even go so far as to suggest that Mark is not referring to the resurrection at all but to a Christian view—perhaps in opposition to Jewish expectations for Jerusalem—that the parousia would take place in Galilee.) This story also hints at the centrality of the resurrection appearance in initiating the mission of the Church—a common feature of many resurrection accounts. Yet the gospel ends with the words ". . . and they said nothing to anyone, for they were afraid."

To understand that ending we must see how Mark uses fear elsewhere in the gospel. Look up the passages in a concordance. Then ask yourself who is afraid and why. You could divide the instances into three groups.

(1) Officials are afraid to act against John the Baptist (6:20) and Jesus (11:18; 12:12). That fear represents recognition of their popularity and is not particularly surprising.

(2) But in chapter 5 we also find people who receive miracles from Jesus being afraid (5:14, 33, 36). The last two instances are instructive because they help us see what the alternative to "fear" is. In both instances, faith is the positive correlate that an individual should display in order to receive a miracle/salvation from Jesus. The type of fear exhibited here is also expressed by another term, amazement or astonishment. We are frequently told that people were amazed at what Jesus did. But before we assume that Mark considers amazement a positive indication of faith, we should read Mark 6:1-6. The people are astonished by Jesus' teachings and works but they do not believe. In fact, their lack of faith limits the miracles Jesus will work. This link between astonishment and disbelief seems to be Mark's way of questioning the automatic validity of the miraculous in producing faith—something that his miracle source would have presumed. He follows this story of rejection with the commissioning of the disciples—they should learn from it what the disciple has to expect.

(3) But the disciples are afraid too. First, the miraculous power of Jesus frightens them (Mk 4:40f; 6:50, they are afraid

even though they have already seen a similar miracle!). Notice that Mark 4:40f. makes the same connection between astonishment and disbelief that we have already seen in the crowd. Out of fear, Peter proposes to set up three tents at the transfiguration and is rebuked by God's revelation that Jesus is Messiah (9:6f.). The disciples are also afraid because of Jesus' teaching—especially his predictions of the passion (10:32, again note the negative connotations of fear/amazement). It seems that people's first reaction to Jesus in Mark is fear or amazement. No one—not even the disciples—has instant faith in him. Even they who have seen all the miracles and have had private teaching from Jesus, journey to Jerusalem in terror and amazement. No one is saved by Jesus unless he or she gets beyond that road block. Both Mark and his readers know, of course, that some people—including the disciples!—were able to do so.

Mark's Picture of Jesus

We can now pull some of these themes together under the two topics that dominate his gospel: Who is Jesus and what does it mean to be his disciple? We have seen that Mark's presentation of Jesus combines two things: great power and authority and hiddenness, secrecy and suffering. The two do not fit together easily yet Mark insists on both. Some interpreters have dissolved the tension by assigning all the motifs of power and glory to Mark's sources or to the theology of some alleged opponents—usually of the 2 Corinthians type—against whom he is writing. We agree with others who refuse to make such a dichotomy. Mark has a more nuanced view of faith than to attribute it simply to the miraculous, but that does not mean that he rejects that side of the tradition. One could argue instead that the power and authority of Jesus point up the true significance of his suffering and death. A person who is obeyed by wind, sea and demons cannot be in the same category as the rest of us—even the great martyrs. He does not suffer because of the evil inherent in the structure of the world and humanity; he suffers only because it is part of a pre-

ordained divine plan, a mode of service that was freely chosen
(10:45). Therefore, his suffering is not a victory for the evil and
demonic powers against which he has been struggling.

Mark's picture of Jesus draws upon the Christian tradition
to provide a complex picture of Jesus as Messiah. This picture
is dominated by the theme that the Son of Man must suffer.
Jewish messianic scenarios sometimes have Elijah precede the
new age. Mark 9:11-13 points to the death of John the Baptist
as proof of two things: (a) Elijah did return; (b) he had to suffer
just as Jesus will have to. The mocking of Jesus at the crucifixion challenges him to perform as the Messiah was expected
to—to save Israel. How could he do that if he could not even
save himself from the Romans?

The same combination of suffering and glory is inherent in
Mark's use of the Son of Man expression to describe Jesus. Both
the revelation that Jesus is Messiah at 8:27f. and that at
14:61f. shift immediately to an assertion about the Son of Man.
The first moves to a prediction of the passion; the second, to his
coming in glory as judge (cp. Mk 13:32). Son of Man is Mark's
favorite designation for Jesus. Recently many complicated
theories have been suggested as to how Christians came to
apply this very elusive metaphor from Daniel 7:13ff. to Jesus.
In Mark's case it is clear that he is relying on earlier Christian
usage. We have seen that the predominant traits of the
metaphor in Judaism are power, glory, heavenly exaltation
and judgment (cf. p. 52). But in Mark after 8:27 the predominant use of the metaphor, 9 of 12 occurrences, is in the
context of suffering and service. Mark 13:26 and 14:62 preserve
the apocalyptic use of the term for the glorious eschatological
judge. Thus Mark is using this symbol to blend authority, glory
and suffering just as he has combined the two themes by following the first passion prediction with the transfiguration
story.

This combination has led some recent authors to emphasize the elements of apocalyptic in Mark's thought. They
refer 16:7 to the second coming; take the apocalyptic discourse
in Mark 13 as the central focus of the whole gospel, and some

even go so far as to interpret the whole of Mark as an apocalypse. Many such presentations are marred by the failure to distinguish traditional materials (like most of Mark 13) used by the evangelist from his own redaction. He is no more or less apocalyptic than Paul or perhaps Jesus himself. Further, it frequently happens that when suffering is an issue—and it was in many of the communities that produced Jewish apocalyptic writings—as it is here (cf. Mk 13:9-13), apocalyptic revelations provide consolation. Mark has edited chapter 13 in such a way as to discourage apocalyptic speculation. *No one* can know when the end will come; Christians are not to be led astray by false prophets and Messiahs trying to tell them it is at hand (13:21f.). But Mark is confident that when it does come it will be a time of salvation for the elect who have suffered in this world (13:37). For Mark, the suffering they must endure is very specific: persecution from both Jews and Gentiles for the sake of the gospel (13:9-13).

Mark's Picture of the Disciples

This emphasis on suffering is central to the Markan picture of discipleship. The disciple is asked to suffer as Jesus has done. Read Mark 6:1-29. The commission of the disciples is placed between Jesus' rejection and the death of John the Baptist. Most of the instruction on discipleship, sandwiched between the passion predictions in chapters 9 and 10, deals with the necessity to reject earthly standards of glory and success in favor of following the suffering Son of Man. But we also saw in our study of fear in Mark that throughout the gospels the disciples are following Jesus but are afraid.

Besides their fear, the disciples do not seem to understand much of what Jesus tells them. He rebukes them for not understanding the parables (4:13); the miracle of the loaves (8:17f.), and the necessity of his passion (8:31f.). They don't even ask about the resurrection (9:10). They compete for places of honor in the kingdom (9:33-35; 10:35-45), and yet are not as good at exorcism in the name of Jesus as an unknown person who is not even a disciple (contrast 9:18f. with 9:38-40). Though they

seem a thoroughly incompetent crowd, they are entrusted with
the mission, and are given the mystery of the kingdom of God
(4:11). We know from the Qumran writings that the expression
"mystery" was used for teaching which God had given the
founder (I QH i,21; ii,13; I QpHab 7:5). These texts indicate
that what is involved is not only his instruction in the eschatological interpretation of Scripture but also instruction
about how the community should please God. Here the disciples have a similar privileged relationship with Jesus.

Some rather extreme interpreters have argued that Mark
must have been opposed to the original disciples to place them
in such a negative light. Even granting the tendency of the
tradition toward hero worship and to idealize the disciples—
note the treatment Paul receives from his disciples in Colossians and Ephesians—the disciples themselves cannot have
been quite as stupid as the Markan narrative suggests. (Or we
might question Jesus' own judgment in choosing them!) Even
when he is most vitriolic about Peter, Paul does not say anything as negative as the portrait of him here. We must ask
what literary purpose Mark had in mind. We suggest that it is
similar to the combination of power, glory and suffering that
we saw in his picture of Jesus. His gospel was probably written
shortly after Peter had suffered martyrdom—others had suffered that fate even earlier. It is unlikely, therefore, that any
Christian reader would not know that Peter, James and John
did indeed drink the same cup as Jesus (10:38f.). But their
martyrdom is not enough to explain the emphasis on suffering
in the gospel.

It seems likely that the Christians for whom Mark wrote
were also being persecuted for preaching the gospel. They
might well have wondered why Jesus did not work miracles for
them. Could he really save those who believed? By stressing
both the glory of Jesus and his own commitment to suffering,
Mark's picture answers such doubts. Jesus is indeed Savior. He
is more powerful than failure, sin, disease and death, but he
does not magically rescue either himself or his followers from

them. The almost ludicrous portrait of the disciples may be seen as encouragement to Christians in Mark's Church. Everyone knows what the disciples eventually became, but people might be tempted to think that they did so because of special endowments since birth—the usual explanation in ancient biography! In fact, Mark says they were even a little "below average." Their success, then, is not due to any native endowments but to the same spirit that assists any Christian under trial (13:11).

STUDY QUESTIONS

1. Briefly describe the way in which ancient biographies were written. How do they differ from modern biographies?
2. How does Mark's picture of Jesus and the disciples differ from the kind of portrait one would expect from an ancient biographer?
3. How has Mark changed the outlook of the miracle source that he used?
4. Describe three literary characteristics of Mark's gospel. Give an example of each one.
5. What are the three scenes in which Jesus is proclaimed Son of God in Mark? What does that sequence of scenes tell us about Jesus' messiahship? About the audience for which Mark was written?
6. What role do fear and misunderstanding play in Mark? How does that motif fit into the purpose for which Mark was written?
7. What is Mark's picture of Jesus? How does he use the Son of Man metaphor to present that view?
8. What is Mark's view of Christian discipleship?

Chapter Eleven

MATTHEW: JESUS, THE TRUE
TEACHER OF ISRAEL

Since many people think of Jesus predominantly in terms of his teaching, you may have been surprised to find so little of Mark devoted to what Jesus actually taught. Both Matthew and Luke add substantially to that dimension of Jesus' activity in their gospels. But the milieu out of which each writes is quite different. Luke is a Gentile writing for other Gentiles. Matthew, on the other hand, seems to have been a Jewish convert writing for a Church that has separated from the synagogue and has made a peaceful non-traumatic—unlike some of the Pauline Churches—transition to including both Jews and Gentiles in one community. You can see one hint of Matthew's Jewish background if you compare his version of the story about plucking grain on the Sabbath (Mt 12:1-8) with Mark's (Mk 2:23-28). Matthew supplies a motive for their action, hunger. Instead of concluding with what appears a general rejection of Sabbath Law (The Sabbath was made for man; not man for the Sabbath.), he only asserts Jesus' authority to interpret Sabbath law. He also includes two additional Old Testament arguments to support the validity of the specific deed done by the disciples: obtaining food to satisfy hunger. In short, he treats the issue as a legal case laid before a Jewish scribe. The citation from Hosea 6:6 is a key one for understanding the difference between Christian and Jewish legislation in

Matthew's view. Christians come down on the side of mercy—
as did some schools among the Pharisees, though one would
never guess it from Matthew's negative portrayal of them!

Sources and Composition

We have already discussed one example of how Matthew
used Mark. (Luke 6:1-5 also smooths out the story but does not
add additional legal argument.) We have also seen that
Matthew and Luke had a common source of sayings material,
"Q," which is sometimes arranged differently by the two
evangelists. Still other material is unique to Matthew. Sometimes the same formal and stylistic analysis as used in source
criticism of Mark can be applied to Matthew to show that that
special material probably derives from oral or written tradition
and is not the free composition of the evangelist. Parts of it
may go back to Jesus himself—each saying or parable must be
assessed on its individual merits.

The most striking literary feature of Matthew is the set of
five discourses that punctuate the work. The Sermon on the
Mount is the most famous. Since they represent Matthew's own
redactional activity in gathering sayings material together,
they may well be taken as a key to the organization of the
gospel. Each one ends with a set formula, "and when Jesus
finished . . ." (7:28; 11:1; 13:53; 19:1; 26:1). We may suggest the
following outline:

Prologue   (chs. 1 and 2): Jesus, Messiah from Galilee.

Narrative   (chs. 3 and 4): Commissioning of Jesus; selection
                             of disciples.

Discourse   (chs. 5-7):   Sermon on the Mount: The Righ-
                             teousness of the Kingdom

Narrative   (chs. 8 and 9): Jesus Messiah heals and teaches
                             on journey.

Discourse   (ch. 10-11:1):   Instruction: teaching and healing
                                 mission of the disciples.

Narrative   (cf. 11:2-12):   Jesus the merciful Messiah in
                                 controversy with Israel.

Discourse   (13:1-53):   Parables of the Kingdom

Narrative   (13:54-17:21):   Jesus Messiah, shepherd of Israel.

Discourse   (17:22-19:1):   Advice to a divided community

Narrative   (19:2-23):   Controversies over Greatness and
                                 Rewards in the Kingdom; Je-
                                 sus, Messiah condemns false
                                 shepherds of Israel

Discourse   (ch. 24—26:1):   The end of the age and judgment

Conclusion   (26:2—end):   Death and resurrection of Jesus
                                 Messiah

This outline does not solve all the problems of understanding
the structure of Matthew. You will notice that the narrative
sections also contain much discourse material. Chapter 23 is
organized as a continuous series of woes. Other outlines have
been attempted. A recent one begins from the expressions
"from that time Jesus began . . ." and suggests a threefold division:

    (1) 1:1-4:16—The Person of Jesus Messiah

    (2) 4:17-16:20—The Preaching of Jesus Messiah

    (3) 16:21-28:20—Trial, death and resurrection of Jesus
    Messiah

The main difficulty with this division is the large number of teaching chapters in part three. Therefore, we are still convinced that some variant of the five discourse scheme is the most adequate way of understanding the structure of Matthew.

However, you frequently read in older books or in popular writers who have not kept up with scholarly developments that the five discourses are a symbolic representation of the five books of the Mosaic Torah. Very few Matthean scholars accept that view today. At best only three of the five discourses could be considered Torah, that is legislation about how Christians should achieve the higher righteousness that belongs to the kingdom. Secondly Matthew never questions the validity of the Torah (cf. 5:17ff. and 23:3). The issue is how the Torah is interpreted now that the Messiah has come (7:12). Matthew even envisaged the possibility of Christian scribes (13:52—a description of Matthew's own role?). Third, and most important, Matthew does not use other common motifs from the Jewish Moses typology to parallel Jesus and Moses. Instead, much of his language about Jesus comes from the Old Testament wisdom tradition. The name Emmanuel, God is with us, can be tied to that tradition as are the expressions used for Jesus in 11:18f.; 11:28-30; 23:34-36, 37-39. You can see that for yourself if you compare the great invitation of Matthew 11:28-30: "Come to me all who labor and are heavy laden and I will give you rest. Take my yoke upon you and learn from me; for I am gentle and lowly in heart and you will find rest for your souls. For my yoke is easy and my burden light," with such Old Testament passages as Ecclesiasticus 51:23-30; 24:19-22; Proverbs 1:20-23; 8:1-21.

There Wisdom calls out to people to receive instruction from her. She promises them rest instead of the toil and labor of human life. Such language has also influenced Matthew's presentation of the miracles of Jesus. Whereas in Mark they were demonstrations of power and authority, in Matthew they demonstrate Jesus' compassion, humility and mercy (cf. 8:17; 9:36; 11:29; 12:7).

A recent study of Matthew's passion narrative has shown

that he uses the picture of the suffering righteous person from Wisdom 2 as a model in his redaction of Mark.Therefore, Matthew's Christology is not based on Moses typology but on a Wisdom typology. Jesus is greater than Moses. He does not give Torah but embodies the Wisdom of God, which is Torah in its most primordial and cosmic form (cf. 2 Bar 3:29-4:4). This understanding helps us reconcile two dominant themes in Matthew: his concern with Jesus as teacher, which has long been recognized, and his interest in the person of Jesus, which is the focus of many recent studies of Matthew.

The Old Testament as Testimony to Jesus

We have already seen that from the beginning Christians claimed that Jesus had fulfilled the prophecies of the Old Testament. Matthew, as might be expected, is most particular about demonstrating that point. Two things about Jesus are clear. He was not directly from the line of Davidic kings; indeed, there was no clear line of succession in this period. Secondly, he is always reported to have been a Galilean and to have carried on his ministry there. But Galilee was considered practically pagan country; Judea was the proper place for a Messiah, and Jerusalem with its temple, the proper focus of his activity. You can see that Matthew goes to great lengths to explain both points in chapters 1 and 2. Jesus is son of David by adoption into Joseph's lineage, and he is said to have originally come from Bethlehem in Judea but to have been brought up in Galilee. (Luke's infancy narrative and geneology preserve quite different traditions. Both Luke and Matthew have been so thoroughly reworked that it is impossible to separate historical fact from legendary elaboration in these stories.)

You will notice that five times in these two chapters Matthew follows a detail in the life of Jesus with an explicit Old Testament quotation set off by some version of the phrase, "This was done to fulfill what was spoken . . ." (1:23; 2:6, 15, 18, 23). These quotations are called formula quotations and occur six more times (4:15f.; 8:17; 12:18-21; 13:14, 35; 21:5; 27:9f.). We know that the Essenes made collections of Old Testament quotations about the Messiah. That discovery led Matthean scholars to suggest that Matthew took his quotations from a similar Christian collection. The point of such quotations is apologetic. Matthew does not mean that anyone who reads the Old Testament would immediately expect the life of Jesus as its fulfillment. Nor does he wish to suggest that Jesus went around with a list of Old Testament passages in his head checking off which ones he had fulfilled. Rather they— like the dreams in the infancy narrative—validate the divine origin of Jesus' mission. Things that seem strange or offensive to the usual understanding of the Messiah are shown to be in accord with what God had revealed in the Old Testament. The messianic identity and origins of Jesus come in for top priority. Now if you look at the other quotations you can see what some of the other problematic areas were:

4:15-16: Jesus' Galilean Ministry. Why didn't he start in Jerusalem. Notice that the quotation identifies Galilee as Gentile country. The Jewish Messiah whose reign was to be a manifestation of God to the Gentiles instead begins his ministry in their territory.

8:17: Jesus' Healing Ministry. In order to understand why that needed explanation, you must remember that the Messiah was not required or expected to be a miracle worker. Once the new age came, death and disease would be abolished along with evil, but that was not necessarily a sign of the Messiah himself. We have seen that miracles are subject to many interpretations. They might prove that a person was a divine man or a magician with a familiar spirit. Mark shows that Jesus' miracles were considered evidence that the kingdom of God was dawning and the power of Satan being broken. We have also seen that Jews were reticent about attributing miraculous powers to an individual. Matthew, therefore, focuses on Old Testament passages about the humility and lowliness of the servant of God and uses them to explain the motivation for Jesus' miracles.

12:18-21: Opposition to Jesus. This quotation applies to the turn that Jesus' ministry takes in Matthew 11:1-12:16. The opposition to Jesus has become such that the Pharisees are seeking to kill him. He is forced to withdraw from where he has been preaching. This passage refers to the anonymity of the servant of God and his preaching to the Gentiles. Matthew understands Jesus' rejection by the Jews as the reason for the Gentile mission. Notice that in Matthew 10:5 the disciples are sent out only to Jews. But the Jews are rejecting Jesus. This quotation explains his withdrawal from where he had been preaching and the fact well-known to Matthew's readers that the Gentiles and not the Jews were the ones to accept Jesus as Messiah.

13:14: Rejection of Jesus. This quotation is taken over from Mark to explain Jewish rejection of Jesus' preaching.

13:35: Matthew then has an additional quotation to make the same point.

21:5: Allusions to this passage (Zech 9:9) are different in different versions of the passion story. It allows public acclamation of the messiahship of Jesus.

27:9-10: Judas. The Old Testament passage may be the source for the tradition about the amount given Judas. It may have originally been used not merely to explain Jesus' betrayal by Judas but his rejection by Israel as a whole. In addition to these formula quotes, many other Old Testament quotes are used within the discourses and controversy stories. We have already seen Matthew add such material to the Markan story about plucking grain. The combined force of this additional Old Testament material is to give Matthew as a whole a distinctly Jewish flavor. But it is Jewishness for a Church that has included the Gentiles and is separating itself from the synagogue. They are the new Israel to whom God has given his vineyard (21:43).

Jesus as Teacher

We have already seen that discourse and teaching material dominate this gospel; that Matthew apparently thought of himself as a Christian scribe, who made the teaching of Jesus accessible and relevant to Christians of his day. Indeed, the gospel ends with an injunction to the disciples to go and teach the Gentiles to observe everything Jesus has taught (28:19). The Messiah was expected to teach the right interpretation of the Torah. Jesus is portrayed as doing just that. Matthew seems to have conceived the messianic function of Jesus to have been teaching a "higher righteousness" than that of the Pharisees. He has formulated his position against two sorts of adversaries:

(1) The Jewish teachers of his own day—Matthew seems to have been aware of the movement toward shaping Judaism in the pharisaic mold that was going on in the decades after the Jewish War and to have opposed it. The picture of Judaism in Matthew is almost entirely assimilated to Judaism of Matthew's time. His Church seems to have been separated from but not totally alienated from Judaism. On the one hand, we find references to the Jews in "their synagogue" (4:23; 9:35; 12:9; 13:54; 10:17). On the other hand, we have a discussion of the temple tax (17:24-27), which suggests that while Christians did not feel obligated to pay, Jewish Christians did so in order not to give *them* (= Jewish authorities) offense.

(2) Christians who would reject the Law entirely—The Christian is not bound by the Law as it is expounded by Jewish teachers. We have seen Paul speak of Christ as the end of the Law. Matthew does not agree (5:17ff.). But there were apparently Christian teachers, Matthew calls them "false prophets," who were dispensing with the Law. Matthew accuses them of empty displays of spiritual power (7:15-23). Notice that in Matthew 3:10 John the Baptist directs an eschatological judgment saying about not bearing good fruit at the Pharisees. Matthew 7:19 has Jesus direct the same saying at the "false prophets." Read the warning against scandalizing other Christians in Matthew 18:5-9. ("Little ones" is Matthew's favorite term for Christians.) That, too, is a warning against false teaching within the community.

How, then, is Jesus the messianic lawgiver? First of all, there is no indication that Matthew understands the Law in any way differently from Judaism. If you again look at his version of the story of plucking grain on the Sabbath, you will see that while Mark almost flaunts Christian freedom from the Law, Matthew treats the whole as a matter of interpretation—as indeed such regulations about keeping the Sabbath were. So many of the Sabbath regulations in that time had no real Old Testament basis that an early mishnaic text says: "The rules for the Sabbath are like mountains hanging by a hair, for Scripture is scanty and the rules many" (m. Hagihah 1:8; T. Hag. 1:9)—and that from Jews who were devoted to the Sabbath. We know that there were widely differing views about how the Sabbath was to be observed in Judaism, and hence Matthew may be quite correct in seeing the dispute as a matter of interpretation, not rejection of the Law.(It is not surprising that almost all Jewish authors write about the historical Jesus as though he were the Jesus of Matthew.) Matthew 23:3 goes so far as to give a positive assessment of pharisaic teaching but to reject their practice.

As the Messiah, Jesus is the authoritative interpreter of the Law. He calls people back to the will of God expressed creation (5:45; 6:26ff.). Like the Pharisees of the Hillel tradition, he invokes the golden rule (7:12) or the twofold commandment of love (20:40) as the epitome of the Law. But his stress on mercy as the chief characteristic of Jesus' interpretation and activity is equally important (e.g., 5:7; 18:33; 9:13; 12:7). The perfect fulfillment of God's will is held up as the ideal by the Law (Lev 19:2 Dt 18:13 cp Mt 5:48) and is realized in following Jesus (19:16-30).

You have doubtless noticed that, like Paul, Matthew speaks of "righteousness." But he does not associate it with faith and the death of Christ in the same way that Paul does. Faith is the mark of the disciple (cf. 8:5-10, 24ff.), but his righteousness is not tied to faith. Righteousness comes through following the true interpretation of the will of God given by the Messiah. Christians stand in continuity with the righteous people of the Old Testament. The disciple is persecuted because of his or her righteousness (5:10f.). Righteousness is equivalent to piety (6:1; 6:33). The disciples must have greater righteousness than the scribes and Pharisees (5:20). The discussion of rewards for prophets and righteous people in Matthew 10:41f.

suggests that Matthew's community may have used the term "the righteous" for Christians.

Matthew wishes to distinguish Christian righteousness from that of the Jews. We should be careful how far we take his language though, since his accusations are certainly unfair to Jewish piety and religious sensibilities—as he doubtless knew. Remember we are dealing with rhetorical polemic that seeks to persuade people that Christian righteousness is superior to what is taught by the Jews. Matthew accuses the Pharisees of hypocrisy, of keeping trivial external details and neglecting the serious matters of the Law (15:1-20; 23:23). He also claims that Christians will engage in those practices shared by the two groups in a different spirit. Read Matthew 6:1-18. Here the three fundamental religious practices of the devout Jew: almsgiving, fasting and prayer are retained. But the Jews are accused of performing them like hypocrites (6:2, 5, 16) or like Gentiles (6:7) for public approbation. True (= Christian) piety seeks to conceal itself.

Matthew's Picture of the Church

One can say that for Matthew Jesus' messianic interpretation of the Law makes it possible for all people to attain the righteousness promised in the Old Testament. We have seen that he shows the Gentiles responding to Jesus more favorably than the Jews (8:10b)—even though the earthly Jesus insists that his mission is to the lost sheep of Israel. Now that the Jews have rejected that preaching, the mission goes to the Gentiles. The judgment sayings in 23:39 and 26:64 claim that the next time the Jews see Jesus it will be as messianic judge.

We have also seen hints that there are problems within the Christian community itself. The "wolves in sheep's clothing" are clearly Christians who are unfaithful to the gospel. Chapter 18 contains various rules for church discipline that give us some insight into the kind of problems encountered in the community. None of them are unusual. They appear in the rule books of the Qumran sect and elsewhere in the New Testament. You will notice that instructions to Peter frame the section. Matthew is generally thought to have been written around Antioch in Syria, an area in which the structures and ideals of the community took shape around the apostle Peter.

17:24-27: Peter is instructed to pay the Temple tax. We have seen that this instruction insisted on Christian freedom from Jewish authority but was willing to pay not to give offense.

18:1-4: The specific instructions are introduced by an example of what greatness in the Christian community should be.

18:5-9: A warning against scandal and false teachers.

18:10-14: Christians are told how to treat a fellow Christian who has gone astray.

18:15-20: This section deals with a common problem: How should Christians deal with disputes among themselves. Remember 1 Corinthians 6 where Paul rebuked the Corinthians for going to pagan courts rather than having a way to deal with such matters themselves. Here we have a description of just such a procedure. There are many legal parallels to the legislation described in rabbinic materials and at Qumran. The expression, "Tell it to the Church" implies a legal proceeding of some kind. (cp. that against the man in 1 Corinthians 5:3-6 which was carried out in a solemn assembly and in the name of Jesus.) Verse 18-20 promises that all such proceedings will have the authority of Jesus.

18:21-22: Instruct Peter on forgiveness between Christians just as Paul reminded the Corinthians that forgiveness rather than judgment was the norm established by Jesus (1 Cor 6:7).

18:23-35: The Parable of the Unforgiving Servant concludes this discourse on a note of warning. Christians who fail to act on the instructions about forgiving a brother may expect to find themselves in the same position as that servant. They have no right to judge other Christians or to treat them harshly.

At the same time that he makes demands upon the Church, Matthew also wishes to encourage them to remain faithful. Compare the stories of Jesus Walking on Water in Mark 6:45-52 and Matthew 14:22-33. You can see that in Mark the disciples misunderstand Jesus from beginning to end. Not so in Matthew, there they begin by being frightened but wind up worshipping Jesus as Son of God. Matthew has a special incident about Peter (vv 28-31). Although Peter does not fare too well, he does become an example of the kind of trust in Jesus that the disciple should have. The rebuke against "being of little faith" occurs elsewhere in Matthew (6:30; 8:26; 16:8). He is using the disciples as negative examples. Christians are not to be of little faith but are to remain confident in Jesus.

Judgment and Christian Life

We have seen that Matthew emphasizes mercy as the norm of Jesus' interpretation of the Law. But his gospel is also full of language about judgment (7:21-23; 10:14f., 40-42; 12:36-37; 13:24-30, 36-43, 47-50; 16:27; 18:23-35). The final discourse deals with watchfulness and the coming of Christ in judgment. His preaching about judgment has two sides to it. First, there is the common apocalyptic theme that the Messiah will judge *the nations*, that is, the sinners and the Gentiles. We have seen that many, both Jews and Christians, held that the righteous were spared that judgment. The famous parable about the sheep and the goats is a parable of how Jesus will judge *the nations*. It is not about how he will judge Christians who believe in him but about how he will deal with non-believers. You may remember that the Jews had different views about whether or not non-Jews would be saved. Some thought that all would be condemned; others that those who did what the Law required without knowing it would be saved. This parable takes that more liberal view. Non-believers will be judged in terms of how they treat "the least of these," which is another of Matthew's expressions for Christians (cp. "little ones"). He makes a similar claim in Matthew 10:40-42. Christ is represented by his followers and non-believers will be rewarded or condemned on the basis of how they treat Christ in his representatives.

But Matthew will not let Christians think for a minute that those in the Church are free from judgment. Before he treated the issue of how non-believers would be judged, Matthew told three parables about faithful and unfaithful servants to warn Christians that they should remain vigilant even if it seems a long time until the judgment (24:45-25:30).

His addition to the story of the wedding feast (22:11-14) warns Christians that it is possible for a Christian not to be saved at the judgment. Christians must produce the fruits of righteousness that belong to the teaching of Jesus. The parable of the unforgiving servant that concluded the instructions to the community is a good example of that demand. The Christians will be held to Jesus' teaching on forgiveness. For the Christian, Matthew's warnings on the judgment are to motivate him or her to carry out the responsibilities inherent in the "higher righteousness" revealed by Jesus. At the same time, Christians should also realize from the merciful forgiveness of the master at the beginning of the story that Jesus did not come just to lay down a new Law with a big stick behind it. He came as the holy and merciful Messiah to seek and save what was lost, both Jew and Gentile.

STUDY QUESTIONS

1. Outline the main sections of Matthew. What does this outline tell us about Matthew's portrayal of Jesus?
2. Explain how Matthew's redaction of the story of Plucking Grain on the Sabbath fits the teaching of Jesus into contemporary Judaism.
3. What is a "formula quotation"? What role do they play in Matthew? Why did the early Christians make collections of such Old Testament quotations?
4. How does Matthew interpret the miracles of Jesus?
5. How does Matthew use the word "righteousness"? What is the importance of righteousness in Christian life? How is

Christian righteousness different from Judaism according to Matthew?

6. Describe two problems facing Matthew's community. How does Matthew give a solution to those problems through the teaching of Jesus?

7. Explain the teaching Matthew derives from the story of Jesus Walking on Water; from the parable of the Unforgiving Servant?

8. What is Matthew's teaching about judgment? Why does he find it necessary to preach judgment to Christians?

Chapter Twelve

LUKE: JESUS, SON OF GOD

If Matthew is the most Jewish of the gospel writers, Luke is the most educated, urbane Gentile among them. The way in which he writes Greek, the literary conventions he employs, the details of the life of Jesus that interest him and even the hints we get as to the type of people who made up his community suggest the relatively well-off milieu of the Hellenistic cities—albeit one in which Christians might still suffer some persecution for their faith. For example, it has long been noticed that the questions of wealth and its proper use play a much larger role in Luke than they do in the other gospels. Commentators have pointed out that Luke does not require such people to sell everything but to give generously to the poor (19:1-10; Ac 4:34-5:11).

While some may object to such a moderate reading of the ethical demands of Christianity, it is important to remember that almsgiving was not an ethical virtue for Luke's audience. The Jewish community from which Jesus and the earliest Christians came had always been instructed to show concern for the poor. But an educated, well-off Gentile would not have received any such instruction. One might be generous to friends from whom one could later expect to receive similar benefits but never to those who could not be expected to reciprocate. Luke must show such people that almsgiving is an important ethical ideal. He does so by portraying the early Christian community and Jesus himself as embodying the Hellenistic ideals of friendship and hospitality. As you read the stories in Luke you will find that he places a great deal of emphasis on details of lodging and how people are entertained. Jesus and his disciples fulfill the ideals of friendship and hospitality.

Another general characteristic of Luke is his optimistic attitude toward the world and the Roman social structure. He does not stress the sinfulness of the world or its impending end. You can see this contrast clearly if you compare the following passages that you read in Matthew with their counterparts in Luke:

Matthew 6:22f.//Luke 11:34-36: Matthew ends with darkness, a metaphor he associates with judgment. For Luke, on the other hand, the promise of light, salvation, is the dominant feature of the saying.

Matthew 7:1f.//Luke 6:37f.: Luke stresses the abundance to be received; Matthew the judgment.

This mood is manifest in yet another way in both the Gospel of Luke and the Acts of the Apostles. There is constant emphasis on the joy or rejoicing of all who hear the message about Jesus. If you turn to the end of the gospel (Lk 24:52f.), you will find joy and praise of God as its final notes (contrast Mark: "And they were afraid"). There are references to suffering and persecution in the Lucan writings but even they are met with triumphant joy (cf. Ac 5:41; 8:39). Thus, Luke's reader gains a picture of the confident and triumphant progress of Christianity. Everything takes place by divine guidance and protection. And, by and large, this triumphant picture of the early Church is the one most Christians grow up with. They are surprised to read of division, disunity and misunderstanding in Paul and Mark because they expect all New Testament writings to reflect the Lucan view of early Christianity. We should remember that although Luke is looking back on the life of Jesus and the early apostles, Christianity was still not the worldwide phenomenon it is today. Therefore, his optimistic picture is still an act of faith not a *fait accompli.*

Sources and Composition

We have already seen that Luke had Mark and Q as sources. He himself refers to previous works. Read Luke 1:1-4. Scholars have realized for a long time that this introduction intends to set Luke's work in the context of secular writings of the day. Of all the evangelists, Luke is most conscious of the literary conventions of general Graeco-Roman literature. Historical works typically had such a dedication and referred to the sources used by the author. Analysis of Lucan style shows him to have been a well-schooled and self-conscious writer. The first two chapters of his gospel are written in the style of the Greek Old Testament. The language of the rest of the gospel is less "biblicized" and that of his second volume, Acts, is even more secular than the gospel. In part, the change in style may be due to the varied sources used by the evangelist. Although the preface is a literary convention it may still tell us something about the evangelist's purposes.

On the one hand, Luke is concerned to make the case for Christianity as a viable religious option for the educated Gentile of his day. On the other hand, the Christian must be assured of the certainty of the faith that he or she has in Jesus. We can find out what Luke has in mind by looking at how he uses certain key terms from the secular vocabulary of the gospel prologue in Acts, where his sources left him freer to compose on his own. You will notice that he continually speaks of eye-witnesses to Jesus. Another of his words "accurately" returns in Acts—usually in legal contexts where someone is supposed to determine the facts of the case about Christianity (Ac 23:15, 20; 24:22). Festus needs to know "certainly" the charge against Paul before he can send him to Rome (Ac 21:34; 22:30; 25:26).

The word "certainly" also occurs in references to Christian preaching (Ac 18:25f.). A key example is Peter's speech in Acts 2:36: "Let the whole house of Israel know *certainly* that God has made both Lord and Christ this Jesus whom you crucified." These speeches may be understood as apology for Christianity—similar to the apology of Socrates. Thus, Luke's introduction suggests to his readers that he will present the kind of defense of Christianity that might be expected in a court or at least in the set speeches made up by students when they studied rhetoric.

But there is another puzzling expression here. He says that he will tell everything "in order." That expression is used of the sequence of prophets and of the sequence of events in a story in Acts 3:24 and 11:4. It is used of the sequence of places in a journey in Luke 8:1; 18:23. The claim to have all in order does not mean that Luke has gone about establishing a chronology that we would find historically reliable. When a student of rhetoric was taught to present his speech "in order," that meant to follow the sequence of topics laid out in rhetorical handbooks for speeches of the type he was to give.

When Luke associates the expression with the journey motif, he clues us in to another important feature of his work. Luke is the story-teller of early Christianity. Not only does he preserve many of the stories about the early apostles, but he uses a type of narrative popular in Hellenistic writings, the journey. It dominates Acts. But it also forms a major structural feature in the gospel. Jesus' journey between Galilee and Jerusalem occupies about a third of the gospel (9:51-19:27). Luke creates that effect by putting stories into the journey narrative that are weakly tied to that context. The motifs of hospitality and meals also belong with a journey account. (One of the favorite expressions for Christianity in Acts is "the way.")

Other features of Lukan composition are a fondness for paired characters and stories. His parables usually have contrasts in them. Often the same story will be told twice—once with a male hero; the second time with a female one. You can get some idea of the parallelism in the gospel by looking at the following chart. The life of Jesus is told in three sections:

(A) *3:21-9:50:* Call at baptism to be Son of God. Collection of witnesses.Galilean ministry.

(B) *9:51-19:27:* Journey to Jerusalem. Discloses the decision to suffer and instructs the disciples.

(C) *19:28-23:49:* Jerusalem ministry and trial of Jesus. Each section has similar themes, for example:

	A	B	C
Rejection:	Nazareth	Samaria	Jerusalem
sends out disciples:	"12" (ch 9)	"70" (10:1-20)	"12" 22:35-38
relatives/ women:	true relatives 8:19-21	mother blessed 11:27f	women Jerusalem 23:26
true greatness:	9:46-48	12:50	22:24-27
Herod:	his opinion 9:7-9	Jesus warned about 13:31-35	Jesus before 23:6-16

Apologetic Motifs in Luke

Our discussion of Luke's literary style already indicates an attempt to write an apology for Christianity on the part of its author. The predominant question about Christianity for a Gentile of the time may have been the death of Jesus as a crucified criminal. For Gentiles, the messianic question would not loom as large as it did in Judaism, since they did not think of salvation in those terms. Scholars have long been puzzled by the fact that Luke has no theology of the cross—unlike Paul, who was consistently preaching it to his Gentile Churches. We have already seen that much of the early theology of the cross is derived from Jewish speculation about the fate of the righteous; the martyrs and the sufferings prior to the messianic age. None of these themes figure prominently in the religious consciousness of those for whom Luke writes. They did know that a good man like Socrates might run afoul of the prejudices of evil political authorities because he criticized them, and that he might suffer a hero's death. This picture has influenced the Lucan account of Jesus' death.

From the beginning, Luke has distinguished the Jewish people who receive Jesus with joy and enthusiasm from their leaders (cf 7:31). The leaders are the ones who get Jesus condemned. Their accusations are lies (23:2). Pilate declares Jesus innocent three times. Herod twice declares Jesus politically harmless (9:7-9; 23:8-11). The Roman involvement in the death of Jesus is considerably underplayed. Herod's men mock Jesus but the Romans never do. Pilate never officially condemns Jesus but turns him over to the Jews (23:25). Even the nationality of the soldiers who crucified Jesus is suppressed. Further, Luke includes a dialogue between Jesus and those crucified with him. (In part a Lukan composition since Luke frequently introduces dialogue into the parables of Jesus.) They admit their own guilt and Jesus' innocence. Finally, Jesus dies with words of piety and forgiveness on his lips.

Not surprisingly, motifs from this picture of Jesus' noble death are reused in the account of Stephen's martyrdom (Ac 7:59f.). The reader of Luke's passion narrative is left in no doubt about Jesus' innocence and the exemplary character of his death. He or she could easily explain that Jesus was not a danger to the state but was a good, innocent person who had fallen victim to the plots of evil people. A similar pattern of political apologetic runs through the various trials of the apostles in Acts. Christians are consistently good citizens but are accused by deceitful leaders of the people. The Roman officials, however, are never taken in by such false accusations. They realize the innocence of the victims and protect them as much as possible.

Universalizing the Picture of Jesus

Jesus in Luke is clearly not a nationalistic political Messiah. The speech at Nazareth in which he opens his ministry in Luke (4:18) is cast in non-political terms. Luke stresses the fact that Jesus brings a message of forgiveness and peace to the whole world. If you turn to the very end of the gospel, you find Jesus commanding that repentance (The NAB erroneously translates "penance." Luke never speaks of penance in the sense in which we use the word.) and forgiveness of sins is to be preached to all nations beginning at Jerusalem. Luke speaks of forgiveness, grace and gratitude more frequently than all the other evangelists. He emphasizes parables that show God's forgiveness and the joyful repentance of sinners. This, then is the basic concept of salvation that he sets before his readers. It is a universal message of forgiveness and peace preached in the name of Jesus.

The most striking way in which Luke stresses the universality of Jesus is his consistent attempt to place all the events of his life within the context of the wider Graeco-Roman world. The infancy accounts are set within the context of Roman, not Jewish, history. Luke's version of Jesus' geneology traces him back not to Abraham as Matthew had but through Adam eventually to God (3:38). Because Luke does not share the apocalyptic preoccupations of other writers, his whole view of history is positive. The world is not a place that has been declining into evil since Adam and is about to end. Rather it contains at least as much of the goodness and care of God as it does of evil. It is not a threatening and hostile place.

People have frequently noted that Luke's perspective on history led him to portray the sweep of events in three periods. Thus, he is often spoken of as writing "salvation history."

The first period was the time of Israel. During that period, God was preparing people to receive Jesus as the Messiah. The infancy narratives of chapters 1 and 2 are used to show the culmination of that preparation. Those Jews who are truly good, pious and devout receive Jesus as Savior with rejoicing.

The second period is the time of Jesus' ministry (Lk 4:16; Ac 10:38). It closes formally with his ascension into heaven. It is a time of peace and success. Notice, for example, that Jesus' miracles in Luke always lead the crowds to praise God. Satan leaves the narrative after the temptation and does not re-enter until the passion.

The third phase is the time of the Church. Luke devotes a second volume, Acts, to recounting how the early Church was moved by the spirit to go out from Jerusalem into the Gentile world. He already hints in his gospel that Jerusalem will lose its status as a holy city because it has rejected the prophets (13:34ff.); rejected Jesus, its Savior, and, in Acts, finally rejects the apostles. This threefold rejection makes it imperative that the message go out to the Gentiles (21:23f.). For Luke, they are the new Israel that has the Spirit of God and transmits the message of salvation from past witnesses to the present. They are no longer bound to Jerusalem or to the fate of Judaism, but are at home in all the great cities of the Mediterranean world.

With such an historical perspective, it is not surprising that Luke downplays the end of the world. Although he does not deny early Christian expectations about the end he de-emphasizes them markedly. The spirit, for example, is not in Luke a sign that the last days are at hand, but God's way of providing for the growth and continuance of the Church— however long it may remain in the world. Similarly the resurrection is not an eschatological event but proof that Jesus is Messiah and that an individual's expectations about judgment and reward are reliable. When Luke speaks of persecution and tribulation, he does not view these as signs of the end, but as part of the ongoing character of Christian life. You can see this change clearly if you compare the Lukan version of the saying about taking up one's cross (9:23) with its Markan source (8:34). Mark's version suggests that the disciple will follow Jesus in suffering and death while Luke has transformed taking up the cross into something the Christian does daily, a following of Jesus in the tribulations of Christian life. Now compare Luke 21 with Mark 13. You will see that Luke has cut down the actual description of the end of the world. He takes some of the tribulations associated with the end in Mark and locates them instead at the fall of Jerusalem. The destruction of Jerusalem and its temple is not the sign of the approaching end that it was in the Markan apocalypse. Rather, it is a prelude to the times in which Luke lives, "the times of the Gentiles" (21:24). Those times have yet to be fulfilled. Until they are, the end will not take place.

Ethics in Luke

The attractiveness of Christianity for Luke, then, does not lie in its message of eschatological deliverance. Instead, Luke collects material in such a way as to show the timeless, ethical goodness of Jesus and the Christian message. Perhaps one of the most striking changes is his picture of John the Baptist. We are used to seeing John as a rather eccentric eschatological prophet who called people to repent before the judgment came. Luke does not deny that tradition but he has John the Baptist take time to give ethical instruction to his converts. Read Luke 3:10-14. Baptism then does not imply salvation from impending judgment as much as commitment to a new manner of life. Luke is not the only person to so transform the Baptist. The Jewish historian, Josephus also described John as a popular moral preacher:

> for Herod had put him (= John the Baptist) to death, though he was a good man and had exhorted the Jews to lead righteous lives, to practice justice towards their fellows and piety towards God, and so doing to join in baptism ... (Ant. xviii, 116)

Like Luke, Josephus was writing an apologetic history of his people using Hellenistic historiographical models. He wished to present an edifying picture of Judaism for an educated Roman audience and makes even more extended use of the clichés of Graeco-Roman philosophizing in so doing than Luke. We can see from this small example that the shift toward ethical preaching was typical of such works.

Further, John's advice in Luke fits in with that given Christians in the rest of his writings. Generosity toward the poor and unfortunate is a persistent theme in Luke. He never suggests that Christians go out of their way to become poor, but they must exercise openhanded generosity, never calculating the gain or loss for themselves. This generosity was also to be manifest in hospitality and sharing among Christians. Luke constantly reminds them of the need to forgive and live in peace with one another.

Another virtue in Luke is one that we do not usually find in our books on ethics—piety. Piety was an important virtue for ancient man. It did not refer to an individual's inner conviction about a god or gods or to his or her emotional state but to his or her respect for the religious traditions of his or her ancestors and his or her city. That respect was shown in public festivals, dedications or acts of worship. If you have ever read

about the philosopher Socrates you know that he was put to
death on a charge of corrupting the youth and not respecting
the gods of the city (Athens). Christians were particularly liable to be suspected of impiety. Not only did they refuse to
participate in any public acts of worship—whether to the gods
of the city or to the emperor—but they clearly rejected the gods
of their ancestors. Jewish refusal to participate in public worship was looked on as odd but understandable as loyalty to
ancestral tradition, and—as long as Jerusalem stood—to their
city. Christians had no such city or tradition.

From his opening pages, Luke takes great pains to show us
that Christians are not impious people, Jesus and his relatives
demonstrate the deepest respect and concern for their city and
ancestral traditions. Throughout his ministry Jesus retires to
pray (5:16; 6:12; 9:18; 22:39, 41, 44). We are even told that John
the Baptist's disciples prayed (5:33; 11:1). But that is not all.
Christians must have some instruction as to how they are to
worship God. Luke has collected teachings on prayer in 11:1-13
and 18:1-8 (which some exegetes suggest is his commentary on
the petition "thy kingdom come"). He stresses the beneficence
and certainty of God's response to prayer. But petition is not
the only type of prayer in Luke. At least as frequently he has
people thanking and blessing God for the salvation he has giv-
en. Frequently they do so in response to one of Jesus' miracles, and the very last words of the gospel touch on these notes
of city, piety, and praise: "and they were in the temple continually blessing God."

No one could read these pages and accuse the Christians of
impiety. Generosity, hospitality, endurance in suffering,
prayer and joy are all marks of the true disciple for Luke. He
cannot, of course, deny that in becoming a Christian he and
other Gentile converts have renounced the traditions of their
ancestry, but he can show that "the way" commits its followers
to lives of responsibility, virtue and piety against which people
could hardly protest. He will go on to show in Acts that the
move from Jewish sect to ecumenical religion was neither an
innovation nor a sacrilege. It took place under divine sanction;

by explicit direction of God—another theme that appears in ancient historiography, the direction of divine providence. Thus the Christians are in fact the only ones who possess the ancestral traditions of Judaism.

Women in Luke

Commentators have frequently noted the emphasis Luke places on women. They occur frequently in the gospel and are numbered among the larger group of disciples who followed Jesus about (8:2-3). There are more stories about women in Luke than in any other gospel, and they are apparently included among the company of disciples who witness the Ascension at the end of the gospel. Therefore, they would seem to be included in the commission to be witnesses. A woman, Anna, is the first person to be described as preaching about Jesus (2:38). You may also notice that while in Matthew all the revelations and instructions about the child Jesus go to his father, Joseph, in Luke, they are all directed to Mary.

Luke 8:2-3 helps us understand the context of this shift. The women there are wealthy enough to provide for Jesus out of their own funds. In Graeco-Roman times Gentile upper class women were much more independent than they had been in classical times. We have already seen that a number of such women played important roles in the Pauline mission among the Gentiles. Frequently, in the eastern part of the empire, at least, girls in such families might also receive some education. Various legal arrangements allowed them to own property. (We find some evidence that this attitude influenced Jews who lived in the diaspora. References to a woman as "ruler of a synagogue" and to prohibiting them from reading Torah in the synagogue hint at more liberal practices in some areas.) Gentiles would have been used to at least some contexts in which women acted as religious functionaries, though we rarely find women directly associated with political or intellectual life.

Therefore, one can say that the picture of women in Luke and Acts is quite normal for his social background. Both in his community and in some of the Pauline Churches, it probably emerged out of the usual roles women played in their communities. There is no evidence that Luke's positive picture of women is a form of proto-feminism. But even less can one force Lukan theology into a 1st-century Jewish mold that would restrict women from roles of religious leadership. (Jews even thought that women were so inferior as to be exempt from study of the Torah.) For Luke, Christian religious obligations and service are equally binding upon all. It is a curious fact that those who wish to distort Luke's portrait of women usually exalt his picture of Mary, while feminist interpreters tend to downplay Mariology. But it is the generally positive view of women that Luke gained from his society and, probably from their work in the early Church, however it was defined—and the New Testament gives us no evidence on this point—that led Luke to paint such a moving portrait of Mary and the other women in his gospel. And I doubt very much that we would have any devotion to the Blessed Mother at all if it had not been for these Lukan portraits.

Finally, Luke's picture of women is really part of the larger perspective of his gospel that we have spoken of as universalizing the picture of Jesus. Luke has applied the ethical teaching of Jesus in such a way that his Gentile Church could perceive its timeless validity. He is going to insist that Christianity is legitimately a world religion for all peoples, not a deviant form of Judaism, and so all those who are joining the movement, Jew and Gentile, rich and poor, men and women find positive ideals of piety and service in the pages of his gospel.

STUDY QUESTIONS

1. What is Luke's teaching about wealth? How does the ideal he sets for Christians differ from what an educated Gentile would be accustomed to hear?

 * 2. Give two or three examples of how Luke makes his picture
      of Jesus a universal one.
   3. What is Luke's view of salvation history? How does it differ
      from apocalyptic views of history such as that embodied in
      Mark 13?
   4. Give two examples of how Luke is using Graeco-Roman
      literary and historiographical conventions in presenting the
      life of Jesus.
   5. What is Luke's understanding of the death of Jesus? How is
      it shaped by his concern with political apologetic?
   6. What is salvation for Luke? How does his presentation of
      Jesus' ethical teaching fit into that view of salvation?
   7. What did ancient man mean when he spoke of piety as a
      virtue? Give two examples of piety from Luke's gospel. Why
      does he emphasize the piety of the early Christians?
 * 8. What role do women play in the Lucan narrative? Why?

Chapter Thirteen

JOHN: JESUS,
THE DIVINE WORD

The Different Gospel

We have seen that the other three gospels are related in that Matthew and Luke used Mark as a source. Since antiquity, John has been a puzzle because it is so different from the other three. Although we still hear about Jesus as a Galilean religious teacher, about some of the same events and about his trial and death, almost everything else in John is different. The ministry is spread over three years instead of one, and John's chronology for other events in the life of Jesus differs from what we find in the synoptics. Jesus cleanses the temple toward the beginning of his ministry rather than just before his death. He dies a day earlier than in the synoptics. He does not institute the eucharist at his final meal with the disciples but washes their feet.

John's literary style is also quite different. There are no narrative parables in John and very few of the short sayings so common in the synoptic gospels. Jesus only works seven miracles here; none of them are exorcisms. Most of the homey details about life in 1st-century Palestine are gone; so is Jesus' preaching about the kingdom of God, ethical exhortation and warnings about the end of the world. Instead, Jesus gives long symbolic discourses. Discussions about the rule of God and keeping the Sabbath have been turned into debates over the identity of Jesus as Son of God. The theme of misunderstanding has been turned from inability to comprehend the suffering of the Messiah to the inability of Jesus' protagonists to understand the symbolic (= Christian) level on which he is speaking.

Finally, while the other gospels have presented Jesus from a variety of human perspectives, the fourth evangelist opens with the divine. Read John 1:1-18. Except for parenthetical remarks about John the Baptist, this introduction proceeds entirely from the heavenly perspective. John has based these verses on an early Christian hymn to Jesus as the divine Word. The reader thus knows that everything he hears Jesus say in the course of the narrative has its ultimate basis in that Word. We are not surprised to find that the evangelist considers the Word of Jesus parallel to the revelation of the Old Testament (2:22).

These differences between John and the other gospels have also led people to diverse theories about the milieu from which this gospel comes. Some have argued that the evangelist formulated his picture of Jesus as revealer in opposition to the pictures of heavenly revealers being formulated by emerging Gnosticism. Others that John's own picture of Jesus so overemphasizes the divine as to border on the heretical. While no one denies that John shows extensive contact with Hellenistic thought—his symbols are found in a variety of religious traditions—nevertheless, the radically Hellenistic, quasi-heretical interpretations of John do not fit well with the overall perspective of the gospel.

Two lines of inquiry have proven most fruitful in recent research. First, the debates with, and allusions to, Judaism in John have provided one context for the formulation of Johannine traditions. They represent the apologetic stance of a community still in serious confrontation with Judaism. Given the harshness of some of its statements about Judaism, the apologetic in the gospel would seem to be internally directed, that is, aimed at bolstering the faith of Christian believers in the face of Jewish opposition rather than aimed at actually converting

Jews. Second, analysis of the contacts that do exist between John and other Jesus traditions suggests that he knows some traditions about Jesus that were similar to, but independent of, the synoptic traditions. Those traditions seem to have been consciously reworked and rethought within the Johannine community to develop the unique theology that we find in the gospel. Both lines of investigation have contributed a great deal to our understanding of John as a theologian.

Sources and Composition

The most influential presentation of the question of Johannine sources was made in the great commentary of Rudolf Bultmann (1921). He hypothesized that the evangelist drew upon three sources for his material:

(1) A signs source, that is, an earlier collection of Jesus' miracles from which he took the seven used in the gospel. He added some of his own remarks and concluding interpretive discourses to those miracles. This hypothesis is widely accepted. Although recent attempts to isolate the contours of that source using form critical and linguistic criteria vary in details, there is enough agreement among them that one can almost speak of a consensus on the issue.

(2) A revelation discourse source. Using later Mandean materials, Bultmann hypothesized that John had derived the discourses of Jesus from Gnostic traditions about a revealer who descends from the heavenly light-realm, reveals to those who have the spark of light within that their true home/ destiny is not in this evil world but in the light, and then returns there. This thesis was attacked both because the comparative material was much later than John and because the language of the gospel does not suggest that the author is copying a source. Since Bultmann wrote his commentary, many new Gnostic revelation dialogues have been discovered that date from mid 2nd century, much closer to the time John was written. They have reopened this question, but so far there is nothing close enough to what we find in the fourth gospel to suggest that the evangelist had such a Gnostic discourse source

before him. Rather the Gnostics—as we knew from the heresiologists—are extremely fond of the fourth gospel because they can interpret it to suit their own purposes.

(3) Passion narrative. We have already mentioned some chronological differences between John's passion account and that of the synoptics. Nevertheless, the evangelist does seem to have reformulated a synoptic-like account of the trial and death of Jesus.

Both the signs source and pre-Johannine passion account are widely accepted sources for the fourth gospel. In addition, detailed investigation of smaller sayings shows the possibility that the evangelist also had synoptic-like oral traditions of the teaching of Jesus. You can see what is meant easily if you compare the following passages: Jn 12:25//Mt 10:39; Jn 13:20//Mt 10:40; Jn 5:9//Mk 2:11; Jn 12:24//3:24. The next three parallels are so important for our understanding of how John reworked early Christian traditions in his picture about Jesus that we will position them next to each other:

John 1:51
Truly, truly I say to you, you will see heaven opened, and the angels of God ascending and descending upon the Son of Man.

Mark 14:62
You will see the Son of Man seated at the right hand of Power and coming with the clouds of heaven.

John 5:27
and has given him authority to execute judgment because he is the Son of Man.

Mark 2:10
that you may know that the Son of Man has authority on earth to forgive sins.

John 12:34
We have heard from the Law that the messiah remains forever, how can you say that the Son of Man must be lifted up?

Mark 8:31
And he began to teach them that the Son of Man must suffer many things . . .

John has reformulated three types of Son of Man sayings: the

first refers to the Son of Man as future judge, the second speaks
of his present authority on earth and the third predicts the
suffering of the Son of Man. Such reformulations are part of the
case for viewing John as a theological interpreter of earlier
Christian tradition.

A striking instance of large scale parallelism between
John and a synoptic source occurs in John 6. When we compare
the sequence of events there with the parallel sequences in
Mark 6 and 8:1-33, we find the following:

	John	Mark
(1) loaves miracle:	6:1-15	6:30-40 (8:1-10)
(2) walk on water:	16-21	45-54
(3) request sign:	22-34	8:11-13
(4) Jesus' parentage:	41-44	6:1-6
(5) Misunderstanding:	60-65	8:16-20
(6) Peter's Confession:	6:66-69	8:27-30
(7) Passion Prediction:	70-71	30-33

Some interpreters take this parallelism and the Johannine Son
of Man traditions as evidence that John had read Mark. However, the mixture of Mark 6 and 8 suggests rather that John
used an independent version of the same tradition used by
Mark, one which had all these points in a single cycle of stories
rather than a double one as we find in Mark.

If you open any extensive commentary on John, you will
find that the evangelist also presents his interpreters with
rather baffling questions of sequence. For example, chapter 7
takes place in Judea and logically follows chapter 5, since it
continues a story pattern that was begun there. But that pattern is interrupted by chapter 6, which takes place in Galilee.
John 14:31 concludes the discourse with an injunction to
leave, yet Jesus continues to speak for another three chapters.
John 20:30f. formally concludes the gospel, but we have
another whole chapter at least part of which was written by
someone who knew of the death of the original evangelist

(21:31f.). In addition, there are smaller units within the gospel that seem oddly situated.

John 3:31-36 does not seem to have been spoken by the Baptist, the last speaker mentioned. Is it a summary by the evangelist? Or part of the discourse by Jesus that was interrupted by the Baptist material? Where does the dialogue with Nicodemus that begins chapter 3 end? At verse 12? Or verse 15? John 12:44-50 seems to be attached to a chapter already concluded. The verses have no setting. The discourse beginning at 8:12 is equally awkward. (John 7:53-8:11 do not belong to this gospel. They are not found in the earliest manuscripts; are not in Johannine style, and in some manuscripts are attached to Luke, whose style and concerns—forgiveness and focus on women—they fit much better.) John 16:5 contradicts 14:5.

One might attribute these problems to careless composition by the evangelist or to a hasty editing of sources if other parts of the gospel did not show signs of careful composition. Look for example at chapter 9. Verses 1-7 are a traditional healing miracle (cp. Mk 8:22-26 or 10:46-52) with some elaboration by the evangelist in verses 3b-5. The rest of the chapter turns that miracle into the occasion for a mini-drama over the identity of Jesus. It can even be divided into scenes if you remember the ancient conventions that not more than two or three protagonists should occupy the stage at the same time. You can see that each one contains an additional revelation of Jesus' identity until the man finally comes to worship Jesus as Son of Man. A coda then condemns the blindness of the Pharisees.

The story of the Samaritan woman in chapter 4:4-42 is another neat dramatic unity where Jesus' identity is revealed in stages until the Samaritans come to confess Jesus as Savior of the world. Scholars think that both these stories may provide clues as to John's milieu. The emphasis on the faith of the Samaritans suggests some association with the Samaritan mission. The bitter controversy over Jesus' identity and the claims made for him in chapter 9 is one of the many hints that John's community suffered opposition from official Judaism.

The man's parents are afraid to testify because they fear exclusion from the synagogue (9:22 cp 12:42; 16:2). Such a ban did not exist in Jesus' day. Paul tells us that Christians were punished by synagogue authorities, not put out. We do know that such a ban was enacted around A.D. 90, but do not know how it was enforced. This passage shows that the claims made for Jesus by Christians were being rejected by Jewish religious authorities on the grounds that he was a sinner and could not have been from God. Elsewhere in John you will find other charges against Jesus. The blind man in this story may be taken as an example of how Christians should behave when challenged about their faith in Jesus.

This peculiar combination of awkward passages and transitions with carefully worked out dramatic episodes and sections of discourse has led to a variety of hypotheses about the composition and editing of the fourth gospel. All agree that some sources and stages of composition are involved. Some think that the text was substantially rearranged by the disciple who added chapter 21. In our commentary on John, we have suggested the following minimal hypothesis as adequate to clarify the composition of the fourth gospel:

(1) *Synoptic-like Traditions about Jesus:* Both oral and written, these formed the backbone of what the Johannine community knew about Jesus. Occasionally the evangelist alludes to a story he never tells. Therefore, we may assume that he expected his readers to be already familiar with some such story of the life of Jesus.

(2) *Johannine Preaching:* The care with which individual sections have been worked out and the parallel farewell discourses suggest that the evangelist had previously worked out some of this material for preaching to the community.

(3) *Evangelist's Gospel:* The evangelist used material from both the previous stages to compose his gospel. In some instances (e.g., chapters 5-8) he may have broken up earlier cycles of material in order to fit his schema of a three-year ministry that alternates between Galilee and Jerusalem. (Cp. John 2; contrast this with the one-year ministry proceeding from

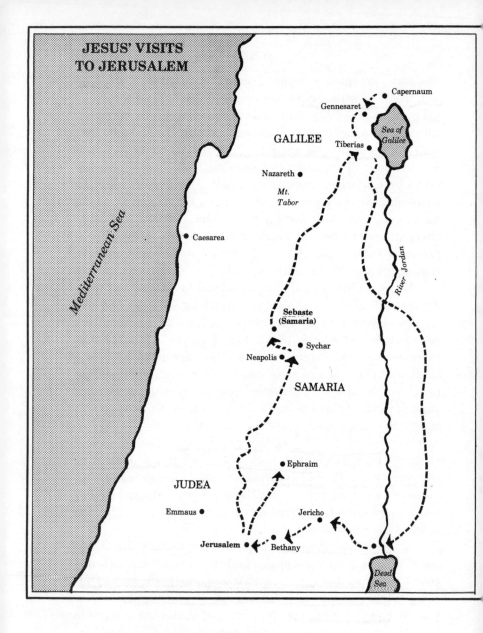

Galilee to Jerusalem of the synoptics.) The magisterial commentary on John by R. Brown in the Anchor Bible holds that the evangelist is responsible for two editions of the gospel; we have not yet been convinced that such a second edition by the evangelist is necessary to account for the gospel as we have it.

(4) *Editing by a Disciple:* After the death of the evangelist, one of his disciples added an explanation of his death and some other material from the preaching of the evangelist (stage 2). We contend that he did not rearrange chapters or compose new sections but that he merely added other material from the preaching of the evangelist at the end of sections where it could be seen to fit (e.g. 3:31-36; 6:51b-58?; ch 8; 12:44-50; chs 15-17; 21:1-18, 20-22).

Since the gospel was written sometime around A.D. 90, the gospel cannot reasonably be attributed to John son of Zebedee as is sometimes done. Beside that, John was martyred (Mk 10:38f.) while we know that the author of the fourth gospel was not (21:21f.). Chapter 21 suggests that the beloved disciple of Jesus was the founder of the Johannine community and the source of its traditions. They looked back to him as on par with the apostle Peter to whom Jesus had entrusted the Church.

Misunderstanding and Irony

We pointed out above that John frequently uses misunderstanding in his stories. Almost no one in the narrative except Jesus and the Christian reader knows what Jesus is referring to when he uses various symbols. Usually those to whom Jesus speaks take his words literally and draw some patently absurd conclusion from them. Occasionally such conclusions have a deeper meaning in themselves, which the Christian reader easily understands. For example, in John 8:22 "the Jews" think Jesus' claim about his return to the Father means that he is going to kill himself. Although he will not commit suicide, their words can be understood to refer to one of John's favorite assertions: no one could take Jesus' life from him if he did not lay it down willingly (e.g., 10:18; 19:11).

This characteristic of author and reader being "in on" the

significance of what is transpiring while most of the actors are not, makes John an ironic work. Recent literary critical studies of irony have pointed out the important role it plays in creating bonds of community between author and readers. Those "in on" the secret or joke are united against outsiders and even certain of the characters. Now look back at John 9. You can see the irony clearly. The Jewish religious authorities claim to be the experts: they know the law of Moses, what God will or will not accept. The blind man should, they think, be guided by them. But their knowledge makes it impossible for them to accept the revelation in Jesus.

John has two other stories about religious teachers that make similar points by using misunderstanding and irony. There the individuals come to a partial understanding of what Jesus is saying. Read the exchange with Nathanial in John 1:45-51 and that with Nicodemus in 3:1-15. We find another important device of Johannine irony in these chapters. He begins with a religious symbol or doctrine that is comprehensible in Jewish terms (designated "lesser" or "earthly" teaching) and moves to one that is paradoxical in that context (frequently some assertion about Jesus as Son of Man). If his protagonist is amazed or cannot understand the former, how is he to understand the latter? Compare the pattern in these two stories

John 1:49-51	*John 3:9-15*
cryptic statement leads Nathanial to confess Jesus as Son of God (= Messiah) (v 49)	cryptic statement Nicodemus cannot understand (v 9)
question: do you believe on that basis (50a)	question: are you a teacher and do not understand?! (V 10)
you will see greater (50b)	if you do not believe earthly things, how heavenly ones (v 11f.)

(statement of the greater or heavenly things)

heavens open	no one has gone up to heaven except the Son of Man (i.e. no one else can reveal heavenly things) (v 13)
angels go up and down on the Son of Man (v 51)	Son of man to be lifted up (= Johannine language for crucifixion)
	so believers have life (vv 14f.)

Now go back to the story in John 9. You can find the same pattern implied there. The Pharisees cannot even see Jesus as a good man to whose prayer God might give an answer (vv 16, 24, 31). They will certainly not see the greater thing revealed by Jesus to the blind man: his identity as Son of Man. These patterns are a key to how John prepares his readers for the rejection that Jesus and Christian preaching encounter among the Jews. He knows that Christians believe many things that Jews find objectionable or even contrary to their understanding of God's will. Here we have seen three: Jesus as the Son of Man from Daniel; Jesus' death as a source of eternal life for those who believe in him, and Jesus as the object of Christian worship (blasphemy in Jewish eyes). These are not things that a person can derive from the Old Testament. John knows that they are dependent upon one's believing that God has revealed himself in Jesus Christ. But the trouble with the Jewish teachers is that they do not even properly understand their own tradition (cf Jn 5:46f.).

The reader is "in on" two levels of understanding then: what is proper to the Jewish religious symbols and what is peculiarly Christian. (Of course, one can argue that a person would have to accept a basic premise of the gospel: Jesus is from God before one could accept its interpretation of the Jewish religious tradition.) In both instances, the irony serves to bind

Christian readers together against those Jewish authorities who might try to convince them that their faith in and worship of Jesus is contrary to the will of God as made know in Scripture. (Another reason for John's stress on the parallel between the word of Jesus and that of the Scripture?)

Controversy with the Jews

Our study of Johannine irony and misunderstanding has already brought out key areas in which Jewish/Christian controversy is reflected. Chapters 5-12 cast Jesus' public ministry as a series of increasingly hostile encounters and increasingly severe threats against his life. In a short work like this one, we can only pick out certain key items in each chapter. Chapter 5 has the only unsuccessful miracle in John. The man does not become a believer. You may also notice that it is the only one that is not given a symbolic interpretation. The original (signs source) story was probably a Sabbath controversy interpreted as a demonstration of Jesus' power to forgive sins (cp. Lk 13:10-17). But the issue taken up in the discourse is Jesus' claim to equality with the father (v 18).

We have already seen that chapter 9 revolves around the related problem of Christian worship of Jesus. To a Jew, such behavior could only seem to be a blasphemous denial of the first commandment. Later Christian theology developed complicated doctrines of God as triune and of the unity of divine and human in the one person of Jesus to try and deal with the problem. The wisdom hymn at the beginning of John played an important role in those later controversies. But John does not appeal to that language here. Instead, he uses a legal metaphor. According to law a person's agent is identical with the one who sent him. The agent can carry on legal transactions just as though he were that person, and he is entitled to the same honor and respect. Jesus here claims authority to act as the Father does, as God's agent: to judge and to give life. He is not claiming an independent sovereignty that would indeed be blasphemous.

Chapter 7 uses the same metaphor—Jesus really is "from

God"—to defend again Jesus' authority to teach as he does. Several formal legal objections are directed against Jesus in this chapter. He is accused of being a false prophet or deceiver whose teaching leads people astray. Deuteronomy mandates the death penalty for such prophets (Jn 7:12, 47). He cannot claim the authority of a Pharisee or rabbi because he has never studied (v 15). Finally, the Galilean origins of Jesus do not fit any of the messianic predictions (vv. 27, 41-42). The answer given to all these objections is that Jesus comes from above with the authority of God who sent him. Chapter 8 returns to that theme in a yet more violent encounter between Jesus and the Jews. It reaches a climax with Jesus' claim to the divine nature, I AM (8:28, 58).

Chapter 6 takes up a different controversy: Christian teaching about the eucharist. Jesus is "from heaven," the true manna. It also includes the claim that we met in chapter 3, the death of Jesus gives life. This chapter insists that a person cannot expect salvation if he or she does not join the Christian community and share its meal. That assertion may have had particular urgency in John's community. Notice the reference to "secret believers" in 12:42f. Nicodemus may also be the type of such a believer. In chapter 11 the revival of Lazarus becomes the occasion for the final decision to have Jesus put to death. With typical Johannine irony, Jesus' gift of life is associated with his death. John 10 invokes the Old Testament images of God as shepherd of Israel to establish that Jesus is her true shepherd and the Jewish leaders, imposters. Once again those claims are validated because Jesus is the agent sent by the Father.

You will also notice that these chapters cast the Jews in an extremely negative light. They are called children of Satan not Abraham. Both Abraham and Moses will condemn their rejection of Jesus. In fact, in rejecting Jesus, they are rejecting God—a logical conclusion from the agent metaphor. Christians today realize that such language cannot be taken as expressing the truth about Judaism. (Paul pointed out in Romans 9-11 that God would not cancel his covenant with them.) In order to understand how such metaphors came to be employed, we should remember that John's Church was the persecuted minority (cf. 16:2). There are hints that anti-Christian polemic was taking its toll among the Christian believers. Look back at the eucharistic controversy. It ends (vv 60, 66) with some of those who had been following Jesus turning away from him. We cannot accept John's language as an objective statement about God's treatment of the Jews, but we can understand the gravity of the polemical situation in which it was formulated. The evangelist had to insure that people did not turn away from their faith under the pressure of Jewish opposition.

The Christology of John

We have already seen that John begins by identifying Jesus with the pre-existent Word of God. That image is not discussed within the narrative, but it would seem that Christian claims that Jesus can be identified with the Father and worshipped were the subject of serious debate between Christians and Jews. Obviously such claims go beyond anything Jews expected of the Messiah. They had developed, as we saw in chapter 5, out of the Church's experience of the risen Jesus. His exaltation into heaven and presence in the community had led Christians to formulate the kind of hymn with which John opens. We pointed out that John tends to move beyond Jewish traditions to Christian affirmations which cannot be derived from them. The divinity of Jesus is one such affirmation.

The first chapter had that movement in reverse. It opened with the hymnic affirmation of Jesus' divinity. Then, the testimony of John the Baptist and Jesus' earliest disciples constitute a collection of messianic titles (1:19-50). But those titles do not tell the whole truth about Jesus. The chapter concludes with a mysterious proclamation of Jesus as heavenly Son of Man (1:51).

This same process of beginning with Jewish messianic titles and moving to a proclamation about Jesus as Son of Man occurs four more times in the gospel (3:3-14; 6:14-53; 7:31-8:28; 9:17-36). In John 4:4-44, a similar process leads from the identity of Jesus as the Samaritan eschatological prophet to the proclamation that he is the Savior of the world. This process suggests that John understands Jesus as transcending all such categories. He uses the mysterious symbol of Son of Man, which we have seen comes from the earlier Christian tradition. He combines three elements from that tradition: the use of Son of Man as self-designation for the earthly Jesus; the coming Son of Man as heavenly judge on the model of Daniel 7, and the predictions of the suffering Son of Man. He combines all of these to describe the earthly Jesus. He does not identify Jesus with the heavenly Son of Man who would come on clouds and judge the world in the future (like Mark 14:62) but speaks of him as the one who brings judgment now. This change is part of extensive reuse of judgment metaphors in the gospel to make the point that judgment is not some future cosmic event but that it takes place whenever a person encounters the message about Jesus (cf. Jn 5:23-30; 12:31, 44-50). A person who believes Jesus' Word has eternal life; one who rejects it is already condemned. If you look at the passage from John 5:23-30 closely, you will see that John has used his lesser to greater scheme in reverse. He begins with the more difficult issue: the presence of judgment in Jesus' ministry and moves to the lesser, a traditional Jewish assertion about resurrection and future judgment (vv 28b-29). For John, then, Jesus is the Son of Man in full glory. Christians are not waiting for some glorious return. Not surprisingly then, he can speak of believers as those who have seen Jesus' glory (cf. 1:14; 2:11).

You may remember that Mark had insisted on the cross as the true revelation of Jesus as Son of God. John has a similar assertion. He never uses negative imagery in association with the crucifixion. Instead he speaks of it as the exaltation and glorification of the Son of Man (cf. 12:28; 13:31). The passion prediction in 8:28 tells the audience that Jesus' identity as agent of the Father will be recognized when he is crucified/exalted.

That prediction also introduces another unique feature of Johannine discourse, the I AM sayings. Here we have an example of what is called an absolute I AM predication (vv 24 & 28). It derives from the divine name in the Old Testament (Ex 3:14; 20:5; Isa 45:5f, 18, 22). A passage from the Greek text of Isaiah 43:10f. shows striking parallels to the language of this passage:

> You are my witnesses and I am a witness says the Lord
> God and the servant whom I have chosen (cp. witness
> language in Jn 8:13ff.)
> that you may know and believe (vv 24, 28)
> and understand that I AM.
> Before me there was no other God,
> and after me there will be none.
> I AM God
> and no one saves except me.

John insists that Jesus is the only Savior and revealer of God. The identity between Son and Father guards such claims against being blasphemy. John 8:28 follows the divine I AM with an immediate assertion that the Son does not act on his own. He is always agent of the Father. These absolute I AM sayings are the culmination of John's understanding of the identity between Jesus and the Father.

However, since John believes Jesus to be Savior of the world and the only revelation of the divine, he uses another series of I AM sayings to identify Jesus and the great religious symbols: bread of life (6:35, 41, 48, 51); life (8:12 cf. 9:5); gate (10:7, 9); good shepherd (10:11, 14); resurrection and life (11:25); way, truth and life (14:6); vine (15:1, 5). Interpreters point out that the effect of these predications is to portray Jesus as fulfillment of all the religious expectations of humanity. This particular set of symbols may well stem from Christian liturgical usage. But the symbols are so ubiquitous that believers from a variety of religious backgrounds could unite in using them.

No one has ever doubted that John portrayed the divinity of Jesus in striking terms. He has been careful to use metaphors to guard his language against the charge of blasphemy against the sovereignty of God the Father. But some commentators, both ancient and modern, find the Johannine Jesus too divine. His humanity seems overshadowed. Luke frequently showed us Jesus at prayer. When he prays in John there is either an assertion that such prayer is not necessary for Jesus but only an example (11:42; 12:30) or a statement of unity between Father and Son (ch. 17). John emphasizes Jesus' knowledge of everyone, his control over his own destiny. Some have even gone so far as to claim that without the exegetical tradition from the 3rd and 4th century that takes John 1:14 to imply physical incarnation, John could hardly be said to have an orthodox view of Jesus. Others have wondered why John continues to be an extremely popular gospel in an age that takes delight in the weaknesses and failures of its heroes—the authors of Jesus Christ Superstar, for example, claimed to be inspired by John. Yet their Jesus shows confusion and uncertainty; he questions God. The Johannine Jesus is never in doubt about his father's will. You may notice that there is no Agony in the Garden and only a small allusion to that tradition in John 12:27f.

The Johannine text allows at least two answers to these questions. First, throughout the gospel we are reminded that Jesus is to be rejected and die. Neither his miraculous power nor his identity with the Father will save him from that fate. John's passion account emphasizes the fact that Jesus really was dead. The soldiers certify his death, and he is buried by two Jewish leaders favorable to him, Joseph of Arimathea and Nicodemus.

A second motif in John that reminds us of Jesus' humanity is that of friendship. We saw in our study of Luke that friendship was an important theme in the Hellenistic world. Luke portrays the early Christian community as an ideal community of friends. For John, friendship characterizes the true relationship between Jesus and his followers. The motif first emerges in the Lazarus story of chapter 11. John 15:12-15 designates the followers of Jesus who obey his command of love as friends. Thus, the story of Lazarus too may be a model for John's understanding of the relationship between Jesus and

the disciple. Ancient treatises on friendship held that there
was to be equality between true friends. John bases his picture
of friendship on Jesus' commandment of love. The supreme
example of that love is found in Jesus' death (cp. a different
application of the same motif in Romans 5:7f.). Death and
friendship are combined as the two motifs that show us the
human side of the Johannine Jesus.

We may say that the emphasis on Jesus' certainty of his
mission and his unity with the Father has two sources. First,
we have seen that liturgical allusions are frequently tied to
assertions about Jesus' identity. The presence of the risen Lord
experienced in the Christian community has had a strong influence on this gospel's portrait of Jesus. Commentators have
often pointed out that Jesus' prayer for the disciples in chapter
17 is spoken as though he were already exalted in heaven (e.g.,
17:11). Secondly, the portrait of Jesus here may serve to reassure those Christians shaken by the persecution and counter-
arguments being directed at them. No one could doubt the
truth of the incarnate divine Word. Jesus' unity with God is so
close that he cannot reasonably be accused of leading people
astray or falsifying the will and revelation of God.

John's View of the Church

You have probably noticed that the disappearance of sayings and parables from the Johannine narrative has meant the
loss of much of the ethical teaching of Jesus. Such paraenetic
material frequently provides us with clues about the concerns
and problems within an author's community. Many have felt
that John is entirely concerned with the individual's faith in
Jesus. Some have gone so far as to suggest that all sacramental
and ecclesial references were the addition of the final editor.
We do not accept that view. You will notice that the fourth
evangelist has a literary tendency to focus on individuals.
Often images that the Old Testament used for Israel are here
concentrated in the person of Jesus. But we have also seen that

John insists on the necessity of joining the Christian community. He does not reduce faith to subjective categories.

Secondly, occasional quotations from the tradition of Jesus' sayings (e.g., 12:25f.) suggest that his Church already knew such teaching. At the same time, the summary of Christ's teaching in terms of the commandment of love seems to have been characteristic of the Johannine Church. The farewell discourses make it the characteristic of Jesus' true disciples. The first letter of John written some time after the gospel shows that it was a main theme of Johannine exhortation.

The discourses that Jesus gives at the last supper are central to John's view of the Church. At his final meal with the disciples, Jesus gives them the example of footwashing to indicate the type of relationship that should obtain between disciples. Chapters 14 and 16 replace the future parousia discourses of the other gospels with a different analysis of Jesus' return. His return does not come to the world. He and his Father come to dwell with the believer, that is, the presence of the risen Christ in and with the community of believers constitutes the true significance of the second-coming tradition. The discourses also show us that Jesus is commissioning the disciples to be his agents or representatives in the world. He first does so in the footwashing scene (13:16-20). The language there reflects the legal principle that when an agent returned to the person who sent him, he could appoint someone else to look after his master's interests (cf v 20). It is in that context that Jesus can promise the believers they will do greater works than his, once he has returned to the Father (14:12). He does not mean that they will do greater miracles. No one could top those reported in the gospel.

John has a special term for miracles, "signs," to indicate that a person must see through the literal miracle to the true glory of Jesus. The term "works" in John covers all the words and deeds Jesus has shown people during his ministry. He speaks of them as witnesses to his truly being from God (5:36). They are given him by the Father who commissioned him. Jesus returns to the Father having commissioned new disciples. They will do greater works because they must carry Jesus' mission throughout the world.

The prayer of commission in John 17 (cf. 17:18) shows that the believers may also be considered one with God. The love the Father has for Jesus is now extended to them (17:26). This prayer extends beyond the immediate circle of disciples to all future believers (v 20). However, the disciples are warned that they cannot expect an easier time than Jesus had. His message brings the judgment of the world. Those who reject it will turn against the message with hatred (15:18-25; 16:1-4a; 17:14). But the Church is told not to flee the world and its opposition. They are not to set up a monastery in some remote desert to escape its hatred (17:15).

Johannine concern with future believers also shows itself in the resurrection stories of chapters 20 and 21. We cannot go into all the details of how John has edited earlier stories here, but a few passages will show you what he wants us to understand: that faith in the risen Jesus is not a matter of seeing him. He wants us to realize that our faith in the risen Jesus is exactly the same as that of the first disciples. He has already instructed us that the presence of the risen Jesus in the community continues his mission and is the true return.

Now look at the stories. The beloved disciple believes even though all he sees are grave clothes—no angels; no Jesus (20:7). Mary is told not to touch the Lord when she sees him because he has not yet returned to the Father (20:17). That is a rewriting of the traditional account in which the women take hold of his feet and worship Jesus (see Matthew 28:9). John wants us to understand that the Christian does not worship the risen Jesus of the appearances but the Lord who is exalted in heaven. Third, the incident with Thomas culminates in a benediction on those who believe without seeing (v 28). A similar motif is introduced into the story in John 21:1-14 in which Peter and the others are commissioned as missionaries. The beloved disciple immediately recognizes the man in the shore

as Jesus (v 7). That faith in Jesus is the key to salvation in the
fourth gospel. The conclusion at John 20:31 sums up the
evangelist's purpose in just those terms.

STUDY QUESTIONS

▶ 1. List three differences between John and the snyoptic gospels.
   2. What sources did the fourth evangelist have for his gospel?
   List the four stages by which the Johannine gospel as we
   know it came into being.
   3. Analyze either John 4:4-44 or John 9. List the stages by
   which the identity of Jesus is revealed. What is the climax
   of the revelation in each case? What area of the early
   Church's experience is reflected in that climax?
▷ 4. How does John use misunderstanding and irony? How does
   Johannine irony fit into his plan of strengthening Christian community in the face of opposition?
   5. How does John present the relationship between Jesus and
   God? How does he argue that Christian claims for Jesus
   are not blasphemous?
   6. How does John use I AM sayings? What do the two types of
   sayings tell us about Jesus?
   7. How does John portray the Jewish religious leaders? Why?
   8. How does John use the Son of Man symbol? How does his
   use of Son of Man sayings differ from Mark?
   9. How has John reinterpreted the traditional Christian
   teachings about judgment and the return of Jesus? Give
   two examples of this reinterpretation from the gospel.
• 10. What do the farewell discourses tell us of the Johannine
   view of the nature and mission of the Church?
   11. Why might John have omitted the Agony in the Garden
   scene from his passion account? How does he remind us of
   the humanity of Jesus?
   12. Now that you have read all four gospels, which portrait of
   Jesus appealed to you most? Why? What features of that
   account made it most meaningful for you?

Part V

CHRISTIANITY AT THE END
OF THE CENTURY

Chapter Fourteen

ACTS: MISSIONARY SUCCESS
AND SALVATION FOR
THE NATIONS

Although Acts is by the same author as Luke and continues many of the gospel's themes, we have chosen to treat it separately from the gospel as one of three quite distinct pictures of Christianity written toward the end of the 1st century. We pointed out in discussing the gospel that Luke takes the time of the Gentiles as a positive historical epoch. But his gospel ended in the temple in Jerusalem. He still has to show us how Christianity moved from its Jewish beginnings to become a Gentile religion spread in all the cities of the civilized world. Acts presents that story under the symbolic guise of the gospel's progress from Jerusalem to Rome. It opens with a programmatic introduction. The apostles are to be Jesus' witnesses "from Jerusalem, throughout Judea and Samaria—even to the ends of the earth" (1:8). Luke will portray this development as divinely ordained and directed by the Holy Spirit. Initially everything flows out from Jerusalem. Persecution there leads to the first move out into the Gentile world, Samaria (Ac 6). Persecution there will send Paul to Rome where the book ends (Ac 21:15-end). As he tells this story Luke will return to many of the themes we found in his gospel.

Sources and Composition

The prologue to Acts is similar to those in other multi-volume works from antiquity. Luke does not tell us anything about sources used for Acts. He cannot have been present at all the events he narrates. You may also notice that the details of Paul's conversion are different each time he tells the story (9:1-22; 22:4-16; 26:9-18)—Paul's own reference to his conversion is much more circumspect (Gal 1:13-17). We also saw in discussing the life of Paul that the Acts account of the Jerusalem meeting (Ac 15) differs from that given by the apostle (Gal 2). Scholars think that Luke may have juxtaposed or conflated accounts of different events. There are also sections of Paul's journeys which suddenly switch to the first person plural (16:10-17; 20:5-15; 21:1-18; 17:1-28:16). Some interpreters think that these "we" sections were derived from a travel diary. Others point out that such shifts into the first person are a standard feature in the novelistic stories of journeys. There is no certainty as to the types of sources Luke used for Acts. Differences between his accounts and Paul's letters make it unlikely that he knew a collection of Pauline epistles, but he may well have had some written sources as well as oral traditions and legends about the earliest apostles.

In his gospel, Luke showed a tendency to introduce dialogue into passages that had none or to shift indirect discourse into direct discourse. Acts has a different version of the same technique. One third of the work is devoted to speeches. Analysis of the style of the speeches shows them to have been composed by Luke himself. You should remember that it was common for historical writers in Luke's time to compose speeches for their characters. The author was supposed to provide his characters with a speech worthy of the occasion. Luke uses speeches in Acts to reveal the meaning of events occuring in the narrative.

One set of speeches are the so-called "kerygmatic" speeches (2:14-39; 3:11-26; 4:18-22; 5:29-32; 10:34-43 all by Peter; 13:16-41, by Paul). These speeches follow a typical outline. Read Acts 2:14-39:

(1) Introduction sets the speech into narrative (vv 14-21).

(2) Schematic outline of the message about Jesus with proofs from the Old Testament (vv 22-26).

(3) Call to penance and conversion.

Luke uses this speech as a turning point in his narrative. Remember (Lk 24:49; Ac 1:4) the apostles had been instructed to remain in Jerusalem until the spirit would be poured out on them. Then they were to begin their mission to the Gentiles, "beginning from Jerusalem." Joel 3:5 (= Ac 2:21) was probably an early Christian proof text to explain the coming of the Spirit. In this speech, Luke uses that tradition as part of an argument that the promise of the Father has indeed been fulfilled (2:39). The apostles are beginning from Jerusalem to preach to the nations because there are people there from every nation listening (vv 5-8). Thus the speech is considered the inauguration of the new phase of salvation history: preaching to the nations. Luke has used traditions and language from older preaching but reworked them to fit his understanding of the history of the early Church. The other type of speeches called apologetic because they are given in defense of the preaching show features similar to these. (7:2-53, Stephen; 17:22-31; 20:18-35; 22:3-21; 24:10-21; 26:1-23; 28:17-20, 25-29, Paul)

The second way in which Luke ties together and advances his narrative is through summaries. Some are only a verse long. But there are three major ones in the early part of the book (2:42-47; 4:32-35; 5:11-16). Read Acts 2:42-47. You can see that the summary presents an idyllic picture of the early Church. It fills out the picture given in the particular incidents by generalizing and claiming that they were typical and frequently repeated. Luke probably had some traditional stories (3:1-10; 4:36f.; 5:1-10); older prayer forms (4:24-30) and the ideals of the apostolic age such as sharing community meals and temple observances to work with. He has put these individual pieces together to give his readers a picture of the earliest community. All the summaries stress the advancement and growth of the Church.

Luke conceives of the growth as an ordered and divinely guided expansion from Jerusalem to Rome, the nations. A simple outline of the book shows that progress:

I. Palestine (1:1-9:43)
    a. Introduction of the mission and preaching (1:1-2:47)
    b. Persecution and apostolic preaching (3:1-4:35)
    c. The ideal community (4:36-5:16)
    d. Persecution and Stephen's testimony (5:17-7:53)
    e. Persecution and mission to Samaria (8:1-40)
    f. Call of Paul (9:1-31)
    g. Peter's mission in Palestine (9:32-43)
II. To the Nations (10:1-end)
    a. Introduction: justification of Gentile mission (10:1-15:35)
    b. Missionary journeys of Paul (15:36-21:14)
    c. Paul in Jerusalem: defense before the Jews (21:151-23:11)
    d. Paul defends the gospel before the nations (23:12-end)
       in Çasesarea (23:12-26:32),
       on journey to Rome (27:1-28:16),
       in Rome (28:17-31).

The whole work is structured to present us with the inevitable progress of Christianity from Jerusalem where it was viewed as a Jewish sect to Rome where it is seen to be a universal religion. You will also notice that Luke has enlisted the two great heros of Christianity, Peter and Paul as the foci for this development.

The Early Church in Acts

We noticed that the summaries in Acts idealize the early community even when the stories report that there were difficulties. It is clear that Luke does not expect Christians of his day to copy the Jerusalem Church. The city in which it was centered and the temple in which its members worshipped have both been destroyed. The strong Jewish Christian wing of the Church that had been centered in Jerusalem has dispersed. The Church in Luke's day had no clear center, though the congregations in the great cities like Antioch played a leading role because their missionaries had founded the communities in many other cities. The picture of the early Church in Acts may be explanatory in that it shows Luke's Gentile audiences the roots of certain traditions such as almsgiving and community meals. At the same time, it saveguards Christianity from the stigma of being a "new religion" by showing that it was rooted in a specific tradition, nation and city.

Given the dispersion of Christian communities at the time Luke writes, we are not surprised that he has no specific doctrine of the universal Church. In his writings the word "Church" designates individual congregations. He sees the apostles—especially Peter—as the source of all the various missionary activities of the Church. Paul is merely picking up on a Gentile mission that had been inaugurated by the apostle Peter before him.

Christian Heroes Peter and Paul

This parallelism between Peter and Paul seems a bit odd when compared with the conflict between the two that Paul reports in Galatians 2. But Luke writes 40 years after Galatians—which he probably had not read—and some 25 years after both had suffered martyrdom for their preaching. For him, the complex problems of sin, Law and righteousness that had bothered Paul, the former Pharisee, do not exist. The Old Testament is viewed simply as a book prophecying Christ. The move to a Gentile mission in Luke is not possible apostasy from Judaism. The apostles who initiate the Gentile mission are loyal Jews. Paul is consistently associated with the Jerusalem group in Acts (9:23-28 contrast Gal 1:15-20). He is even willing to have Timothy circumcised because of the Jews in a region where he is working (16:3 contrast Gal 5:11!) These loyal Jews are led irresistibly by God to start the Gentile mission. The will of God is revealed in miraculous signs and visions (9:1-19a; 10:1-11:18; 13:1-4).

While the controversy stories in the gospels and the Pauline letters suggested that much Jewish Christian controversy centered on Christian teaching about the Law, the Law never emerges as an issue in Acts. All the early Christians, who were converts from Judaism, keep the Law as a matter of course. In Acts, the tensions arise over the Christian preaching that Jesus is risen. Thus scholars have suggested that Luke's picture tells us what the issues were in Luke's day. It may also be the case that Luke has based his construction in Acts on those elements of early Christian preaching that have been preserved in his predominantly Gentile environment.

Both Peter and Paul are portrayed in the same way. Scholars have observed that their two careers are almost parallel. Look at the following examples:

Acts 2-12 (Peter) Acts 13-28 (Paul)

1. Spirit initiates his preaching:	2:1-40	13:1-40
2. Heal lame man:	3:1-10	14:8-13
3. Speech follows healing:	12-26	15-17
4. Stoning/persecution leads to wider mission:	(of Stephen) 6:8-8:4	(of Paul) 19-23
5. Spirit in a vision instructs apostle to broaden mission; he must explain to Jerusalem:	chs. 10-11	chs. 13-21
6. Imprisoned at Jewish feast, no information about his ultimate fate:	12:4-7	21:16-28
7. Conclusion: success of Word of God:	12:24	28:30f.

Besides these parallels in the events of their life stories, we find other parallels in the activities of each:

1. Counter magician:	8:9-24	13:6-12
2. Gentiles try to worship him:	10:25f.	14:13-15
3. Raise the dead:	9:36-43	20:9-12
4. Delivered from prison:	12:6-11	16:24-26

5. Gives spirit by lay- ing on hands:	8:14-17	19:1-6
6. Appoints others with prayer and laying on of hands (apostles)/ fasting (Paul):	6:1-6	14:23
7. Defended by Pharisees in Sanhedrin:	5:34-39	23:9
8. Accused of acts vs. temple, laws, customs of Moses:	6:13-14 (Stephen)	21:20f.; 25:8
9. Risen Christ designates witnesses:	1:21-22	23:11; 26:16

Both apostles, of course, are shown to be eloquent speakers. A naive view might suppose that the lives of Peter and Paul actually did follow the same course. But such a view becomes even more unlikely when we notice that not only are the lives of the apostles similar to each other, they also show striking parallels to the life of Jesus as it is set out in the gospel of Luke. Here are some examples:

	Luke	*Acts*
1. Spirit given in physical form:	3:21f	1:14, 24; 2:1-13
2. Opening sermon on fulfillment of Old Testa- ment and rejection of Jesus:	4:16-30	2:14-40
3. Examples of preaching/ healing prove fulfill- ment of promise; conflict leads to rejection:	4:31-8:56	2:14-12:17
a. Heal lame:	5:17-26	3:1-10
b. vs leaders:	5:29-6:11	4:1-8:3
c. Pious centurion:	7:1-10	ch 10
d. Widow and resurrection story:	7:11-17	9:36-43
e. criticism from Pharisees:	7:36-50	11:1-18

Jesus' journey to Jerusalem may be paralleled by Paul's own

journey there. Both are punctuated with statements about the necessity for the journey; the danger that awaits the hero in Jerusalem, and his resolve to go through with it (Lk 9:51ff.//Ac 19:21; Lk 13:22//Ac 20:22; Lk 13:33//21:13; Lk 19:11, 28//Ac 21:15, 17). Further similarities occur when each arrives in Jerusalem:

	Jesus	Paul
1. Enthusiastic reception:	19:37	21:17-20a
2. Enter temple:	19:45-48	21:26
3. Sadducees do not believe in resurrection; scribes support hero:	20:27-39	23:6-9
4. Bless/break bread:	22:19a	27:35
5. Seized by mob:	22:54	21:30

There are some similarities in the trials of the two men. Each undergoes four of them: Sanhedrin; Pilate # 1/Felix; Herod// Herod Agrippa; Pilate # 2//Festus. Both are slapped at the High Priest's (Lk 22:63f.; Ac 23:2). Both are declared innocent three times (Lk 23:4, 14, 22; Ac 23:9; 25:25; 26:32). In both cases, the Jews cry "away with him" (Lk 28:18; Ac 21:36), while a Roman centurion expresses a favorable opinion of them (Lk 23:47; Ac 27:3, 43). Those details of the passion of Jesus that Luke derived from his sources, i.e., the abuse by the High Priest and the centurion—were probably introduced by him into the story of Paul. He always stresses hostility of the Jewish leaders as the reason for action against Christians. Both the people and the Roman officials give the heroes a warm welcome.

These lengthy parallels show that Luke has cast the lives of his three heroes in the same mold. Such stylization is typical of ancient rhetoric, historiography and biography. But scholars have not reached any consensus as to what types of ancient biography might have served Luke as a model. Some have proposed the popular lives of the philosophers. Others, the fictional heroes of ancient romances. Whatever his models were, the set of correspondences between the lives of Jesus, Peter and Paul provided Luke's readers with a stable pattern for the life of the Christian hero.

The Theology of Acts

The theology of Acts continues to be a matter of some debate. For a work that is one third speeches, there seems to be little emphasis on the kinds of theological concerns that moved Paul or John. Some observations about the theology of Acts merely reiterate what we have already seen in the gospel: the cross is not part of a necessary plan of salvation; it is presented as a judicial error by Jewish authorities, who thereby fulfill Old Testament prophecies about the Messiah. Nor does Luke emphasize the eschatological teaching of early Christianity. Christians expect the resurrection and the return of Jesus. That judgment is treated as a motif for repentance (Ac 17:31f).

In comparison with the fourth gospel, for example, the Christology of Acts seems underdeveloped. God the Father predominates. He is clearly creator, responsible for miracles and directing all that happens through the spirit. Even Jesus is under the direction of the Spirit. We never find any of the images that led early Christians to speak of the pre-existence of Christ as Son of God in Luke-Acts. You may also contrast the end of Luke and beginning of Acts with the endings of Matthew or John. You will notice that while Matthew and John emphasize the abiding presence of Jesus with the Church, Luke emphasizes his absence. The succession of witnesses must continue to testify about him. For Luke, the resurrection is a doctrine of future eschatology, something to which the believer looks forward because Jesus has already been raised. Who is Jesus then? In Acts, he emerges as a good man who having died a martyr's death has been exalted by God to be Lord and Savior of all and eventually judge. There are two ways in which the presence of the divine influences the community. The name of Jesus is viewed as an active salvific power. And the Spirit guides the continuing life of the Church. We are shown that every Christian receives the Spirit at baptism. It may also give

individuals the ability to perform specific tasks. The Spirit is
guiding the community just as it had guided Jesus.

At the same time, Luke's readers may have found themselves transported back into the time of Jesus and the earliest
apostles by his narrative. We have seen that Luke has drawn
the lives of Jesus, Peter and Paul in the same colors. The
reader, then, might infer that the life of Jesus is made present
again as it is embodied in his disciples.

Acts as Apology for Christianity

We noted that many of the speeches in Acts are apologetic;
they seek to provide a reasoned defense of Christianity. Two
key elements in that defense are explaining the transition
from Jewish to Gentile movement and making Christianity
itself intelligible to a Gentile audience. On the first point look
at Paul's speech in Acts 22:1-21. This speech does not touch on
the accusation against Paul: defiling the temple. Rather it de-
fends Christianity's move out to the Gentiles. So, Paul's Jewish
heritage is stressed, as is that of Ananias (v 12). He did not
attain his position as apostle to the Gentiles out of disrespect
for or lack of instruction in, the traditions of his fathers. The
whole movement is directed by the God of the fathers (v 14).
Finally, the rejection that Paul suffers from the Jews is given
as the reason for the mission to the Gentiles (22:21).

While that argument might answer the objection that
Christianity is an apostate Jewish sect, not a religion for Gentiles, it does not explain why a Gentile might want to join the
movement. Acts 17:22-34 shows us Luke's positive view of
paganism and its religiousness. (It contrasts strongly with a
typical Jewish view such as the one Paul gives in Romans
1:18-3:26.) Archaeologists have not discovered any altar to *an
unknown God* in Athens. Literary traditions (Paus. i.1,4;
Philostr. *Vit. Apol.* vi, 3,5) mention Athenian altars to unknown gods, i.e., altars not dedicated to any particular god.
Perhaps Luke is dependent on such literary remarks in formulating the introduction to this speech. He can then present
Christianity as the fulfillment of pagan religiousness. Univer-

salism and monotheism of a sort, were as we have seen, common enough themes in popular philosophical speculation of this period. Luke's presentation draws both on the Old Testament and on the common pagan tradition. He then continues with a stock Old Testament argument against paganism (Isa 40:18-20; 46:5-6; Wis 13:10). But a pagan philosopher might well agree with some of these comments since they could be just as critical of the anthropomorphism of popular religious mythology.

Thus, the first two parts of the speech are similar to what one might hear from any wandering preacher or philosopher. Christianity would be understood as fitting the mold of enlightened, popular religious thought. Such a pagan listener might then expect to be called to a life of philosophic virtue as the realization of kinship with the divine. Instead repentance and judgment (v 28) are preached. The resurrection is God's guarantee that Jesus will be the judge. Such traditional Christian eschatology does not fit the mold of a philosophic sermon. We have already noted that Luke does not seem to have given any theological reflection to such assertions. They seem to be traditional assertions from the Gentile mission that Luke has inserted in this context. Perhaps he views them as representing the key difference between Christianity and its pagan competitors. At the same time, the crowd reaction (vv. 32-34) makes that the crucial point of misunderstanding. It may be possible to preach the Christian doctrine of God the Father in terms familiar to pagans just as it was possible for Luke to present Jesus as popular miracle worker and universal ethical teacher, but the Christian doctrine of judgment resists assimilation. The case for Christianity can be made only to a point. Then Luke turns to a recital of conventional eschatology.

The positions represented in his speeches are part of Luke's overall apology in this work. He shows Christianity to be a non-threatening, religious movement. One whose progress has been carefully guided by divine providence. Christians did not abandon ancestral traditions or invent some new religion. Rather the people to whom those traditions had belonged violently rejected the purposes of God both in rejecting Jesus and in rejecting the great missionaries who continued to bear witness to him. Gentiles, on the other hand, respond to the message enthusiastically. The Areopagus speech points to Christianity as the logical fulfillment of the best of pagan popular religious speculation. The Gentile Christian reading Luke's two-volume work might well look upon his religion as part of the universal history of humanity and himself or herself as a citizen of the wider *oikumene*. He or she is not portrayed as the devotee of some unusual sect, a follower of a religious group frequently despised in the Graeco-Roman world. He or she is heir to the great heroes, Peter and Paul, and a devotee of the religion that is God's plan for the whole world.

Those today who find Acts overly triumphalistic should be reminded that Luke's Church was still a small minority; still persecuted sporadically. The large numbers of converts in the opening stories may be as much hope of the future as exaggerated tradition about the first days. The absence of both Jesus and those first apostles may have been keenly felt. The community must now take its inspiration and hope for the future from the past as Luke has portrayed it: a past of trial and persecution to be sure, but also one of success, divine guidance and rejoicing.

STUDY QUESTIONS

1. How does the outline of Acts reflect the author's purpose in writing?
2. What role do speeches play in Acts? How does Luke use summary statements?
3. What is Luke's picture of the early Jerusalem community? What is the significance of that picture for Christians in Luke's day?
4. What is Luke's explanation for Christianity's shift from Jewish sect to Gentile religion? How does it compare with

the picture given in the Pauline epistles?

5. Give three examples of how the lives of Peter, Paul and Jesus are made parallel in Luke.

6. What is Luke's picture of the "hero apostle"? What virtues would it teach his readers?

7. What is the Christology of Acts? How is the Church guided now that Jesus and the apostles have died?

8. What, according to Luke, is the relationship between Christianity and pagan religious thought?

Chapter Fifteen

HEBREWS: THE NEW ISRAEL, A PILGRIM PEOPLE

Since antiquity people have realized that the theology and language of Hebrews are not Pauline. You will also notice that Hebrews is not formally a letter. Only the conclusion, vv. 13:18-25, has that appearance. It may have been added by someone who included Hebrews in a collection of early Christian letters and who assumed that Paul was the author of the treatise. Hebrews was not accepted as canonical in the West until the 4th century. It is a moving and learned homily by an anonymous Christian. His Greek style and vocabulary are among the best in the New Testament. He uses a method of allegorical and typological exegesis of the Old Testament that is represented among Alexandrian Jews as well as philosophical concepts from middle Platonism. (The Jewish philosopher Philo also combines both these characteristics.) Since Hebrews is quoted in First Clement (*ca.* A.D. 96), it must have been written before the turn of the century.

Two of the images from Hebrews have had an abiding influence on Christian spirituality and liturgy: that of the Church as a wandering people of God, and that of Christ as high priest after the order of Melchisedek. Yet, most Christians cannot tell you what Hebrews meant by using those images. A quick look through Hebrews reveals that apostasy is one of the author's major concerns (2:1; 3:6, 12-14; 4:11; 5:11; 6:4-12; 10:23, 29, 39; 12:4-17, 25). It seems that some who had been Christians (10:32f.) were abandoning their faith. Perhaps they are returning to Judaism, since the author's energy has been channelled into demonstrating the inferior and transitory character of Judaism. Whenever we are reading a passage from Hebrews we should ask how it fits into the author's aim of exhorting Christians to remain faithful.

Metaphysical Assumptions

Most of the New Testament does not require any philosophical background. Even Paul's Areopagus speech does not go beyond the popular, "street corner" philosophy of the Graeco-Roman world. Hebrews is different. The author consistently presupposes the world-view of middle Platonic philosophy. That speculation contrasted the unchangable, perfect world of the divine, which can only be grasped by the mind, with the transitory, imperfect world of sense perception. The author of Hebrews consistently applies this contrast to the Old Testament and Christianity. Jewish exegetes like Philo had also applied this scheme to the Old Testament, but their purpose was to show that the material imagery of the Old Testament was simply an allegorical way of describing what is divine and unchanging. From the ethical perspective, that included descriptions of the way in which the soul of the wise could progress toward the divine by advancing in virtue. Abraham's wanderings, for example, exemplify the progress of the individual soul. Clearly, Hebrews does not take over this type of interpretation of the journey motif.

Now look at Hebrews 12:12-29 and you will see how he does use this metaphysical system to interpret traditional, Christian eschatological language.

Hebrews 12:12-17 introduces the problem: Christians who are becoming "weary." If you look at the cross references in your Bible, you will see that the author is frequently quoting the Old Testament (e.g. v 12, Isa 35:3). The interpretation of the Esau story is an example of *typological* interpretation of the

Old Testament. The Old Testament figure, Esau, is a type of the future Christian believer. Also notice the doctrine of no repentance—the author has earlier argued that there is no "second chance" for apostates (10:31). Here the Esau story is said to teach that doctrine.

Hebrews 12:18-29 then contrasts the salvation of Israel and the Sinai theophany with Christian salvation and the revelation of God to come at the last judgment. But notice that there is another term introduced, the heavenly Jerusalem, which is not linked with the events of the second coming and judgment as it would have been in traditional Christian and Jewish eschatology and as it is in the book of Revelation. If we were to put the author's categories in columns as we did in studying Paul's typological interpretation in Galatians, we would have to have two Christian sections: one for the underlying heavenly realities and one for the events still to affect earth, for example:

	Old Covenant	*New Covenant*
on	Sinai theophany	
	thunder, earthquake	shaking at the end of
earth	voice of God	the world
	fear of Moses	(fear at the judgment)
	blood of Abel	
abiding in		heavenly Jerusalem,
heaven		unshakable
		voice of Jesus speaking
		blood of Jesus

Notice how the author has reinterpreted traditional eschatology in v 25. The apocalyptic view was that heaven, and earth would be shaken and destroyed prior to a new creation. Hebrews tells its readers that the material world will disappear and the heavenly one remain. Because Christians belong to that heavenly world, their kingdom is unshakable. Platonic philosophy held that the material world was an imperfect copy of the heavenly archetypes existing in the mind of God. (Some-

times these archetypes were interpreted as numbers.) Jewish
exegetes might apply this system to the Old Testament by
saying that earthly liturgy was only symbolic of heavenly
reality or the progress of the soul that must become perfect in
virtue in order to see God. Then the house or temple would be
understood to be the soul, which was to be purified of all passions and attachments to the material world. You will notice
that in our chart of the Hebrews passage there are no Jewish
heavenly realities. All correspondences are drawn to Christianity. The perfection/stability of the divine realm can only be
found there.

Such metaphysical assumptions play an important role in
religious traditions. They assure believers that their convic-
tions and values are grounded in the structure of reality itself;
that there is an unbreakable connection between the way one
ought to live and the structure of the universe. Within this
context the famous motif of the wandering people of God takes
on a different coloring from that usually assigned to it. Wandering is a necessary condition of life in this material world. In
the philosophical tradition, the soul wandered while it sought
the perfection that was the goal of the wise man. In Hebrews,
the goal is described as "rest"—the rest or promised land lost
by the Old Testament people of God because of their apostasy
(3:6-4:13). Notice that the author insists that the stability of
that rest must be paralleled by the stability of the people. The
Old Testament exodus stories serve as a warning against apostasy (3:7-19). The apostasy of the Israelites could not cancel the
promise of such a rest because the rest is not a temporal
phenomenon but part of the divinely established order, itself
(4:3f.).

Liturgical Imagery in Hebrews

Hebrews does not interpret liturgical language in ethical
categories as a reflection of the progress of the soul. Rather
Jesus' exaltation into the heavenly sanctuary marks the end of
the earthly cult. Notice that Hebrews is not describing earthly
Christian cult. All its Christian cultic language is associated

with the heavenly sanctuary and the offering of Christ. We do hear of some Christian liturgical practices in the list of elementary doctrines, which the author says he will not discuss (6:1-8). Both baptism and laying on of hands are included (v 4f.). But Hebrews does not interpret those practices as successors to the Old Testament, unlike other New Testament authors we have read (e.g., 1 Cor 10; Jn 6). His contrast is drawn between Old Testament sacrifices and its covenant and the covenant made through the death of Christ. The former share the transitory character of all earthly phenomena. They are not permanently efficacious but must be repeated. This intensive devaluation of Old Testament liturgical language suggests that the temptation to apostasy was coming from Judaism. He implies that no perfection can ever be attained through its rites and ceremonies. Perhaps he even formulates this polemic against the type of philosophical interpretation of liturgy found in people like Philo.

Hebrews not only presents the sacrifice of Jesus as the only heavenly liturgical reality, but throughout the letter emphasizes the superiority of Jesus to all other heavenly beings who stand as intermediaries between God and the material world. Middle platonic philosophy stressed the transcendence of the divine. A whole hierarchy of intermediary beings stand between God and his creation. Frequently the expressions "word," "son" or "wisdom" are used of such intermediaries. Jewish authors could treat figures like Aaron, Moses, Levi and the High Priest as exemplars of perfection. As guides to others, they might also be said to mediate the perfection of the divine world. The soul was to become "like God," i.e., a son of God.

Hebrews shares much of the language of that tradition, but it does not treat the progress of Christians as a progress in virtue in the same way as such Jewish authors do. He seems to be alluding to that tradition when he argues that only Christians attain the goal. They can do so because Jesus is greater than all these other intermediaries and has established the true, eternal covenant of salvation. The work opens by designating Jesus as the "Son," intermediary through whom God

maintains the cosmos (1:1-4). But notice that the perfection of
the Son is not based on his metaphysical status as "Son" but on
his liturgical act of making purification for sin (vv 3f.). Hebrews then moves on to argue that the angels cannot/do not
mediate perfection. Their rank in the hierarchy is much lower
than that of Jesus to whom the whole cosmos is subject (1:5-
2:8a). This hierarchical scheme allows the author to answer an
objection, "We do not see the universe subject to Jesus" (2:8b).
You remember that apocalyptic writers expected to see the
subjection of all to the Messiah when he established his rule
over the new creation. But in Hebrews the created order is not
going to last; the glorious exaltation of Jesus as Son is not
something to be seen there. Instead what can be seen in the
created world is the earthly humiliation of Jesus who became
lower than the angels in order to become the source of perfection for others (2:9-18).

A variety of arguments are used throughout Hebrews to
show that Jesus is superior to others who were understood to
mediate perfection in the Jewish tradition. Hebrews 3:2-6 establishes his superiority to Moses. The polemic there is not
clear until you realize that "house" was used in the Alexandrian Jewish exegetical traditions as part of a set of symbols:
God's house = temple = universe = soul of the wise. The goal of
perfection was to make one's soul "house." Hebrews says that
Jesus is superior to Moses because he is over (= mediator of
creation) the house (= cosmos) while Moses was only a servant
in the house (= temple). We become house of God (i.e., receive
perfection) through hope. You can read other liturgical arguments in Hebrews such as chs 8-10 and see that the same
hierarchical schema is being employed to assert the superiority
of Jesus and to warn Christians that they had better not become apostates since they can only attain perfection through
Christ.

At the same time it was clear to all New Testament authors that Jesus was not and could not have been a priest like
Aaron or Levi or the founder of the Qumran sect or the messianic priest as he lacked the appropriate geneology. Hebrews

6:13-7:28 deals with that problem by arguing that Christ belongs to a superior order of priesthood that of Melchizedek. He uses that strange story in Genesis to argue that Abraham, Aaron and Levi are all subordinate to the order (= rank in the hierarchy) of Melchizedek. Like Jesus, Melchizedek is without geneology and like Jesus—but unlike the others—is eternal.

Scholars are less puzzled by what seems a forced argument since the discovery of Melchizedek texts at Qumran. There, Melchizedek is conceived as a heavenly figure who would take dominion and execute judgment in the messianic age. They understand his eternity and heavenly status as a guarantee to Abraham and through him to Jewish priests of the Levitical line that their priesthood would be eternal and that he would have a share in "heavenly things," be heirs to God—that is the messianic kingdom. Now you can see what Hebrews has done. It has taken that tradition and turned it around. Because Jesus is eternal and not a mortal man he is the true heir to Melchizedek. Melchizedek guarantees or prefigures his priesthood not the Levitical priesthood of the Jews. Therefore, those who will gain the inheritance of God are those who have been made sons through the priesthood of Christ.

Christ the Faithful High Priest

We have seen that Hebrews uses metaphysical and liturgical language to establish the superiority of Christ and his salvation to other alleged mediators of salvation and that he is doing so in reaction to a real threat of apostasy. Some interpreters would even suggest that the problem is brought on by polemic on the part of those who were expounding a liturgico-philosophical interpretation of Judaism. We have also seen that although Hebrews uses much of their language, he does not use the philosophical categories of middle Platonism to define what Christian salvation can mean. Wandering in the wilderness is not a type of the progress of the soul to God; it is merely the image of the necessary existence in this world while the people are away from the abiding heavenly reality that constitutes their destiny.

A look at Hebrews' description of Jesus' functions as High Priest will provide a clue to its understanding of salvation. Perfection and permanence are the marks of divine heavenly reality. Hebrews 7:15-28 argue that the old covenant and priesthood were imperfect and transitory because of the sinfulness, weakness and mortality of those who held the office of High Priest. We have seen, of course, that he is contradicting Jewish traditions that saw the High Priest, especially as exemplified in Moses, Aaron and Levi, as a model of perfection and that argued that the Melchizedek story was a guarantee of the permanency of the Levitical priesthood. They would not agree that the old covenant did not bring perfection (7:18f.). Chapters 8 and 9 portray Christ as minister in the heavenly sanctuary that he has entered through his death. The Jews would have agreed with Hebrews 8:5 that the earthly temple is a copy of the heavenly pattern, but they would not agree with the Christian claim that the death of Christ enabled him to enter the heavenly one (e.g., 9:23-28). They might argue that the death of Christ is like the earthly rites that Hebrews rejects because they are limited to the natural, bodily realm and not that of the conscience (9:9-10).

You can see that the monkey wrench in the system is the traditional Christian preaching of the death of Christ as effecting salvation and forgiveness of sins. Hebrews must reformulate the liturgical-philosophical language he has adopted in order to express that reality. He repeatedly stresses the perfection of Jesus and the uniqueness of his sacrifice as indications of the superior character of the covenant it establishes. But he cannot avoid the peculiarity—for a platonist exegete—of having the blood and flesh of Jesus as what opens the way into the heavenly sanctuary for the believer (10:21f.). Hebrews is not expounding a theology of the eucharist but describing the permanent cosmic efficaciousness of a specific event, the death of Jesus.

We have already seen that the material world is one of imperfection and weakness for the Platonist for whom perfection means drawing near the divine by abandoning the body, its passions and senses. In Hebrews we have someone presented as heavenly and perfect, who is said to have gone in the other direction and even to have become perfect in the offering of his body (1:3f.)! Hebrews does not deny that the material (flesh and blood) realm is the realm of sin, temptation, imperfection, weakness and ignorance. But if you read Hebrews 2:10-18 and 5:7-10, you can see what he has done with these categories. Jesus' suffering and death were established by God for his perfection. Jesus' humanity implies his solidarity with us in temptation, suffering and death. Notice that apocalyptic language about deliverance from Satan is now associated with the redemptive character of Jesus' perfection through suffering (2:14-15). Hebrews 5:7-10 makes it clear that Jesus first achieves perfection through his steadfast obedience in suffering and death. Then he is designated High Priest according to the order of Melchizedek and is a source of salvation for others who obey him. In this way, Christ's heavenly perfection is neither something he possesses by some kind of divine nature nor something he has gained by fleeing the material and bodily realm through philosophic contemplation and perfection of soul. Rather, he has gained perfection within the realm of the created and imperfect by steadfast obedience; by suffering all the temptations, passions and weaknesses of the flesh without sinning (4:15).

The notion that suffering and martyrdom could be understood as an "education" leading to perfection was not foreign in Hellenistic Judaism. It occurs in accounts of the Maccabean martyrs and of the suffering of the people of God (cf. Wisd 11:9-10; 12:22; 2 Macc 6:12,16, 27f, 31; 4 Macc 10:10f.; cp Hebr 5:7-10; 2:10; 7:28; 12:1-11). Such traditions have been influential in other Christian formulations of the meaning of Jesus' death as we saw with Romans 3:24-26. Hebrews has utilized them in a unique way by stressing the idea that Jesus has been educated through his sufferings.

You may also notice that his view of Jesus' perfection implies that Jesus himself must be "saved" or perfected. He genuinely endures temptation and trial. Most Christians find the humanity of Jesus "unreal" because they do not take it with full seriousness as Hebrews does. They do not think of Jesus as "being perfected," as being tempted in such a way that he might actually have failed, but they think of him as already perfect, as possessing the kind of freedom from passion and bodily weakness that the philosophic tradition admired. Such a person is not tempted because his soul is entirely cleansed of passion. Hebrews rejects that understanding of Jesus' perfection as incompatible with the tradition of the suffering and death of Jesus in Christianity. Therefore, he cannot accept the liturgico-philosophical categories of the understanding of salvation without radically modifying their notion of perfection.

But his modification goes even beyond his account of the earthly life of Jesus. One might suppose that once Jesus is appointed High Priest after his trials, that his soul is cleansed of all "passion"; that he then achieved the passionless state associated with the eternal abiding nature of the divine just as the Maccabean martyrs were said to do in 4 Maccabees 13:19-14:20. Not so. Hebrews provides a rationale for this peculiar process of perfection, which implies that even as heavenly high priest Jesus has not abandoned the realm of imperfection. The reason for the process he went through was to provide a sympathetic and merciful High Priest (2:16-18; 4:14-5:3). You could say that Hebrews views the perfection of Jesus as exemplified in his feeling (*pathos*) for his brothers who remain in the realm of weakness, temptations, sin and pilgrimage.

Christian Salvation in Hebrews

This profound reformulation of both the liturgico-philosophical interpretations of Judaism and of earlier Christian traditions of perfection has implications for the life of the Christian as well. We have already noted the consistent polemic against apostasy: the exhortations to endure in confidence that Christians are to inherit an unshakable heavenly kingdom. We have seen that Christians are warned that there will be no salvation at the judgment for those who do abandon this promise. You have probably noticed that endurance, faith and hope are key words that Hebrews uses both in his exhortations to Christians and in his description of the career of Jesus. Read 6:19f. Jesus' entry into the heavenly sanctuary as High Priest guarantees the Christian hope of salvation. He even speaks of hope as entering that unseen heavenly sanctuary. That modification is important. Hebrews does not say that Christians are only suffering and enduring to wait for some future afterlife or some future end of the world. He constantly says that they can now enter the sanctuary, rest, approach the throne, etc., (3:6, 14; 4:7, 11, 16; 6:4-5; 9:11; 10:19-20). They are to do this through faith and hope. They are what give the Christian the immediacy and access to God that the liturgico-philosophical language of the epistle promises.

Now read the famous verses on faith in Hebrews 11:1-2. You can understand the question being answered. Hebrews is not answering the question, "What is faith?" He is answering the question, "How can we hope in or possess an unseen salvation." Most translations obscure the significance of what is being said here: "Faith is called the *hypostasis* of what is hoped for and the proof of what is not seen. The RSV translation of hypostasis as assurance does not get at the full significance of what is being said. Hypostasis means substance or essence. The Greek word *elegchos* (proof), rendered "conviction" in the RSV, is much stronger than conviction. It refers to an actual demonstration. It can be used, for example, of a mathematical proof or of the proof (= evidence) in a legal case. Thus Hebrews is not presenting a subjectivist interpretation of faith that would make it a kind of hyper-conviction of the soul. It is presenting faith as really getting ahold of, as proving the promised salvation. The transitory and temptation-ridden character of life in this world does not deprive us of perfection any more than it hindered Jesus from becoming the source of perfection of others with whom he still sympathizes. In fact, temptation and testing are part of the process of perfection as the Old Testament examples in chapter 11 show. But there is a crucial difference between their faith and that of the Christian. They did not receive what was promised (11:13-16). Unlike Paul,

Hebrews does not make Abraham's faith Christian faith. Abraham does not receive the covenant/promise that comes in Christ. Why? Because there can be no perfection before the perfection achieved by Christ (11:39f.).

Hebrews has argued consistently that Jesus' sacrifice is the only one that forgives sins; that before him the way into the heavenly sanctuary, the holy of holies was closed. Nonetheless the Old Testament can and does provide Christians with both positive and negative examples of how people are to live in this world. But the supreme model is Jesus himself. Hebrews 12 and 13 apply that model to Christian exhortation. The Christians must also be "educated" (RSV: discipline) to the perfection that makes them true sons of God. That education/discipline is embodied in the variety of moral precepts by which the Christian is "trained" (13:1-17). He or she must follow the lead of Jesus who is "founder and perfector of faith" (12:2).

STUDY QUESTIONS

1. What is the major practical problem faced by the author of Hebrews? How does the doctrine of no second repentance fit in with that problem?
2. What basic metaphysical assumptions underlie the argumentation of this epistle?
3. How does Hebrews use the Old Testament? What significance does the Old Testament have for Christians?
4. How does Hebrews argue for Christ as the only mediator of salvation?
5. How is the death of Jesus interpreted in Hebrews?
6. Why are faith and hope key virtues in Hebrews? How does Hebrews interpret faith?
7. What is "perfection" for Hebrews? How is its view of Jesus' perfection different from that in the philosophical tradition?
8. How does the priesthood of Christ differ from all other priests according to Hebrews?
9. How does the present life of the Christian relate to that of Jesus according to Hebrews?

Chapter Sixteen

REVELATION:
THE MARTYRED SAINTS

Both Hebrews and Revelation exploit liturgical language to describe the certainty of salvation. But Revelation uses apocalyptic and visionary traditions about the heavenly liturgy, not a liturgico-philosophical understanding of the Old Testament. The problems confronted by the two authors are also different. Hebrews told us that most of its readers would not be tested to the point of shedding blood (12:4). Revelation, on the other hand, is dominated by the motif of martyrdom. The book can be said to revolve around the poles, death/life. Paradoxically one can only gain eternal life through death.

The book of Revelation continues to be one of the most puzzling books in the New Testament. Many of its images and symbols have a long history in Judaism and in surrounding religious cultures. Readers in the 1st century shared that heritage of images and therefore could understand Revelation much more directly than we can in the 20th century. To get some feel for the types of tradition involved turn to your Old Testament and read the visions of Daniel 7-12 and Ezekiel chs 1-9; 26-27; and 39-44 and Zechariah 9-14. The most important thing to remember is that Revelation is not an allegory. Rather, the author is using a long tradition of religious imagery and poetry to make a picture of Christian life and salvation. It is not possible to predict the end of the world from Revelation by identifying each symbol with an historical person or event, past or present. But you will often find people doing just that. I have frequently met people who had been thoroughly scared by preachers. Revelation does not doubt that there will be a judgment and that it will be preceded by all the catastrophes mentioned in the Old Testament prophets. It apparently shared the conviction of many early Christians that the judgment would occur soon. That conviction has, of course, been shown to be incorrect. But the value of the book does not stand or fall with the timing for the end of the world. As a work of imagery and poetry, it may still inspire visions of the world and the problems Christians encounter as they try to live in it.

In the past year two books on Revelation have appeared, both by lay theologians who were trained as lawyers. They have tried to use the imagery of Revelation to explore the questions of society, the state, evil and justice that face us today. We cannot go into their observations here, since they do not treat the historical interpretation of Revelation. But the appearance of these works shows that Revelation is still a significant source of Christian theology and reflection, quite without literalistic, fire and brimstone preaching that so often characterizes popular interpretations of this work.

Sources and Composition

We have already pointed out that the Old Testament is an important source for the languages and images of Revelation. Parallels with other visionary literature of the 1st century and careful analysis of the language of Revelation suggest that the other used and perhaps even copied other sources in composing this work. For example, we find the following patterns of older material being reused:

(1) The inaugural vision (1:12-20) combines features of Daniel and Ezekiel.

(2) Chapter 5 depicts the heavenly assembly of the gods, an ancient mythological motif used in the prophets as the divine council of Yahweh.

(3) Holy war, when the god defeats the monster of chaos and death and brings forth a new creation, was used of Yahweh in the Old Testament and returns here in Revelation 19:11-22:5.

(4) Other apocalyptic visions speak of judgment as recorded in books; so here (20:11-15).

(5) Contrast of heavenly and earthly cities is common (14:8-21; chs 17-18; 21).

(6) The Exodus plagues (8:1-11:4; 15:5-19:10).

(7) The mythological pattern of conflict with the chaos dragon in order to save the divine child (12:1-14:5; 19:11-20).

(8) Revelation 6:1-7:17 reuses traditional material about world cataclysms.

(9) The actions of Revelation 9:1-11:4 recall the symbolic actions of the Old Testament prophets.

(10) The motif of the winepress of God in Revelation 14:9-20; 19:13 is a prophetic one, Isa 63:3; Jl 4:13.

Besides these older traditions, Revelation uses a variety of literary forms that come from the prophetic and visionary traditions. There are prophetic announcements; words and promises from God's commands; beatitudes, and lists of virtues and vices. The visionary tradition also stressed the presence of an angelic interpreter. Chapters 2-3 are typical of the prophetic messenger speech. The prophet in Revelation has three commissioning visions (1:12-20; chs 4-5; 10:1, 11,14). In addition to these prophetic materials the work is punctuated with antiphonal hymns (4:9-11; 5:9-12; 7:10-12; 11:15b-18; 16:5b-6, 7b; 19:1b-3, 4b, 5b-6b, 8a).

This book uses another form that seems to have been more characteristic of early Christian literature. Although it is a visionary revelation, it is introduced as letters to seven Churches. These letters have a set pattern:

(1) Address and command to write.

(2) the formula, "he says these things . . ." This formula is similar to the messenger formula of the Hebrew prophets.

(3) An exhortation introduced by "I know," which includes some or all of the following:

   a. Situation: "I know that . . ."
   b. Censure: "but I hold it against you . . ."
   c. Call to repentance.
   d. Revelatory sayings and introduction "see . . ."
   e. Announcement of the Lord's coming.
   f. Exhortation.

(4) The saying, "Let him hear . . ." makes it clear that these letters are really addressed to all the Churches.

(5) Each letter ends with an eschatological promise.

While there is widespread agreement as to the nature and extent of such individual units, interpreters find it more difficult to outline this work. Three basic compositional techniques are obvious. The book has two scroll visions. It uses a variety of patterns of seven. And the author likes to interlock material from one section with the next. If we take the patterns of seven as the key to Revelation, we might outline the book as follows:

   a. Prologue (1:1-8)
      Preface (vv 1-3)
      Prescript and sayings (vv 4-8)
   b. Seven Messages to the Churches (1:9-3:22)
   c. Seven Seals (4:1-8:5)
   d. Seven Trumpets (8:2-11:19)
   e. Seven Unnumbered Visions (12:1-15:4)
   f. Seven Bowls (15:1-16:20)
      Babylon Interlude (17:1-19:10)
   g. Seven Unnumbered Visions (19:11-21:8)
      Jerusalem Interlude (21:9-22:5)
   h. Epilogue (22:6-12)
      Sayings (22:6-20)
      Benediction (22:21)

An important question for interpreters of Revelation is whether or not each set of seven represents a linear sequence of events or is a repetition of the same theme. If you look at what you read in Daniel 7-12, you can see that Daniel has a series of visions (7:1-28; 8:1-27; 9:1-27; 10:1-12:13) each of which overlaps with the others. The first introduces us to four empires,

Babylonian, Medes, Persian, Greek, in the form of beasts. The last and most elaborate details the history of the last two, Persian and Greek, and brings the whole to an apocalyptic conclusion in Daniel 12:1-3. Other non-canonical visionary writings show the same system of repetition and elaboration. Therefore many interpreters assume that the visionary sections of the work form a series of overlapping visions and reapplication of the same material. Just as you can be suspicious of any interpretation of Revelation that does not pay attention to the traditional, mythological, symbolic character of its imagery, so you should be suspicious of any interpretation that treats each vision as a new event that has not been alluded to before. You notice that both here and in Daniel each repetition has variations. In Revelation, the various metaphors of destruction and salvation are intensified as we move through the cycles. They are building up to the climax: the vision of the new Jerusalem.

If you now look at the visions in detail you can discover a progressive movement within each one. They all begin with some indication of the persecutions being suffered by the saints. A description of the wrath, judgment or destruction to come upon evil follows. We then return to heaven for a scene of salvation, usually one that includes a hymn or some description of the heavenly liturgy. If you did your reading attentively, you will have noticed that the reader is viewing everything from the perspective of the seer and the martyrs, that is, looking down on earth and later into Hades. He or she is not down among the plagues and beasts but above them. Awareness of this perspective is extremely important as we try to understand the impact this work would have had on those who first heard it.

The Opening Letters

Our outline of the book has shown that the visionary sections are set off by new scenes of prophetic commissioning. The first section is dominated by the seven letters to the Churches, each of similar structure. These letters are introduced as the message from Jesus, the Son of Man, who has died but is alive and is now ruler of the earthly kings. Certain problems emerge in each letter. False apostles and prophets are leading Christians astray; the Churches are not showing the same enthusiasm they did in the beginning; some are following a Judaizing heresy; others must be encouraged to remain steadfast under persecution. You will also notice that each letter ends with a promise of glorious eternal life for those who remain faithful and endure (2:7, 10f., 17, 26; 3:5, 12, 21). We cannot tell with much precision exactly what the false teachers were doing. The reference to not learning the "depths of Satan" (2:24) reminds one of a similar reference to the "depths of God" (1 Cor 2:10). There, Paul argues against the Corinthians that only the Spirit searches the "depths of God" (cp. Rm 11:33). Here the opponents probably claimed knowledge of the depths of God that the author of Revelation is calling knowledge of the depths of Satan. Some scholars have interpreted both passages as allusions to a Gnosticizing heresy, since "depths" appears as a technical term in Gnostic mythology. However, both Romans 11:33 and 1 Corinthians 2:6-10 are using language more reminiscent of apocalyptic writings. In that context the "depths of God" could be an expression similar to the "mysteries of God" (Rm 11:25; 1 Cor 2:7 etc). The Qumran scrolls have shown us clearly that "mystery" in apocalyptic language meant the secrets of God's plan for the end of the world. In Romans, that refers to God's plan for allowing Israel to be hardened against the Messiah for a time in order to allow the Gentiles to be included in salvation. In 1 Cor 15:51, it refers to the transformation of the living at the end-time. The secret wisdom of God in 1 Cor 2:7 is the crucifixion of the Messiah.

Such parallels suggest to us that the issue is not Gnosticizing but the claims by Christian prophets to secret knowledge about the end-time. Perhaps this eschatology denied the types of reward for endurance, or martyrdom promised in these letters. If eschatological speculation was the issue raised by the false teachers and prophets, it is easy to see why the letters are only a preface to the larger whole: a revelation of "what is and what is going to happen after these days."

Besides the doctrine of such false teachers the Christians have a more serious problem to face: external persecution for their faith. In the letters, the persecution at the Churches of Smyrna and Philadelphia is attributed to Jews (2:9ff; 3:9). We know that the Jews represented a strong independent group in Smyrna at this time. We also know that they played a role in the martyrdom of Polycarp of Smyrna some fifty years later. The author of Revelation fully expects that the Christians at Smyrna will experience further persecution (2:10f.). You should remember that persecution of Christians in the first two countries was not on an empire-wide basis. Persecution was regional and the result of private individuals bringing charges against Christians. Correspondence between the governor Pliny and the emperor Trajan (*ca.* A.D. 110) makes the character of such persecutions clear. Pliny has Christians being brought up before him and does not know how to handle the cases, since there is no imperial policy on the matter. He is told not to go looking for Christians and not to accept anonymous accusations against people. Those who say that though they once were Christians but are so no longer and are willing to demonstrate their loyalty to Rome and the emperor by offering incense before the emperor's statue are to go free. Later in Revelation we learn that refusal to worship "the beast" (emperor/empire) is leading to martyrdom (13:8f.). Therefore, it seems likely that the same type of judicial procedure was being applied in the Churches with which Revelation is associated.

Interpreting Myth and Symbol

When we turn to the visionary sections of Revelation, it is important to be aware that mythical and symbolic language is being used. We have already seen some of the myths and traditions being used. A lengthy commentary on Revelation would be required to trace all the various allusions there. But even with such background—and the notes in your Bible will help you with the Old Testament allusions—we would still have to have some key as to how to interpret such language. We have already pointed out that literalistic readings that try to tie each symbol to a specific historical event are widely recognized to be a fallacious procedure.

In recent years, both anthropologists and literary critics have been stressing the importance of myth in human social and religious life. They have weaned us away from the endeavor to find literal and rational meanings in myths: to find concrete events or abstract ideas behind them. Some schools of psychology see myth as a basic component in the development and transformation of the human psyche. We cannot address the details of the various approaches that have been suggested. French anthropologists—Claude Levi-Strauss, for example—find the meaning of myth as a way of thinking in the concrete. Certain basic dilemmas of human life are symbolized by pairs of binary symbols that emerge within the story. The dilemma is resolved as the story introduces pairs between the original antitheses, which can produce reconciliation or mediation. Revelation lends itself to such binary analysis. Just from the first three chapters, you can see that the basic antithesis is life/death and that the supreme reconciling symbol is Christ, the one who has died and yet lives. You can make a chart of these antitheses and see how they are reconciled or overcome.

Another type of analysis is derived from French structuralist literary critics. They argue that every narrative will have (or imply) characters (or objects) that fulfill basic functions. These functions can be schematized in a diagram:

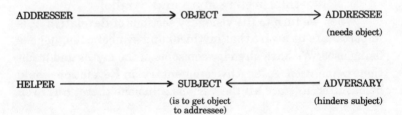

These roles do not need to be expressed by characters; objects, emotions or attitudes may be used. Sometimes a narrative is ambiguous because we are not clear how to distribute the various roles.

They go on to suggest that narrative follows a set sequence. Complexity and variety are added by having various subsequences. The story may end at any point in the series if the required sequence does not reach a satisfactory conclusion.

I. Contractual Syntagm

Contractual Utterance (CU) 1: The subject accepts or rejects the task before him, which will provide the basis for the narrative. The introduction often alludes to previous failures to carry out the same mission.

CU 2: If the subject accepts, then a helper must be provided.

II. Disjunctional Syntagm

The subject must leave his or her normal environment and relationships if he or she is to carry out the contract.

III. Performance Syntagm

PU 1: The addresse is confronted by the subject's need for the object.

PU 2: The subject must subdue the adversary.

PU 3: The subject must deliver the object to the addressee.

IV. Disjunctional Syntagm

The subject returns to the environment and relationships he or she left at the opening of the narrative. Many ambiguities arise within narratives. Sometimes it is not clear how to determine the subject. Is it the main actor? The person from whose viewpoint the story is told? The subject of most of the sentences? The subject may vary if a narrative has several subsequences.

However, one decides these questions for a given section of Revelation, the conclusion in heaven indicates that the narrative is meant to be one of success. One might argue that Revelation is not intending to reconcile opposites in a renewed world order—unlike say the vision of the Old Testament prophets—but ends with a radical disjunction between heaven and hell. All the positive forces, good life, etc., are ultimately gathered in heaven while all evil is relegated to hell. Earth as the place of mediation or confrontation between the two spheres will disappear. The new heaven, earth and Jerusalem (ch 21) have none of the characteristics of the old. They are so unambiguously the dwelling place of the divine that not even the temple (a traditional religious symbol of the mediation between heaven and earth) is needed (21:22; contrast the Ezekiel visions of a new temple). When you read Revelation from this perspective you will see that it is filled with symbols of disjunction and separation.

A recent article has proposed the following two diagrams of the functions within revelation:

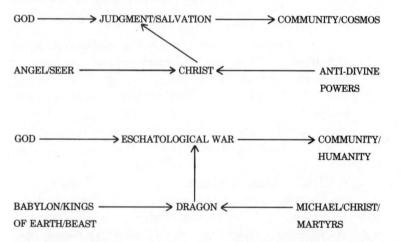

We should ask ourselves what the impact of such a tale would be on those Christians who heard it read. The constant repetition of cycles that end up in heaven would certainly reinforce the earth/heaven disjunction. Not only is salvation not possible on earth but everything that happens on earth follows upon a decision taken in heaven. Since the listener views everything from the perspective of heaven, he or she may feel transported into those realms. Life really belongs to that higher sphere.

Continuing life on earth is of no importance—hence one should not fear martyrdom.

Martyrdom

We have seen that persecution and martyrdom are central facets of Christian life in Revelation. In the cycle of stories about the beast, the martyrs are the only ones who oppose him. They seem a small number compared to the multitudes who go along worshipping him. Our first introduction to Jesus speaks of him as faithful witness (martyr) (1:5). The martyrs first appear in the vision of the fifth seal (6:9-11). They ask how long the persecution will continue and are commanded to "rest" until the number is "fulfilled." The company of martyrs reappears in the next chapter where we learn that it is a vast multitude from all the earth. The next sequence of seven visions has the antithesis to the martyrs in its fifth section: those who wish to die because the apocalyptic tribulations are too much for them. They seek death, but death will not come to deliver them from that tribulation (9:6).

Chapter 11 describes the death/resurrection and ultimate destruction of the enemies of two Christian martyrs. We have already seen that the martyrs are the adversaries of the dragon and the beast. Chapter 14 pronounces blessings on the whole company of martyrs. Revelation exalts the martyrs because of their faithful testimony, that testimony gains them access to heaven. But Revelation does not attribute independent significance to their deaths. (During the great persecutions of the 3rd and 4th centuries all sorts of powers would be attributed to the martyrs. An elaborate cult of the martyrs came into being. Some claimed that those awaiting execution had the ability to forgive sins—a clear expansion of the "martyrs blood" of Christ that cleanses from sin. Some people even sought to become martyrs. Revelation avoids such excesses.) It insists that a person must endure whatever persecutions come but should not seek them! The blood in which the martyrs are washed is not that of their own sacrifice but the blood of the lamb (7:14; 12:11).

Jesus

We have already seen that Jesus is presented as the victorious martyr (cf. 1:18). His victory over death delivers others from its power and created the new Israel to glorify God (1:6)—a function that we see them perform in the heavenly liturgies. The picture of Jesus as slain lamb on the throne (5:6-20) has become a persistent motif in Christian art from stained glass windows to the lamb cakes consumed at Easter. But Revelation does not begin with an image of the slain Christ. It begins with him as the heavenly and glorious son of Man from Daniel 7 (1:7-16). The reader is never to forget that Jesus has triumphed over death.

This victorious image leads into other images of Christ in the book, which some people find disturbing or unworthy. We meet the wrathful lamb (6:6; 17:14) and the warrior Christ (19:11-16). These visions conclude with acclamation of Christ as "King of Kings" and represent a vision of what was more prosaically stated in Revelation 1:4: Christ is Lord of the kings of the earth. These images too have a long history in Christian art and spirituality. They are unpopular now because they have so often been invoked to support holy wars and crusades. But they are not being used to encourage Christians to such militant action in Revelation. This work has to assure its readers that Christ is king against terrific odds and seeming evidence to the contrary. The Christians are in no position to fight any of their enemies. Nor are they given any role here in the final war with Satan—unlike the Essenes who had a War Manual for how the elect were to be drawn up for those battles. The Christian really has only two choices. He or she can renounce Jesus or suffer martyrdom. Without a strong conviction that Jesus is king, it would not be possible to endure such suffering.

The State and Judgment in Revelation

Recently, theologians have interested themselves in Revelation as a critique of the state and its abuse of power. Certainly the bestial images taken from Daniel and the description of Rome as "whore of Babylon" paint a negative picture indeed. The Christian must be discouraged from cooperating with imperial policy and ideology. The Trajan-Pliny correspondence on the Christian question makes it clear that educated pagans could not see the issue at stake on the Christian side. They considered Christians victims of a peculiar obstinacy and of a superstition. Why should they not at least nominally show loyalty to the Roman imperial order? Trajan was not trying to wipe out Christians. But he did want to be sure that they were not members of some disloyal and subversive group. Revelation makes it clear that Christians saw the issue differently. For them, the question was, "Who shall rule? The state or God through Christ?" Note that the Church as a monolithic, powerful institution did not exist. It could not have challenged the power of the empire on the same level. Christians were certain that there could be no compromise on the question of who rules the cosmos and so chose to die rather than to recognize what seemed to be idolatrous claims on the part of the state.

They did not suppose that they were to set up some sort of rival government or political system. Indeed, they would not even be involved in the termination of the existing empire of the beast. All they are to do is to bear witness by their refusal to bow to the power of Rome that there is one who is "King over the kings of the earth." It is also clear that the vivid descriptions of destruction and judgment are not aimed at the faithful Christians. They will view it all from the perspective of heaven but aimed at those who refuse to acknowledge the sovereignty of God and follow the beast. Thus, Revelation is not a book written to scare Christians but one to encourage them in the difficult task of bearing witness that confronts them. It is a book of Christian hope, not of Christian triumphalism.

STUDY QUESTIONS

1. What must the interpreter of Revelation remember about the language in which it is written?

2. Describe three types of traditional material found in Revelation and give an example of each.

3. What does the perspective from which the seer views events in Revelation tell us about the purpose of the book?

4. How is the number seven used in Revelation?

5. Where do we find descriptions of heavenly liturgy in Revelation? What is the effect of those descriptions on the reader?

6. Why is the opposition between life and death predominant in Revelation? What solutions does the narrative give to that opposition?

7. What do the opening letters tell us about the situation of the Church in which Revelation was written? Why do you think the author opens with letters?

8. What is it that "the saints" in the story need? How do they obtain that object (or salvation) in the narrative?

9. How does Revelation view martyrdom? Should Christians seek to become martyrs?

10. Describe two of the images of Christ given in the book. What does each one tell us about him? Why would that message have been important for Christians?

11. What is the view of the state presented in Revelation? Do you agree/disagree? Why?

12. Make a list of the different noises mentioned in the book on earth and in heaven. What is the difference between the sounds in the two realms? What kind of music would you choose for heaven? For earth?

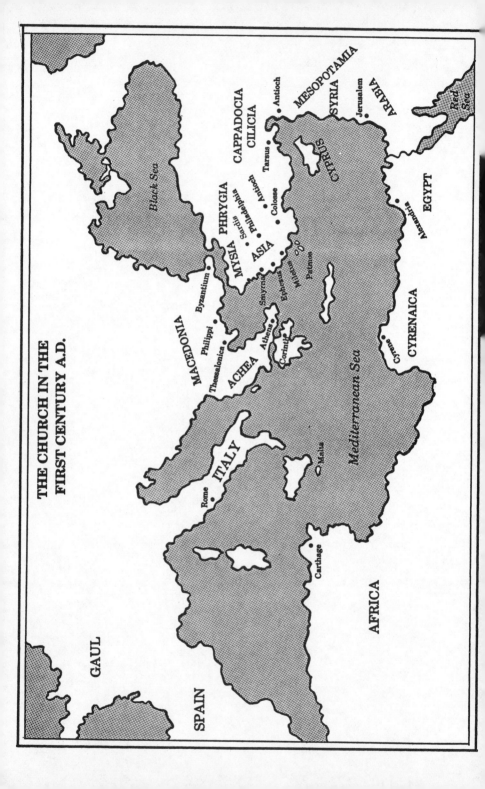

Chapter Seventeen

PRESERVING THE APOSTOLIC TRADITION: CHRISTIANITY BECOMES AN INSTITUTION

We have now read all the major works in the New Testament. Three collections of short letters remain: the pastoral epistles (1 and 2 Timothy; Titus); the Johannine epistles (1-3 John), and the catholic epistles (1 and 2 Peter; James; Jude). They do not present any strikingly new theological developments, but they help fill out our picture of the next stage in the life of the young communities. We have seen that Christianity exploded with tremendous energy and diversity. But in order for it to endure, some consolidation had to occur. All religions go through such a process in their development. Three important factors went into the process as we observe it here. Christians lost their expectation that the second coming of Jesus would occur in the near future. The movement became large enough that its communities required some standardized organization. And Judaism has been definitively lost as the "parent" religion. In these letters, "Jew" can be used as a term of slander for a Christian heretic regardless of an individual's ethnic background or the doctrinal content of his teaching. Questions of identity inevitably arise. The Christians must define more clearly who they are and how they are different from other people and religions. They must establish the organization of their communities and must define the norms of Christian tradition and behavior.

These letters are not by the apostles to whom they are attributed. Their language is that of a later generation. What their authors want to do is to preserve the apostolic tradition that has been given them by the great apostles. Thus, the letter of Jude concludes with the injunction that Christians remember the predictions of the apostles of Jesus Christ (v 17). 1 John shows the loss of Judaism as the opponent for Christianity—contrast the gospel!—when its final injunction is that Christians are to keep themselves from idolatry (5:21). 2 Peter has to remind its readers that Paul's letters are hard to understand and that they can easily be misinterpreted by false teachers (3:15-17). Speaking in the name of the apostle, the author of 1 Timothy admonishes his associates against heretics (1:3-7). 1 John, written perhaps by the disciple who prepared the final edition of the gospel, must also warn against heretics who would deny the human reality of Jesus. They may even have been basing some of their claims on the gospel. These letters then are not trying to break new theological ground. They are written as though from the great apostles to preserve their tradition against misinterpretation.

Ethics in Average Christianity

But questions of doctrinal tradition take up relatively little space in the whole collection, or even in a letter like 1 John. Ethical questions predominate and the advice given in these letters provides us with a picture of "average Christianity." We are able to see what most Christians—not the great theologians or those undergoing persecution—at the turn of the century found their religious ideals to be. These letters are not so much addressed to specific problems as to the community in general. James, for example, is addressed "to the twelve tribes." The picture that comes through these letters is that of a small group that seeks to impress the world by its behavior (cf 1 Pt 2:12).

If you compare James and 1 Peter you will discover that

some of the metaphors in these letters belonged to common Christian preaching. The Old Testament metaphor of withering grass, quoted in 1 Peter 1:24, is applied to the rich in James 1:10. Proverbs 10:12 is quoted in 1 Peter 4:8 and James 5:20. God's opposition to the proud appears in 1 Peter 5:5 and James 4:6. We already saw in Luke-Acts that hospitality was an important virtue. Now look at Hebrews 13:2; 1 Peter 4:9; 1 Timothy 3:3. This emphasis clearly indicates the communal character of early Christianity. In James 2, Christians are warned that faith without works is dead, and hospitality is one of the works referred to (2:25).

Other communal concerns are reflected in James 2:1-7. The passage condemns partiality in Christian assemblies. Rabbinic law forbade litigants from appearing before the court in clothing that showed one to be rich and the other poor. It also forbade one to be allowed to sit while the other had to stand. Usually both were required to stand and only the judge sat. These laws suggest that the context for this passage in James is a Christian court, an assembly to render judgment like that described in 1 Corinthians 6, and not an assembly for worship. We also saw that Matthew 18 outlined specific procedures for Christians to use in settling disputes. The legal nature of the passage in James is badly obscured by a mistranslation in the RSV. James asks the rhetorical question, "Have you not become judges with evil *dialogismoi*, a word translated "thoughts," but in a legal context the word has the meaning "decisions"—that is the legal decisions of a court. Both this passage and other references to the rich in James show that the problem of rich and poor affected the community not only from without but also from within. This passage indicates that partiality toward rich Christians was a problem within the congregation. Verses 5-7 make an ironic argument: the Christians who claim to be the elect have themselves suffered from the rich (= outsiders). And they are dishonoring a name by which they are called. That name was probably derived from the Old Testament *anawim*, "the poor" or "the elect poor." That expression also appears as a designation for the community of the

redeemed in the Qumran writings. Thus James is warning
Christians that partiality in their community life belies their
calling as Christians.

Rabbinic legislation against partiality also continues with
specific rules about judging one's neighbor, that is, another
member of the chosen people and with the citation of Leviticus
19:15 just as James continues with the Leviticus rules about
judging a neighbor. Thus it seems that the Christian community for which James writes considered the Old Testament law
valid, holy and binding just as a Christianized interpretation of
the Torah was upheld by Matthew's. Chapters 4 and 5 of James
may even draw on some collection of the preaching of Jesus
like the Sermon on the Mount. The "law of liberty" in James
1:22-25 refers to the Old Testament as interpreted by Christians; not to some new Christian code. These parallels remind
us that the transition from Jewish sect to Gentile religion did
not take place in the same way and with the same intensity
everywhere. (Jude, which alternates with James in early
manuscripts is almost entirely Jewish apocalyptic.)

But other letters from this period are almost entirely Gentile. The Old Testament has been taken over by the Gentile
Christians as their holy book, and they call themselves by
Jewish terms for the chosen people. You can see how this shift
effects the Pauline tradition if you turn to 1 Timothy 1:8-11.
The first thing you should notice is the non-Pauline tenor of
the language here. Whenever Paul uses Law he is talking
about the Old Testament as a means of salvation. Here Christians are being told to be good, law-abiding citizens (cp. the
teaching on prayer for public officials 2:1-7). Law means secular law. You will also notice another typical feature of these
letters in this passage. Expressions that reflect profound
theological concepts are not used for the purpose of reflecting
on the significance of the Christ-event but in order to bolster
the ethical injunctions of the author. Compare the use of the
suffering servant theology in 1 Peter 2:18-25 to enjoin slaves to
suffer unjust masters.

As you read through these letters, you can see that the

sources of early Christian ethical teaching were varied. The teaching of Jesus, the Old Testament, and popular ethical maxims of the time are all intermixed. You should also observe that there is some distinction between conduct required within the group and conduct toward outsiders. Toward those outside, Christians must prove themselves good, law-abiding people so that the non-Christians will be edified by their behavior. One might say that such "edification by conduct" is the way in which these Christians understood their universal mission to convert others (cf. 1 Pt 2:12).

One of the requirements for a bishop or "overseer" of the community is that he be well thought of by outsiders (1 Tim 3:7). Look at the list of great theological topics in 1 Peter 3:14-22: Christ's suffering; his preaching to the spirits (which means his victory over the cosmic and demonic powers; it has nothing to do with preaching to souls in hell. That comes from later traditions.); Christian baptism, and Jesus' resurrection. All this theological "heavy artillery" has been drawn up to encourage Christians to maintain a clear conscience and always to do good even if they must suffer for it. This intricate interlocking of themes from Christian kerygma and ethical exhortation is particularly striking in 1 Peter.

You will also notice that most of the ethical teaching in these letters applies within the Christian community. In 1 John, for example, the love command concerns the love of the "brethren" (= fellow Christians); not relationships with outsiders. James insists that the works that give life to faith involve showing charity to fellow Christians (2:14-17). All these letters manifest a phrase that has been used of 1 Peter. They are an "ethic for exiles." James addresses himself to the "twelve tribes *in the diaspora*" just as 1 Peter is addressed to the "*exiles of the diaspora*." We should not condemn these authors for failing to deal with larger questions of social injustice. They were hardly in a position to affect such issues. But what they have done is to insist contrary to the impression one might have gained from Paul, Mark or Luke, that the Old Testament is a valid norm for Christian ethical reflection and action. Therefore, although they do not explicitly pick up those points, there remains for Christian theology a large corpus of reflection on issues of national and social justice.

The pastoral epistles provide discreet catalogues of duties for the various types of people in the community. A brief look at them provides clues to the general instruction given in Christian communities at the turn of the century: on prayer, 1 Timothy 2:1-7; for bishops, 1 Timothy 3:1-7, Titus 1:7-9; for elders, 1 Timothy 5:17-20, Titus 1:5-6; for men, 1 Timothy 2:8; for women, 1 Timothy 2:9-15; for widows, 1 Timothy 5:3-16; for the elderly, Titus 2:2-3; for young people, Titus 2:4-8; for slaves, 1 Timothy 6:1-2, Titus 2:9-10; for the rich, 1 Timothy 6:5-10, 17-19. Less systematic lists can also be found in 1 Peter 2:11-5:11. Such catalogues of duties were common in popular philosophical preaching of the period. These lists show us what people considered ideal Christian behavior to be.

Concern for Tradition

We pointed out that these letters were written to preserve the tradition of the apostles for later generations of Christians. Both the Petrine and Pauline writings hold up their respective heroes as models. 2 Peter invokes the image of the apostle (cf. 1:12-15; the apostle's death is referred to and we are told that the letter is to help later Christians remember his teaching) and early Christian apocalyptic traditions (note the parallels with Jude) to warn Christians against heretics. This letter makes explicit what we suspected was true in the Johannine tradition as well: that the problems of heresy are caused by deviant scriptural interpretation (2 Pet 1:20f.). 2 Peter 3:3-7 tells us that at least some people took the delay of the parousia as an indication that all Christian eschatological teaching was false. Its concluding description of false interpretations of Paul (3:14-18) suggests that the letters of Paul have now become normative Scripture on a par with the Old Testament. Perhaps a reference to the transfiguration in 1:16-18 is a clue that a gospel already (ca. A.D. 110) functioned in that way as well.

The tendency to idolize Peter and Paul was already present in Acts. There, their missionary sufferings and triumphs were the themes of the story. In the Petrine and Pauline traditions as represented in these letters, their example as martyrs comes to the fore (cf. 2 Tim 4:6-8; 2 Pt 1:12-15). 1 Timothy 1:12-17 makes a very un-Pauline use of the story of his conversion. It is not the source of his unique call from God to be an apostle but an example for the repentance and conversion of sinners. Other examples of this exemplary personal exhortation may be found: 1 Timothy 1:18-20; 4:6-16; 5:21-25; 6:11-16; 2 Timothy 1:3-14; 2:1-13; 3:10-12; 3:14-4:2, 5).

The concern for preserving the tradition against heresy looms large in these letters. We have seen that 1 John is primarily concerned with docetism, those who deny the humanity of Christ. In many cases, the condemnation of heretics is so general that we cannot be sure what was involved. We met a similar problem in reading the seven letters that introduce the book of Revelation. The combination of invective against heresy and apocalyptic traditions that we found there and in 2 Peter may be observed in the other letters as well (cf. 1 Tim 4:1-5, 7; 2 Tim 3:1-9; 4:3f). When you read condemnations of heretics in the pastoral epistles (e.g., 1 Tim 1:3ff.; 6:3-5, 20f; 2 Tim 2:14-26; Tit 1:10-16; 3:9-11), you should know that the heretics did not do all the things of which they are accused. There were ways of slandering one's opponent that were common rhetorical practice just as we have set forms of political slander. Read 2 Timothy 3:1-7. Now compare that passage with the following attack on wandering cynic philosophers written by the satirist Lucian. In this passage, philosophy is speaking. She is bemoaning the swarms of cynic philosophers who infest the land:

> It wouldn't be so bad if they offended against us by only being what they are. But, although they appear very reverent and stern in public, if they get a handsome boy or a pretty woman in their clutches, it is best not to mention their conduct. Some even carry off the wives of their hosts, pretending that the women are going to become philosophers. Then they offer them as

common property to all their friends and think that
they are carrying out a principle of Plato's when they
do not know on what terms that holy man thought it
right for women to be so regarded. What they do at
drinking parties, how intoxicated they become would
make a long story. And while they do all this, you
cannot imagine how they condemn drunkenness and
adultery and lewdness and covetousness. Indeed, you
could not find any two things so opposed to each other
as their words and their deeds.

You can see that most of the accusations in 2 Timothy are
standard rhetorical polemics.

The pastoral epistles betray their post apostolic origin by
their concern with preserving the "deposit of faith." Faith is no
longer always a state of confidence in God and the salvation
wrought by Jesus. It is frequently used as a synonym for the
body of tradition and doctrine that is to be preserved (2 Tim
2:18; 3:8; 1 Tim 4:1; 6:21; Tit 1:1, 13; 2:2, 10); for the common
ethical traditions of Christianity (1 Tim 5:8, 12—where the
RSV translates it "pledge"—; 6:10); or for Christianity as in
the expression "the faith" (1 Tim 1:2; Tit 1:4). Maintaining
sound Christian doctrine is listed as one of the ethical duties of
the Christian (Tit 2:2, 10).

"The faith" that Christians are exhorted to keep is reflected in the many pieces of earlier hymns and creeds that are
quoted in these letters. Often they occur in contexts quite different from their original usage. For example, 1 Timothy 2:5: a
credal affirmation of Christ as mediator between God and humanity occurs in the middle of an ethical exhortation to lead a
peaceable life (cp. 1 Tim 3:13-16, a creed mixed with exhortation; 2 Tim 1:10; 2:8-13; Tit 2:11-14). The longer citations
clearly suggest credal or hymnic origins (cp. also 1 Tim 3:16,
1:15; Tit 3:3-8). You may also notice indications of traditional
origin in the little expressions attached to some formulations
like that in 2 Timothy 2:11, "This is a trustworthy saying," or 1
Timothy 3:16, "And confessing that great is the mystery of our
religion." These formulations are presented to the reader as
objects of belief.

Church Order

Our discussion of ethics and tradition in these letters has constantly run up against problems of deviant behavior and teaching. There are unauthorized teachers; false interpretations of Scripture and of teachings about Jesus and eschatology. On the one hand, you could say that this group of epistles tries to deal with the problem of regulating Christian behavior and doctrine by appealing to the apostolic tradition. The life, example and teaching of the apostles is codified for use in instruction. On the other hand, as 2 Peter shows, that move will not solve all the problems. Even if the pastoral epistles are meant as a normative guide for interpreting Paul, they can be interpreted along with other "difficult passages in our brother Paul." The question that must be thrashed out is: Who has the authority to interpret the traditions? These letters only stand on the threshold of some very crucial developments that answered that dilemma.

In the pastoral epistles we find a codification of church offices. Qualifications for bishop/overseer and deacon are given (1 Tim 3:1-13). We also read of a system of church order in which elders cared for the flock in 1 Peter (5:1-5) and James (5:14f, in the context of anointing of the sick and forgiveness of sins). 1 Peter 5:5 makes it clear that the office of "elder" still implied an age distinction. Acts 14:23f. presupposes the system of elders, since it has Paul and Barnabas appoint them in all congregations. (Paul's own letters have the founder-apostle as supreme authority and the intra-community offices as a matter of spiritual gifts to a variety of individuals.) 1 Timothy 5:17-22 includes rules for taking disciplinary action against an elder who exercises the office unworthily. Some historians think that these rules were formulated when the system of elders was in effect and that the office of *episkopos* (bishop/overseer) was a later development. Timothy is said to have been given office through the laying on of hands of the elders (1 Tim 4:14), but he is clearly designated "bishop." However, both titles may be early.

The Essene community had an overseer who functioned

something like a steward. Titus 1:7 refers to the bishop as steward and 1 Timothy 3:4-5 makes such ability part of his duties. The overseer at Qumran also had to instruct candidates in the sect's interpretation of the Law and see to it that they keep the rule. Both Qumran and 1 Peter 5:2-4 refer to the overseer as shepherd over the flock. (Cp. Paul's discourse to the elders at Ephesus in Acts 20:28-31.) Therefore, other scholars hold that elder/bishop was a single office with two designations just as the Essenes had two designations, *mebaqqer/paqid*, for a similar functionary. Timothy, however, is only called bishop/ overseer. They suggest that that terminology developed when age was no longer a requirement for the office—perhaps close to the time 1 Timothy was written, since the epistle makes a point of claiming that Timothy's youth is not an impediment to his ministry (1 Timothy 4:12).

In 1 Timothy, Timothy succeeds to the office through the elders. But the implication of the epistle is that his ministry is based on apostolic sanction, since he receives explicit instructions of all phases of his duties from Paul. 2 Timothy 1:6 makes that implied sanction explicit by claiming that Paul laid hands on Timothy and encouraged him to an apostolic ministry in imitation of his own. When we turn to the functions of the bishop in these letters we find that they are primarily instructional. Cultic and judicial functions are only rarely mentioned. Clearly the problem being solved by these instructions is that of preserving the Pauline tradition. The bishop is responsible for ethical admonishment and judgment within the community. He must be a person of recognized civil and family virtue. He must also preserve the tradition against heretics (1 Tim 1:3-11; 4:1-5). Thus, instruction is his major function: He is to guard the tradition and the proper interpretation of Scripture. We now clearly find ecclesiastical office mentioned as a career to which a person might aspire. At the same time it rests on apostolic commissioning and provides for the preservation of apostolic tradition.

Toward the Ancient Church

The episcopal system is still in its infancy in these letters, but they already show the driving force behind the development of the episcopate. The communities found it necessary to have clearly defined succession to church offices. Someone had to be the definitive interpreter of the tradition and had to set the norms for Christian life and conduct. Of course, we have seen that the problem of unworthy elders also existed. People were not naive about the problems implied in such offices. The concern with traditional formulations of faith provides another important norm against which divergent forms of Christianity could be measured. Such concerns would lead to the formal credal summaries of Christian belief.

2 Peter hints at yet another development that will be solidified in the controversies that the Church will face in the next century: the problem of a clearly defined Christian canon to stand alongside the Old Testament as "Scripture." All these aspects of church life and organization have many phases to their evolution as do the occasional allusions to penance and discipline of elders, before they come to be what we know today. Liturgical order has yet to be fixed as other Christian writings from about the same time show. On the one hand, *Didache* 10:7 has instructions for the celebration of the eucharist by wandering prophets. On the other, the letters of the bishop, Ignatius of Antioch, show that eucharistic praxis was consolidating in the hands of the bishop or those delegated by him. Thus, the association of elder/bishop as sole celebrant of the eucharist did not occur everywhere in the Church at the same time. Remember, there was no central authority to pronounce on such matters. What these letters do not yet envisage is the development of more detailed theological systems to meet the challenge of heresy and divergent understandings of Christianity. Liturgical discipline, canon, creed and church office will all be necessary but not enough for the future life and growth of the movement. The Spirit will also raise up in the

Church creative thinkers to meet the challenge of articulating what this carefully preserved deposit of faith and tradition means.

STUDY QUESTIONS

1. What phase of Christianity is represented in the pastoral and catholic epistles?
2. Describe the threats that led these authors to their concern with preserving the apostolic tradition.
3. Explain how these letters meet those threats.
4. How would you describe the ethical advice given in these letters? Which advice do you agree with the most? Which do you disagree with? Why?
5. 1 Peter holds that Christians should influence others by their conduct. Do you agree/disagree? Why?
6. Draw up a table of duties like those in the pastoral epistles for someone your age and in your situation. What led you to list each of the duties you did? Is there anything that makes your list specifically Christian?
7. Why was it necessary for Christianity to develop beyond the stage of consolidation reached at the end of the New Testament period? How do Christians today concern themselves with preserving the tradition?
8. Suppose someone today were to write a letter to help Christians interpret and preserve the tradition. What topics would he or she have to discuss? How does that list compare with those discussed in these letters?

SELECTED BIBLIOGRAPHY

This bibliography is to help you find more information about topics discussed in this book. Those marked with an asterisk (*) are intended for the general reader. The others are more specialized. "O.p." indicates books which are out of print.

Methods Used In Interpreting The Bible

Harrington, D. *Interpreting the New Testament: A Practical Guide.* Michael Glazier: 1979. (Clear discussion and illustration of the various methods of NT interpretation with additional bibliography.)

Jesus And His Times

*Toynbee, A. ed. *The Crucible of Christianity.* World: 1969. (A large, beautifully illustrated volume with articles by leading scholars on all aspects of NT backgrounds. Worth finding in a library just to look at the photographs.)

*Freyne, S. *The World of the New Testament.* Michael Glazier: 1980.

*Grant, M. *The World of Rome.* New American Library: 1960.
(Excellent survey of the period with particular attention to the religious dimensions of Graeco-Roman culture. O.p.)

*Hades, M. *Hellenistic Culture.* Norton: 1959.
(An information treatment of how hellenistic culture spread.)

*Kee, H.C. *Christian Origins in Sociological Perspective.* Westminster: 1980. (Discussion of how social science helps scholars understand the early Christian movement.)

Peters, E.F. *The Harvest of Hellenism.* Simon and Schuster: 1972.

Dodds, E.R. *Pagan and Christian in an Age of Anxiety.* Norton: 1966. (An interesting treatment of the "psychological mood" in the period just after the NT.)

Festugiere, J.M. *Personal Religion Among the Greeks.* University of California: 1962 (o.p.).

Nock, A.D. *Early Gentile Christianity and its Hellenistic Background.* Harper. Reprinted in his *Essays on Religion and the Ancient World. Vol. 1.* Harvard University: 1972, pp. 49-133.

Finley, M.I. *Ancient Slavery and Modern Ideology.* Viking: 1980.

Finley, M.I. *The Ancient Economy.* University of California: 1972.

Sarton, G. *History of Science 2: Hellenistic Science.* Norton: 1959.

Safrai, S. & Stern, M. eds. *The Jewish People in the First Century.* 2 vols. Fortress: 1974/76. (A massive collection of articles on all aspects of Jewish history, life and culture.)

*Stone, M. *Scriptures, Sects and Visions: A Profile of Judaism from Ezra to the Jewish Revolts.* Fortress: 1980.

Hengel, M. *Judaism and Hellenism.* 2 vols. Fortress: 1975.

*Neusner, J. *From Politics to Piety.* Prentice Hall: 1973. (A reconstruction of the development of Pharisaism.)

*Rhoads, D.M. *Israel in Revolution 6-74 C.E. A Political History Based on the Writings of Josephus.* Fortress: 1976.

Russell, D.S. *The Method and Message of Jewish Apocalyptic.* Westminster: 1964.

Nickelsburg, G. *Resurrection, Immortality and Eternal Life in Intertestamental Judaism.* Harvard University: 1972.

*Ringrenn, H. *The Faith of Qumran.* Fortress: 1963 (o.p.).

*Vermes, G. *The Dead Sea Scrolls. Qumran in Perspective.* World: 1978.

*Jonas, H. *The Gnostic Religion.* Beacon: 1963.

Perkins, P. *The Gnostic Dialogue: The Early Church and the Crisis of Gnosticism.* Paulist: 1980.

Sourcebooks:

These books provide selections from the religious writings of the NT period.

Lewis, N. & Reinhold, M. *Roman Civilization Sourcebook II: The Empire.* Harper Torch: 1966.

*Barrett, C.K. *The New Testament Background: Selected Documents.* Harper Torch: 1961.

*Dungan, D. & Cartlidge, D. *Sourcebook of Texts for Comparative Study of the Gospels.* Fortress: 1979.

*Kee, H.C. *The Origins of Christianity.* Prentice Hall: 1973.

*Grant, F. *Hellenistic Religions.* Bobbs-Merrill: 1953.

*Gaster, T. *The Dead Sea Scriptures.* Doubleday Anchor: 1977.

*Vermes, G. *The Dead Sea Scrolls in English.* Penguin: 1975.

Foerster, W. *Gnosis: A Selection of Gnostic Texts.* 2 vols. Oxford: 1972/74.

Robinson, J. ed. *The Nag Hammadi Library in English.* Harper: 1977.

Gospels and Acts

"Mark," in the *Jerome Biblical Commentary.* Prentice Hall: 1967.

*Achtemeier, P. *Invitation to Mark.* Doubleday Anchor.

*Harrington, W. *Mark.* Michael Glazier: 1979.

"Matthew," *Jerome Biblical Commentary.*

Meier, J. *Matthew.* Michael Glazier: 1980.

Meier, J. *The Vision of St. Matthew.* Paulist: 1979.

*Senior, D. *Invitation to Matthew.* Doubleday Anchor.

Conzelmann, H. *The Theology of St. Luke.* Harper: 1961.

*LaVerdiere, E. *Luke.* Michael Glazier: 1980.

Tiede, D. *Prophecy and History in Luke Acts.* Fortress: 1980.

"Acts," *Jerome Biblical Commentary.*

*Crowe, J. *The Acts.* Michael Glazier: 1980.

Hengel, M. *Acts and the History of Earliest Christianity.* Fortress: 1980.

*Karris, R. *Invitation to Acts.* Doubleday Anchor: 1980.

Barrett, C.K. *The Gospel According to St. John*^{2} *Westminster: 1978.*

Brown, R.E. *The Gospel According to John.* Anc. Bi. 29 & 29A. Doubleday: 1966/70.

Life and Teaching of Jesus

*Bornkamm, G. *Jesus of Nazareth.* Harper: 1960.

*Flusser, D. *Jesus.* Herder: 1969 (o.p.).
(By a Jewish scholar.)

Perrin, N. *Rediscovering the Teaching of Jesus.* Harper: 1967.

Carleston, C. *The Parables of the Triple Tradition.* Fortress: 1976.

*Jeremias, J. *Rediscovering the Parables.* Scribner's: 1966.

*Perkins, P. *Hearing the Parables of Jesus.* Paulist: 1981.

*Smith, C.W.F. *The Jesus of the Parables.* Pilgrim: 1975.

Fuller, R. et al. *Essays on the Love Command.* Fortress: 1978.

Brown, R.E. *The Birth of the Messiah.* Doubleday: 1977.

*Brown, R.E. *Virginal Conception and Bodily Resurrection of Jesus.* Paulist: 1973.

Brown, R.E. et al. *Mary in the New Testament.* Fortress/ Paulist: 1978.

*Stanley, D. *Jesus in Gethsemane.* Paulist: 1980.

Dunn, J.D.G. *Christology in the Making.* Westminster: 1980.

Hengel, M. *The Son of God.* Fortress: 1976.

Jeremias, J. *The Eucharistic Words of Jesus.* Scribner's: 1966.

*Houlden, J.L. *Ethics and the New Testament.* Oxford: 1977.

Schnackenburg, R. *The Moral Teaching of the New Testament.* Seabury: 1975.

*MacRae, G.W. *Invitation to John.* Doubleday Anchor: 1978.

*Perkins, P. *The Gospel of John.* Franciscan Herald: 1978.

*Brown, R.E. *The Community of the Beloved Disciple.* Paulist: 1979.

Pauline Studies

*Bornkamm, G. *Paul.* Harper: 1971.

*Fitzmyer, J. "Life of Paul;" "New Testament Epistles," and "Pauline Theology," in *Jerome Biblical Commentary.*

*Hooker, M.D. *A Preface to Paul.* Oxford: 1980.

Kaesemann, E. *Perspectives on Paul.* Fortress: 1971.

*Keck, L. *Paul and His Letters.* Fortress: 1979.

Munck, J. *Paul and the Salvation of Mankind.* John Knox: 1959.

Schoeps, H.J. *Paul.* Westminster: 1959.
(Classic treatment by a Jewish scholar.)

*Stendahl, K. *Paul Among Jews and Gentiles.* Fortress: 1976.

Commentaries on New Testament Epistles

Fitzmyer, J. "Romans, Galatians and Philippians," *Jerome Biblical Commentary.*

*Houlden, J.L. *The Pastoral Epistles.* Penguin: 1977.

Kaesemann, E. *Commentary on Romans.* Eerdmans: 1980.

*Harper Commentary Series, Harper & Row:

Barrett, C.K. *1 Corinthians; 2 Corinthians; Romans.*

Houlden, J.L. *The Johannine Epistles.*

Laws, S. *The Epistle of James.*

Hermeneia Series, Fortress:

Betz, H.D. *Galatians.*

Conzelmann, H. *1 Corinthians.*

Dibelius, M. (Greeven), *James.*

Dibelius, M. (Conzelmann), *Pastoral Epistles.*

Lohse, E. *Colossians and Philemon.*

*New Testament Message Series, Michael Glazier:

Maly, E. *Romans.*

Murphy-O'Connor, J. *1 Corinthians.*

Fallon, F. *2 Corinthians.*

Osiek, C. *Galatians.*

Swain, L. *Ephesians.*

Getty, M.A. *Philippians and Philemon.*

Rogers, P. *Colossians.*

Reese, J. *1 & 2 Thessalonians.*

Karris, R. *The Pastoral Epistles.*

Casey, J. *Hebrews.*

Kugelman, R. *James and Jude.*

Senior, D. *1 & 2 Peter.*

Perkins, P. *The Johannine Epistles.*

Apocalypse

Collins, A.Y. *The Apocalypse.* Michael Glazier: 1979.

Sweet, J.P.M. *Revelation.* Westminster: 1979.

AUDIO-VISUAL BIBLIOGRAPHY

The following is a select bibliography of audio-visual material for each chapter of the text. Teachers are advised to preview any material before using it with a class. Please consult the distributor's listing at the end of the bibliography for information about ordering material.

Chapter 1: *Why Study the Bible?*

Reese, Rev. James M., O.S.F.S. "God's Revelation in the Bible" and "What is biblical 'Inspiration'?" Talks 1 and 2, Tape 1, *Toward Understanding the New Testament*, Paulist Press (cassette). Fr. Reese discusses two key concepts in biblical studies, presenting basic information about each and their relevance to Christians today.

Chapter 2: *The World of Jesus*

"The Exodus" (Color, 28 min., 16mm film), available from Mass Media Ministries. An account of God's chosen people's desert experience with a visual portrayal of the birthplace of the Judaeo-Christian tradition.

"Where Jesus Lived" (Family Films, Color, 14 min., 16 mm film), available from Roa Films. The places of Jesus' life, death and resurrection with references to the lifestyle of Jesus' time.

"The Passover" (Gospel Films, Color, 30 min., 16 mm film), available from Roa Films. An introduction to the Jewish feast in which the Christian Eucharist is rooted.

"Nomad Life of the Hebrews" and "Religious Life of the Hebrews" in *Old Testament Life and Times* (K-82), Alba House (35 mm filmstrip with record).

"The Geography of the Holy Land," (K-28), Alba House (35mm filmstrip with record).

Chapter 3: *The Life of Jesus*

"Archaeology and the Living New Testament" (Film Services, Color, 25 min., 16mm film), available from Roa Films. The setting of the last week of Jesus' ministry and the work of his first followers.

"The Great Mystique Shatterer" (5 min., 35mm filmstrip with record), available from Teleketics. Various artistic representations of Jesus are the backdrop as two women discuss their images of Jesus.

"It's About this Carpenter" (13 min., Black and white, 16mm film), available from Roa Films. A modern parable about a carpenter who delivers a cross to a church and encounters many different responses on his journey.

Perkins, Pheme, Ph.D. "Who Is Jesus?" *FAMILY Parish Religious Education*, (Paulist Press, 35mm filmstrip with cassette), available from Paulist Press. An examination of the many images of Jesus found in the Synoptic Gospels.

Chapter 4: *The Preaching of Jesus*

"The Parable" (22 min., Color, 16mm film), available from Mass Media Ministries. An award winning film that presents a Christian parable in contemporary terms.

"The Greatest Dinner Party" (35mm filmstrip with record or cassette), available from Teleketics. A retelling of the Lucan banquet parable that stresses our invitation to be part of God's Kingdom.

"The Cure of the Crippled Man" (35mm filmstrip with record or cassette), available from Teleketics. The story of Jesus' cure of the cripple that shows the power of faith and Jesus' challenge to the Pharisee's law.

"Sermon on the Mount, Now" (19 min., Color, 16mm film), available from Mass Media Ministries. A reading of the Sermon on the Mount with modern images that highlights the ethics of Christ.

Chapter 5: *The Risen Christ: Beginnings of Christology*

"Pentecost" (35mm filmstrip with record or cassette), available from Teleketics. A light-hearted narration that emphasizes the Apostles' change from frightened persons to courageous disciples.

La Verdiere, Rev. Eugene A., S.S.S. "The Nature of 'Gospel'." Talk 4, Tape 2, *Toward Understanding the New Testament*, Paulist Press (cassette). A discussion of the roots and implications of Jesus' proclamation.

"Right Here, Right Now" (Teleketics Films, 15 min.,Color, 16mm film), available from Roa Films. An "average" man changes the lives of six troubled people, who continue in their new way of life after his death.

Chapter 7: *The Life of Paul*

"The Conversion" (Cathedral Films, 30 min., Black & white, 16mm film), available from Roa Films. The story of Paul's persecution of Christians and his subsequent conversion, based on Acts 9.

"Archaeology and the Living New Testament" see notes on Chapter 3.

Keegan, Rev. Terence J., O.P. "St. Paul's Life and Ministry in Acts 12-28." Talk 7, Tape 4, *Toward Understanding the New Testament*, Paulist Press (cassette). A discussion of Paul's life and work and an outline of his letter to the Thessalonians.

Chapter 8: *Christians: Jew and Gentile*

Keegan, Rev. Terence J., O.P. "St. Paul's Epistles to the Galatians and Romans" and Turro, Rev. James, "The Epistle to the Philippians." Talks 9 and 10, Tape 5, *Toward Understanding the New Testament*, Paulist Press (cassette). A discussion of the background and main points of these three epistles.

Chapter 9: *The Gentiles Interpret Christianity*

Keegan, Rev. Terence J., O.P. "St. Paul's First Letter to the Corinthians." Talk 8, Tape 4, *Toward Understanding the New Testament*, Paulist Press (cassette).

Turro, Rev. James. "The Epistles to the Colossians and Ephesians." Talk 11, Tape 6, *Toward Understanding the New Testament*, Paulist Press (cassette).

These tapes provide an exploration of the particular Pauline epistles mentioned in the titles.

Chapter 10: *Mark: Jesus, Hidden and Suffering Messiah*

Keegan, Rev. Terence J., O.P. "Mark—Christian Kerygma," *Service Evangelists Filmstrip Series*, Paulist Press (35mm filmstrip with cassette or record). A portrayal of the events of Jesus' life as recounted in Mark's Gospel.

Freyne, Sean, Ph.D. "Faith in the Gospel of Mark." *Family Parish Religious Education*, Paulist Press (35mm filmstrip with cassette). An examination of the responses to Jesus characterized by people in Mark's Gospel.

LaVerdiere, Rev. Eugene A., S.S.S. "The Gospel of Mark." Talk 5, Tape 3, *Toward Understanding the New Testament*, Paulist Press (cassette). The structure and content of Mark's Gospel.

"The Gospel According to Mark," *The Four Gospels* (K-98), Alba House (35mm filmstrip with record).

Chapter 11: *Matthew: Jesus, the True Teacher of Israel*

Boadt, Rev. Lawrence, C.S.P. "Matthew—Discipleship." *Service Evangelists Filmstrip Series*, Paulist Press (35mm filmstrip with record or cassette). An examination of the nature of true discipleship seen in the Sermon on the Mount.

LaVerdiere, Rev. Eugene A., S.S.S. "The Gospels of Matthew and Luke." Talk 6, Tape 3, *Toward Understanding the New*

Testament, Paulist Press (cassette). An exploration of the structure and content of these two gospels.

Reese, Rev. James, O.S.F.S. "Reconciliation in the Gospel of Matthew." *Family Parish Religious Education*, Paulist Press (35mm filmstrip with cassette). A look at Jesus' call to his followers to be peacemakers in the world.

"Matthew 5:5" (5 min., Color, 16mm film), available from Teleketics. A poetic presentation of images related to this gospel text.

"Theirs is the Kingdom" (5 min., Color, 16mm film), available from Teleketics. A look at what it means to put the beatitudes into action in the contemporary world.

"The Gospel According to St. Matthew" (136 min., Black & white, 16mm film), available from Audio Brandon Films. A simple but profound presentation of Matthew's account of the life of Jesus.

"The Gospel According to Matthew," *The Four Gospels* (K-98), Alba House (35mm filmstrip with record).

Chapter 12: *Luke: Jesus, Son of God*

LaVerdiere, Rev. Eugene A., S.S.S. "The Gospels of Matthew and Luke." See notes on Chapter 11.

Keegan, Rev. Terence J., O.P. "Prayer of Jesus in the Gospel of Luke." *Family Parish Religious Education*, Paulist Press (35mm filmstrip with cassette). An examination of the Lukan portrayal of Jesus' prayer.

Perkins, Pheme, Ph.D. "Luke—Prayer and Social Apostolate." *Service Evangelists Filmstrip Series*, Paulist Press (35mm filmstrip with cassette or record). The relationship of prayer and social action in Luke's portrayal of Jesus.

"The Gospel According to Luke," *The Four Gospels* (K-98), Alba House (35mm filmstrip with record).

Chapter 13: *John: Jesus, the Divine Word*

Dillon, Rev. Richard. "The Gospel of John, Part I" and "The Gospel of John, Part II and the Johannine Letters." Talks 15 and 16, Tape 8, *Toward Understanding the New Testament*, Paulist Press (cassette). The themes and discourses in John's presentation of Jesus' life.

Hellwig, Monika, Ph.D. "Eucharist in John's Gospel." *Family Parish Religious Education*, Paulist Press (35mm filmstrip with cassette). A look at what it means to say that Jesus is the Bread of Life.

Malatesta, Rev. Edward, S.J. "John—Spirituality and Sacrament." *Service Evangelists Filmstrip Series*, Paulist Press (35mm filmstrip with cassette or record). An understanding of Jesus' mission through a look at John's accounts of Jesus' personal interactions with others.

"The Gospel According to John," *The Four Gospels* (K-98), Alba House (35mm filmstrip with record).

Chapter 14: *Acts: Missionary Success and Salvation for the Nations*

Rohr, Rev. Richard, O.F.M. "Community in the Acts of the Apostles." *Family Parish Religious Education*, Paulist Press (35mm filmstrip with cassette). How the early Church lived the Gospel message.

Reese, Rev. James, O.S.F.S. "The early Christian Community in Acts 1-9." Talk 3, Tape 2, *Toward Understanding the New Testament*, Paulist Press (cassette). Luke's purpose in writing and his examination of the marks of the early Church.

Keegan, Rev. Terence J., O.P. "St. Paul's Life and Ministry in Acts 12-28." See notes on Chapter 7.

"Many Different Gifts" (50 min., Color, 16mm film), available from Mass Media Ministries. Portrait of the celebrations of a non-territorial Catholic community.

"Works of Fatih" (Kino Films, 12 min., Color, 16mm film), available from Roa Films. How the early Christians differed from the dominant culture in daily living and business practices.

Chapter 15: *Hebrews: The New Israel, a Pilgrim People*

Bourke, Msgr. Myles M. "The Epistle to the Hebrews." Talk 17, Tape 9, *Toward Understanding the New Testament*, Paulist Press, (cassette). Background and content of this epistle with application to today's world.

Chapter 16: *Revelation: The Martyred Saints*

Boadt, Rev. Lawrence, C.S.P. "The Book of Revelation." Talk 18, Tape 9, *Toward Understanding the New Testament*, Paulist Press (cassette). A study of the structure, characters and symbolism of this unique New Testament writing.

Chapter 17: *Preserving the Apostolic Tradition: Christianity Becomes an Institution*

Dillon, Rev. Richard. "The Gospel of John, Part II and the Johannine Letters." See notes on Chapter 13. Of particular concern in the present chapter is the material on the Johannine epistles.

Tambasco, Rev. Anthony, S.M.M. "The First Epistle of St. Peter" and "The Epistle of St. James." Talks 13 and 14, Tape 7, *Toward Understanding the New Testament*, Paulist Press (cassette). Major themes of these two pastoral epistles.

Turro, Rev. James. "The Pastoral Epistles to Timothy and Titus." Talk 12, Tape 6, *Toward Understanding the New Testament*, Paulist Press (cassette). The authorship and teachings of these epistles are explained.

FILM DISTRIBUTORS

Some of the audio visual material cited is available for rental; some material is not. Where rentals are not obtainable through publishers or distributors, teachers are advised to try their diocesan religious education offices. Many dioceses purchase AV material and rent them to religious institutions and schools at reasonable rates. Below are the locations of publishers and distributors mentioned in the bibliography. Their catalogues are available on request.

ALBA HOUSE COMMUNICATIONS
Canfield, Ohio 44406

AUDIO BRANDON FILMS
34 MacQuesten Parkway So.
Mount Vernon, N.Y. 10550
914-664-5051

3868 Piedmont Avenue
Oakland,Ca. 94611
415-658-9890

1619 North Cherokee
Los Angeles, Ca. 90028
213-463-1131

2512 Program Drive
Dallas, Texas 75220
214-357-6494

8400 Brookfield Avenue
Brookfield, Ill. 60513
312-485-3925

MASS MEDIA MINISTRIES
2116 N. Charles Street
Baltimore, Md. 21218
301-727-3270

1720 Chouteau Avenue
St. Louis, Mo. 63103
314-436-0418

PAULIST PRESS
545 Island Road
Ramsey, N.J. 07446
201-825-7300

ROA FILMS
1696 North Astor Street
Milwaukee, Wis. 53202
414-271-0861
800-558-9015

GLOSSARY

APOCALYPTIC — From the Greek word for "revealing/ uncovering", *apokalypsis*. The word is used for those Jewish and Christian writings which claimed to reveal the secrets of how God was to bring the world/history to an end. Such writings are usually said to be by ancient holy men or prophets and to describe a revelation directly from/of heaven. Often an angel interprets highly symbolic visions for the seer. In the Old Testament, the book of Daniel chs. 7-12 is an apocalyptic work. In the New Testament, the Apocalypse or Book of Revelation.

CANON — From the Greek word for "rule", kanon. This word is used to designate a list of writings accepted as Sacred Scripture.

CHRISTOLOGY — Literally "teaching about Christ." It refers to the statements and doctrines which Christians developed to describe the person of Jesus Christ and his relationship to God the Father.

DEAD SEA SCROLLS — See ESSENES

DIASPORA — The Greek word for "dispersion." It is used to refer to Jews living outside of Palestine.

"DIVINE MAN" — A term used in studying religions of the time of Jesus to describe those religious

329

preachers and prophets who claimed or were thought to possess divine powers. These powers were frequently displayed in miracle-working. When we speak of a "divine man Christology" we are referring to views of Jesus which emphasize his miraculous powers as the basis for belief in him.

ESCHATOLOGY From the Greek for end, *eschaton*. Literally teaching about the last things—usually the end of the world and judgment. When we speak of "realized eschatology", we are referring to the view that judgment is not some future event but is determined in the present by how a person responds to the preaching of/about Jesus Christ.

ESSENES A group of pious Jews which existed from the mid-second century B.C. until the 70's of the first century A.D. They formed special communities which were separated from the world so that they could follow the Law of God perfectly until the end of the world. A collection of their writings and biblical manuscripts known as the Dead Sea Scrolls and the remains of an Essene community were found near the Dead Sea at Qumran. These writings have provided us with a wealth of information about Jewish religion in the time of Jesus. They also represent our earliest copies of Old Testament texts.

GNOSTIC (Gnosticism). From the Greek for knowledge, *gnosis*. It refers to an ancient religious group (later a Christian heresy) who believed that those who had insight into their inner divine nature—who realized that they really belonged to a divine world beyond this one—would be saved. They claimed that the god who created this material world was an evil being, fallen from the divine realm, who was jealous of humanity and sought to keep them from realizing their true destiny. Revealers from the heavenly world were said to have brought true knowledge of that destiny. They came into conflict with Christianity not only over the doctrine of God and creation but also because they claimed that Jesus was such a revealer and that the real meaning of his teaching was to direct the soul to the gnostic light world. Many gnostic writings were discovered at Nag Hammadi in Egypt about the same time as the Dead Sea Scrolls. One of these, The Gospel of Thomas, is a collection of sayings and parables of Jesus—many of them also found in our canonical gospels. Some scholars wonder if sayings from the Gospel of Thomas not found in the canonical gospels might also have come from Jesus.

GOSPEL From the Middle English "good spell", good news. A translation of the Greek word, *euangelion*, good news.

HELLENISTIC (Hellenism). From the Greek word, hellenismos, "imitation of the Greeks". It refers to the adoption (and adaptation) of Greek language and cultures by peoples of the east after their conquest by Alexander the Great.

KERYGMA Greek word for "proclamation." It is used for passages which summarize or proclaim the basic message about Jesus Christ.

PARAENESIS The Greek word for "exhortation" or advice. A term used to describe passages which give the ethical teaching of the early Christian communities.

PAROUSIA   Greek word for presence. Used as a technical term for the second coming of Christ at the end of the world.

PASSION NARRATIVE   The account of the suffering and death of Jesus.

Q   First letter of the German word for source *Quelle*. It is used to designate the collection of stories, sayings and parables of Jesus that was used as a source by both Matthew and Luke.

QUMRAN   *See* ESSENES.

SEPTUAGINT (LXX)   The translation of the Old Testament into Greek made by diaspora Jews. This translation was the Bible of most of the early Christians, since they were largely Greek speaking and was the basis of the later translation into Latin.

SOTERIOLOGY   Literally "teaching about the Savior", soter, in Greek. It refers to Christian explanations of how the life, death and resurrection of Jesus brought about the salvation of humanity.

SYNOPTIC GOSPELS   "Synoptic" is Greek for "look at together." Matthew, Mark and Luke are called the synoptic gospels because they tell the story of Jesus in much the same fashion. The gospel of John, on the other hand, is quite different.

INDEX OF SUBJECTS

INDEX OF
BIBLICAL
REFERENCES